Advance Pr.
A Death in Peking

"In this brilliantly researched account, Graeme Sheppard looks again at the violent murder of Pamela Werner in Peking over eighty years ago. Digging in archives in the UK and the USA, Beijing and Rome, he corrects previous accounts and offers a mass of new evidence in an attempt to unravel the truth at last."
—Frances Wood, author of *The Lure of China*

"Who murdered and mutilated Pamela Werner? The combined efforts of Beijing Police Colonel Han Shi-chung and ex-Scotland Yard detective Richard Dennis hit a dead end. Now, Graeme Sheppard has taken a forensic scalpel to the political intrigue and rumours of sexual excess surrounding the case. His investigation goes deeper than any that has gone before. Using new material, he has come up with compelling answers to this old mystery."
—Chris Emmett, Retired Senior Superintendent, Hong Kong Police

"This book presents a meticulous investigation of a brutal cold case murder. The historical and cultural backdrop adds to the intrigue. With an attention to detail the author has produced convincing conclusions."
—Chief Inspector Adrian Denby, London Metropolitan Police

"Sheppard is the experienced investigator - systematic and convincing. His conclusions are well-founded and to the extent possible, supported or at least not contradicted by the (at the current time) available case information."
—Frode Olsen, Danish National Police

A DEATH IN PEKING

Who Really Killed Pamela Werner?

Graeme Sheppard

EARNSHAW
BOOKS

A Death in Peking

By Graeme Sheppard

ISBN-13: 978-988-8422-94-4

© 2018 Graeme Sheppard

HISTORY / Asia / China

EB103

Published by Earnshaw Books Ltd. (Hong Kong)

INTRODUCTION

THE BRUTAL MURDER of Pamela Werner in 1937 in pre-communist Peking horrified the foreigners living in the ancient walled capital, and many others besides. The appalling injuries the young British woman suffered were as barbaric as they were mysterious. Months later, China was engulfed by war with Japan and the macabre crime remained unsolved with the murderer still at large. *A Death in Peking* investigates this cold case using primary source material hitherto un-examined.

In recent years, there has been a rekindling of interest in Pamela's death owing to the publication of *Midnight in Peking* by Paul French, an account stemming principally from the murder theories of her idiosyncratic adoptive father, E.T.C. Werner, a renowned sinologist and long-time member of the China consular service. That was how I, a retired London police officer with thirty years of experience, first learned of the case. But reading the book, I immediately saw that the narrative and its conclusions were deeply flawed. Evidentially, the conclusion didn't stand up and, with my professional curiosity aroused, I set about investigating the crime myself. For three years I painstakingly gathered evidence and eventually turned the case on its head. Clearly, there was far more to the murder than had ever before been revealed. *A Death in Peking* is the result.

This book dissects the crime, utilizing a broader range of historical sources - British, Chinese, Canadian, Italian and American. The context of Pamela Werner's death and its investigation are examined. The many suspects to the murder, including names both old and new, men whose lives intersected with that of the victim, are scrutinised, and their characters and motivations put under the spotlight. Allegations of a political motive for Pamela's death are considered using secret correspondence - which I discovered in the British National Archives - between the enigmatic Sir Edmund Backhouse and the British Embassy. In this manner, *A Death in Peking* also illuminates many of the extraordinary lives led by foreigners in a China long since vanished.

Who killed Pamela Werner? Is it possible that the solution, the true identity of the murderer, has been overlooked? Yes, I believe it has.

Graeme Sheppard
London
July 2018

Contents

1

THE DISCOVERY

A BODY BY THE CITY WALL

The Times newspaper edition published in London on Saturday, January 9, 1937 carried a short but sensational news item:

> **British girl's death in Peking; Murder Suspected**
> The British authorities and the Chinese police are investigating the mysterious death last night of Pamela Werner, a 17-year-old British girl, the daughter of Mr. Chalmers Werner, the author and former British Consul at Foochow. She disappeared yesterday evening after skating at the French club rink.
>
> The body was found this morning inside the city wall and 250 yards from the girl's home, at one of the loneliest spots in the city. It had been so badly mauled by stray dogs as to be unrecognisable and to make it difficult, except after a careful medical examination, to hazard a guess how she met her death, but in view of the lack of evidence that an accident had happened murder must be suspected.[1]

The Times was impressively quick off the mark with its report

1 "British girl's death in Peking; Murder Suspected," *The Times*, January 9, 1937.

from its own correspondent in Peking, but the article contained two errors. Pamela Werner was nearly twenty, not seventeen, and her father's name was Edward Theodore Chalmers Werner. It was a sensational international story with a strong British angle, and newspapers and news agencies for a short time covered the story on an almost daily basis. But in Peking (then officially called Peiping), Pamela's murder was front page news for much longer, and at much greater length. On the morning after the crime's discovery, the city's only English-language newspaper, *The Peiping Chronicle* ran the following headline and strapline above its story:

Dead Body of Young Foreign Woman Found in Gully
along City Wall
Victim believed to be Pamela Werner, daughter of Mr. E.T.C.
Werner; Post-mortem Examination Made; Inquest This Morning.[2]

Accompanying the report was a grainy photograph showing where the body was found in a ditch at a desolate spot directly under one of Peking's immense city walls.

The foreign community was appalled by the news that one of its own had been murdered. Detached from Chinese society as most of them were, foreigners in Peking were rarely touched by serious crime. As details of rape and mutilation were leaked to the press, shock changed to horror. Few on that day could have imagined how many of their number—diplomats, doctors, journalists, soldiers—would sooner or later be implicated as either murderer or conspirator in the crime.

In the first days after the body was discovered, correspondents of international news services including the London-based

2 "Dead Body of Young Foreign Woman Found in Gully along City Wall, *Peiping Chronicle*, January 9, 1937.

2

Reuters News Agency and the American news organizations the Associated Press and United Press filed stories regularly. On January 8, the day Pamela's corpse was discovered, the United Press filed its first story with a first and highly speculative scenario of how it happened, one involving feral dogs:

Daughter of Retired Consular Agent Found in Ditch; Identification Not Positive

PEIPING, Jan 8, United Press - The mutilated body is a 17-year-old British girl was tentatively identified today as Pamela Werner, daughter of a retired veteran of the British consulate service in China.

Identification was made by the discovery of a stocking and one shoe, found with the body in a ditch near the Tartar city inside the walls of Peiping.

However, the girl's other clothing and a bicycle which Pamela was riding when she disappeared yesterday were missing, and identification was not positive.

The father, Edward Theodore Werner, well-known in the Far East, had been a member of the British consulate service for many years.

The body of the girl was found near the Werner home at a spot haunted – Chinese legend says – by the ghost of a suicide. Chinese shun the locality, which is an isolated part of Peiping.

One theory was that what girl's death was caused by scavenger dogs which run in droves in the ancient capital – lean, gaunt, all but wild creatures. Mutilation was apparently caused by these beasts which infest the city, and it was believed the girl was first set upon by the dogs and bitten to death.

An inquest will be held tomorrow.

3

The following days brought further reports of varying accuracy. This was a hot story of significant interest across the board, but particularly to foreigners living in China. And the biggest foreign population in China was in the city of Shanghai to the south. The *North-China Herald*, published in that city each Sunday, had a report in its next edition:

No Clue Found

Peiping, Jan. 10 - No clue to the person responsible for the death of Miss Pamela Werner, 19-year-old daughter of Mr. E. T. C. Werner, former British Consul, has yet been uncovered, according to word from the Chinese police who are in charge of the case.

Miss Werner's mutilated body was found in a ditch beside the road which runs under the Tartar City wall, early on the morning of January 8. An inquest was held on Saturday and adjourned to this week, pending the

Crime scene: the ditch where Pamela's body was found beside the Tartar Wall.
(Published in contemporary newspaper reports)

conclusion of an autopsy and the
gathering of medical evidence.

It is revealed that the autopsy
will reveal that it was a case of
premeditated murder. This view is
held because of the severe mutilation
of the whole of the upper part of the
girl's body, especially the face. This
mutilation was apparently done
with a knife, in order to conceal the
identity of the victim from those who
found her remains. It is believed,

*Pamela Werner, a studio
photograph taken shortly
before her death*

further, that the murder was committed indoors, the body
being taken later to the spot where it was found. This
theory, however, has raised the question of why the victim's
skirt was found near her remains, though no other clothing
was discovered in the vicinity.

So far, the movements of Miss Werner after she left the
French Club skating rink at 7.30 p.m. on January 7, remain
untraced. Investigations are entirely in the hands of the
First District of the Chinese Police under Captain Han.
Considerable reluctance is being shown by them to divulge
their activities, though it is understood that there is still no
clue which would indicate a possible murderer.

The same day, the Chinese newspaper *Ta Kung Pao* published
a report headlined: "Western female corpse case - No Chinese
Involved".

"The body was yesterday transported from the Xiehe Hospital
(Peking Union Medical College) into the British Legation before
an autopsy was performed, as a result of which it is assumed that
the case is unrelated to Chinese people and the British authorities

have decided to handle the investigations themselves."[3]

Two days later, the *Peiping Chronicle*, carrying a Reuters news article, expanded on the 'committed indoors' theory with the addition of the use of a motor car, and also reported the arrival of British policemen in Peking to investigate:

Still no Clues Found to Murder Of Miss Werner

Girl Believed Murdered in House and Taken by Car To Ditch

Two Foreign Detectives arrive Here from Tientsin to assist

Chinese: Inquest Delayed

Peiping, January 12, Reuter - The Werner murder mystery appears to be no nearer solution today, according to reports from foreign and Chinese sources.

The inquest, adjourned from Saturday, was not continued today up to 3 p.m.

As further information becomes available it becomes apparent that the crime was an even more complicated affair than was first thought. It is stated reliably that indications now are that the murder was committed elsewhere than in Wall Street, probably in a house, and that the body was afterwards deposited in the ditch where it was found on Friday morning.

It is presumed in some quarters that it may have been taken there by car from the place where the murder was committed.

Speculation is rife and theories of the crime increase in number daily, much discussion centring on the possible nationality of the murderer, whether he was a foreigner or Chinese.

The Chinese police authorities here now have the

....

3 Ta Kung Pao newspaper, Jan 10, 1937

assistance of two detectives from Tientsin in trying to solve the mystery, these include a Russian detective and a detective from the British municipal police in Tientsin.

A Chinese police official interviewed today indicated that the police were no nearer a solution and remarked that the crime was a very complicated one.

The victim's father, Edward Werner, was more forthcoming to a Reuters reporter:

Mr. Werner Interviewed

Peiping, January 11, Reuter - Interviewed by a reporter of this paper yesterday Mr E. T. C. Werner admitted that the body of the young foreign girl found in the ditch along the city wall between the Hata Men and the German cemetery was that of his daughter, Pamela. The face was mutilated beyond identification but the clothing on the body was exactly the same as his daughter wore in her lifetime.

Continuing, Mr. Werner said that although Peiping was a big city with a large population, the number of foreigners was small and the fact that no one else had come forward to claim the body to the foreign girl during the last two days whilst his daughter was missing, was a strong presumption of the dead girl being his own daughter.

Mr. Werner further said that he had received a preliminary report of the autopsy performed by the P.U.M.C. on the body of his daughter and that further investigations were going on. He would not be able to take delivery of the body during the next few days. He intended to bury the body in the British Cemetery outside the Hsichih Men beside his wife.

Mr. Werner also said that Captain Han Shih-ching,

Chief of the police station on Morrison Street, had come
to see him and ask about her daily movements prior to
that fateful afternoon on Thursday, and also about her
correspondence and friends.

Captain Han was at the house when the reporter called.
Interviewed, Captain Han said that the case was extremely
complicated but so far no important clues had been found.

According to another report Chinese detectives working
on the case have secured several clues and the murder
mystery is expected to be cleared up in a few days. - Shih
Chieh Jih Pau.

The next day brought more news reports with a heady mix
of facts and hearsay, including a Reuters dispatch which said:
"Rumours are plentiful, including one that a ricksha man has
been arrested in connexion with the crime. This however is not
confirmed in official circles."

Dogs, motor cars, houses and rickshaws. Rumours were
indeed plentiful. The difficulty, then as now, was how to sift
substance from speculation.

George Gorman, Liverpool-born and Irish by descent, was
editor of the English-language cultural magazine *Caravan*, and
well-placed to offer the Peking community a unique perspective.
He knew the Werners personally and, indeed, *Caravan* had
included a profile of E.T.C. Werner just the previous month.
Pamela had, in fact, visited the Gormans the day before she died.
Gorman used this closeness to full advantage and published an
exhaustive report in the February edition, the text of which is
reproduced below. It provides a valuable insight into the crime
from a contemporary source.

The Pamela Werner Case

Peking Wall Mystery Baffles Foreign and Chinese Detectives

Slim, fairhaired, grey-eyed, gentle English schoolgirl, Pamela Werner, was murdered in Peking on January 7th under horrifying circumstances. As the magazine goes to press three weeks later the crime is no nearer solution than it was when the corpse was discovered in the shadow of the Tartar Wall, although every resource and ingenuity of Chinese and British detectives, together with the wholehearted cooperation of the native and foreign community has been employed in a determined effort to solve the mystery and apprehend the slayer.

Here are the facts:

Pamela Werner, the adopted daughter of Mr. E.T.C. Werner, notable British scholar and sinologue, a former consul in His Britannic Majesty's service, was home from Tientsin Grammar School, having just completed her course there, taking the Cambridge final examination with honors, and parting from old school friends with fond farewells. She was returning home permanently. She had come in time for Christmas and New Year holidays.

Pamela resided with her foster father, in the East City of Peking, about half a mile from the Legation Quarter. Although close to her twentieth birthday (January 26th), she looked no more than fifteen. She was a slip of a girl about five feet four in height, with yellow-brown hair brushed back from a broad

E.T.C. Werner in January 1937

9

brow to a natural wavy mass behind very small ears. Her manner was reserved, shy; but she had a self-contained way with her, possibly the result of having no women in her household during the formative years of her youth. For her foster mother died in 1923. And Mr. Werner lived alone with her and two Chinese servants. Previously Pamela had attended the White Franciscan convent in Peking, but in order to complete higher studies her father sent her to Tientsin two years ago. During the school term she resided with a missionary family where she was beloved for her gentle ways. She took her vacations with her father in Peking, and in the summer months went with him to the seaside resort of Peitaiho.

During the week previous to her death she came home to Peking and with her father made one or two social calls on families who had known the Werners for several years. She brought her bicycle and skates with her, using the 'wheel' rather than the rickshaw in going about the old city she knew so well. She accepted the advice of friends and joined the French club skating rink on January 6th, the day before her death. The French club is an ice rink set up under a p'eng or matshed for use of the French Embassy Guard, whose barracks are immediately opposite the club in a quiet street of the safe Legation Quarter. At the request of a large number of foreign families of various nationalities the guard commandant permits the general use of the rink to ticket holders, a convenience much appreciated.

SEEN FOR THE LAST TIME

On the Wednesday of her first visit to the rink to buy a membership ticket and enjoy her first skate, she left her bicycle at the home of friends in the Quarter, about five hundred yards from the rink. When she returned for it about seven o'clock she said she was delighted to have joined the club because she had met an old school friend and had been invited to tea with her the following day. Moreover, she said it would no longer be necessary to leave her bicycle at the house, presumably because she would use her friend's nearby house for garage purposes in future.

Caravan magazine

The following afternoon (Thursday), her last day on earth, she told her father of her intention to take tea with her girl friend. He left the house for a walk between three and four o'clock in the afternoon. Pamela was then writing a letter to some friend, evidently outside of Peking, because the k'aimendi (gatekeeper) remembered posting it, and the envelope carried a five cent stamp.

Mr. Werner never saw his daughter again. The girl, it subsequently developed in testimony to detectives, went to her friend's house for tea, and when that little ceremony was over Pamela cycled away to the rink where she was seen by several persons. The exact hour of her departure has not been determined, but the general opinion is that she went away on her bike, carrying her skates, about 7.30 p.m. It was pitch dark at the time. There was no moon.

Miss Werner's homeward way would lie by two routes, parallel streets leading East from Hataman street near the famous Hatamen Tower. Whether she went down the larger

street or hutung (to use the Chinese name) is not verified.
But she was found dead on one of them the following
morning, brutally murdered, disfigured and horribly
mutilated. Subsequent medical testimony said she had been
sexually assaulted by a man.

The hutung where the body was found runs
immediately north of the Tartar Wall which separates the
Chinese City from the Tartar City. It is like a long, bleak
tunnel, with the wall rising sixty feet high on one side, and
the lower walls of a Chinese school on the other. That lane
is one of the loneliest in the city; there are no residences or
shops except at the west end where it joins on to Hatamen
Street, and the lower end where it sweeps around the
German cemetery. The place is ghost-haunted according to
Chinese legend. It is a paved hutung, with no sidewalks, of
course, as is the way with all but the main thoroughfares.
The way is bumpy for cars, rickshaws and cycles. On its
south side the roadway dips into a depression used for
dumping refuse, and it was in this hollow, beyond hailing
distance from the nearest residence or patrol, little Pamela's
body was found.

FIRST TO SEE BODY

At dinner time that night Pamela had not appeared to
join her father; he presumed she was skating late with her
school friend. When she failed to turn up by nine o'clock
Mr. Werner made a tour of the neighbourhood. He sent a
servant to inquire at the skating rink. Though uneasy, he
was not alarmed, assuming Pamela had remained with the
other family. He retired late that night and next morning
hurried off to the home of Mr. W.P. Thomas, the Secretary
of the Legation Quarter Commission under whose
supervision come the Quarter police. Having reported the

disappearance he proceeded home. Down that bumpy hutung he made his way until he noticed a little knot of Chinese standing in the depression alongside the wall.

"Is it a Chinese case?" he asked a native policeman whom he knew.

The policeman turned away and motioned with his arm towards the group of onlookers. Mr. Werner made his way through the ring and saw the body of a girl whom he could recognize only by the clothing and hair. It was his adopted daughter. The shock to Mr. Werner (aged 73) was enough to send him reeling, and he staggered away to his home, hardly knowing what to do. Soon there arrived on scene Mr. W.P. Thomas, Mr. Fitzmaurice the British Consul and Mr. Pearson the British Embassy constable and business manager. Here is what they saw:

Pamela was lying among the stones and debris, her head to the West. She was almost completely disrobed. She was wearing her shoes and stockings, knickers and brassiere. Nothing else. Near by were some of her other garments, shirt and chemise. In fact the chemise was under her body.

Overcoat and sweater were missing, but there is some doubt about the description of these because Mr. Werner was not familiar with clothing brought up from Tientsin. Bicycle and skates were not there. But she was wearing her wrist watch. Whether it had stopped was not divulged by investigators.

HEART TAKEN AWAY

When the authorities examined closer they discovered the terrible nature of the injuries. Her face was almost unrecognisable. Most of the surface flesh had been scraped, gnawed or cut away. Some heavy cleaver, knife or axe had been used in a terrible orgy of mutilation. There were deep cuts or slashes in the upper part of the cadaver. The lower trunk had been cut open. Her heart was missing. Several bones had been smashed through. Her head had been terribly bashed and it is believed she may have been knocked unconscious or killed outright before she was otherwise attacked.

Mr. Pearson obtained a temporary coffin from a Chinese undertaker, in which he placed the body and the clothing. Obviously it would have been too much to expect Mr. Werner to have the constant reminder of his affliction before him and instead of housing the box in his home he placed it in a Chinese temple nearby, with a Chinese guard to keep watch. Mr. W.P. Thomas then arranged to have it removed to the P.U.M.C. (Rockefeller) hospital, the most modern hospital and medical college in Asia, and with few peers in the world. At the request of the British authorities the pathologists began the post mortem examination for the coroner. Mr. Fitzmaurice, as consul, was the coroner.

The hue and cry was sounded for the murderer. The case aroused universal horror and determination to find the perpetrator. First investigations were undertaken by Mr. Thomas and Colonel Han, chief detective of the Morrison Street police station, who has spent his life chasing criminals. Mr. Thomas questioned Mr. Werner about the movements of his daughter and the Chinese chief laid down the routine lines before launching the particular inquiry, that is he sent word to all stations about the missing bicycle and skates. He caused inquiries to be made along the route the girl may have taken from the skating rink to the lane of death. Then in company with Mr. Thomas, a Russian detective from Tientsin and another member of his Chinese staff, he called at Mr. Werner's that night.

CORRESPONDENCE SEEN

A foreign friend who had called to offer Mr. Werner the hospitality of his home as some escape from the depressing environment, found the little group standing in the Werner yard. The gatekeeper was with them. It was explained to the visitor that Mr. Werner had retired, locking the door of the house behind him as was the custom. Like other native houses the Werner residence consists of a main dwelling divided into several rooms, two other buildings for servants, the whole enclosed by a wall. A small garden plot is in front of the house. A verandah leads along the front, on which the various windows give out.

It was decided that Mr. Werner should be roused; there was some fear that anything might have happened to him, aged and overcome with grief. But he responded with a tap on the window. After declining to move to his friend's house he offered to let the detectives look around Pamela's bedroom; especially to discover if there was anything in her correspondence to offer a clue.

Pamela had slept in a small room on a camp bed, comfortably made up adjoining her father's bedroom. There was no other entrance to it, as the windows opened onto a trunk room which had outside windows. And there were two windows opening directly to the compound. The room was just as would be expected as a temporary but comfortable place for a short sojourn. Mr. Werner explained that the furniture had been partially disposed of many months before in preparation for the sell-up when he and his daughter would say farewell to China. This would be as soon as some literary work, requiring researches on the ground, was completed. Nothing of clue interest was found in Pamela's room; no light could be thrown on the crime by the bereaved father. In a short while Mr. Werner was able to retire to his saddened room.

By this time the news of the crime had spread like a cotton fire throughout the city and was already in the London papers. That evening several residents of Peking heard their first reports on the mystery by radio from England. Speculation ran wild with the range of imagination and conjecture, but the police were unable to find evidence pointing to the killer. Coincidental with the intense inquiry in Peking were investigations in Tientsin where Pamela had spent two school years. Nothing cogent was discovered there as far as the authorities would reveal. They had in charge of the hunt Mr. R.H. Dennis, Chief of British Municipal Police and Mr. R. Botham, Detective Inspector. On Sunday the latter was transferred to Peking to assist the Chinese Police, on whom rests the onus of finding the murderer. Both are old "graduates" of Scotland Yard. Assisting them were Russian agents.

On the Monday the inquest opened with formal identification of the clothing by Mr. Werner, and his story of the grim discovery. Inasmuch as the autopsy was not complete the inquest was postponed. Interest centred about the findings of the pathologists. Their work was strictly confidential. Nothing was permitted to reach the public nor the Press. Owing to the fearful conditions of the body the doctors had a difficult task in verifying the direct cause of death, the probable hour of the fatal blow, whether the criminal assault had occurred before or after death (if there had been such an assault); the purpose of the mutilations; traces of poisoning if any; the state of the girl's health; anything and everything of a physiological nature bearing on the crime and likely to assist in a solution of the case. Photographs were taken too, but to the regret of the detectives none had been made as the body lay alongside the road.

SCOTLAND YARD METHODS

Despite the reticence of the hospital people odds and ends of information, or conjectures, managed to leak out. One of these findings was that Pamela had been violated, traces having been found. Another that a blunt instrument had been used to batter her head. A third that the ghastly operations had been performed with a cleaver or heavy knife by a person having some anatomical knowledge. Until the written findings of the pathologists are available (if the coroner decides to let them be known) these statements cannot be verified, but from the confidences of competent people who saw the body before it entered the hospital items two and three certainly are correct, although the surgical knowledge was not observed.

The hunt was speeded up with the arrival of Inspector Botham and the periodical visits of Chief Dennis. Scotland Yard methods were employed; the inquiry settled down in the most painstaking examination of everything and everybody likely to have knowledge or valuable opinions. An appeal was issued in the foreign and Chinese newspapers, asking that anybody with the merest thread of data should make a call on the foreign inspector. The radio was used for the same end. Several callers interviewed the police at the station on Wang Fu Ching Ta Chieh (Morrison Street), near the Legation Quarter, which Inspector Botham made his headquarters.

A thrill of expectation ran through Peking on the Wednesday, one week following the murder, when a

Early 20th century image of the Tartar wall. A view looking east, from the Hataman Gate. Pamela's body was found to the left and half way to the distant tower

foreigner was detained in the police investigation. How the police came to link an elderly foreigner, who had been out of regular and profitable employment for a long time, with the Werner case is not known. But they searched his residence and found bloodstained boots, a sheath knife with blood marks on the handle and a piece of rag with a similar discoloration. At first the man refused to give any information about himself or the ominous marks, but after two days under observation he volunteered a statement that the marks on the boots may have been made in cutting liver for his cat; the rag had been used to wipe a jagged razor which had cut his face. Nothing was said about the knife marks. At any rate it was deemed that the man could not legally be held further and he was set free.

FRIENDSHIPS FOLLOWED

Numerous other clues were followed up. One local paper went as far as to say that the inquiry would be carried among "society stars" who had social intercourse with Pamela Werner, but as the girl was known to be out of touch with local "society", because of youth and other interests, the suggestion was not taken seriously.

After the release of the first and only man under scrutiny the police and public came slowly to the realization that there was the dreaded possibility of the case passing into the fog of unsolved mysteries. This did

not abate the chase, but it did go to show that there was
little or nothing to chase after. No encouraging beginning
could be addressed. There were no clues or helpful signs.
Nevertheless hope was not abandoned nor effort relaxed.
Well established lines of inquiry were followed, such as
old friendships of the dead girl. Everyone who had seen
her before the fateful evening was canvassed; every effort
was made to discover who had been with or near her in the
skating rink, who had seen her leave, who had noticed her
along the route. If these efforts did not yield results, at least
they satisfied the authorities and the public that no stone
was left unturned in an effort to show, not only what might
lead to the murderer, but to reassure a nervous population
of Peking that proper safeguards were applied. This is an
appropriate place and time to mention that Peking long
has held the enviable record as the safest city in the world.
Violence is almost unheard of; robbers a matter of surprise
and swift and severe punishment. The native police
have such a long record of efficiency that, when the new
national capital was established at Nanking, a hundred of
the local force were drafted there to form a nucleus of the
safety corps. Their equal could not be found in China. It
is a matter of common knowledge that a foreigner could
go anywhere in the city at any time of night, unattended,
in any condition (this applies to the occasional convivial
wayfarer) without fear of attack or robbery. The rickshaw
pullers, poor to the edge of direst distress, have a name for
kindness, consideration and dependability almost beyond
belief. For the most modest payment they undertake
incredible labors cheerfully and reliably. Mothers entrust
children to their care without the slightest fear; women use
the tireless and patient pullers in the loneliest and darkest

lane in the fullest trust, for the working rickshawman is
in a class by himself. He is also the server par excellence.
Nothing escapes his notice, and when and if the Werner
crime is solved it would surprise none that the tip will
come from a class of see-all know-all.

SOME OF THE THEORIES

Considering the facts as they are known here are the
principal theories reached:

1. Pamela was waylaid by some person made desperate
   by poverty who killed the girl to quieten her.
2. Attacked by a sadist.
3. Slain and mutilated in revenge.
4. Followed along the route from the skating rink and
   attacked by more than one person.
5. Trapped by an insane person.
6. Invited by someone she knew to visit a house where
   the deed was done.
7. Victim of a sex ritual.

Take these in order:

Waylaid - The night was dark and cold, with a bitter
wind blowing. The way was dark and deserted. Even
the poorest of the poor could not expect to find anything
or anybody there. An ordinary murderer would not
commit the horrible excesses. Her wrist watch was on
her arm. Skates and overcoat and bicycle are difficult
to dispose of. Chinese in the most abject poverty would
not do this work. How would this theory account for the
rape? But the mutilations must have taken a considerable
time. Supporters of this theory contend much of the
disfigurement was the result of scavenger dogs and rats
in this district dump. Dogs could not break the bones nor
remove the heart.

Attacked by a sadist - Appearances are strongly in
this direction. The horrible appetite of the lunatic who
hurts for pleasure might have been indulged. Medical and
police history is replete with cases of this kind, from the
Stuttgart murderer who took a score of lives to a notorious
Frenchman back in the days of Joan of Arc who tortured
and killed hundreds of people and was himself hanged. But
even sadists do not lurk in freezing places on the off chance
of finding a victim. Of course he might have known that
Pamela was due to take that way home, (her usual course)
which narrows the field of inquiry for the police. But the
ghoulish orgy of a sadist could not well be carried out in
almost total darkness, as the street is hardly lighted at all.
The sadist theory may well be true, but the terrible work
was not done on the spot.

Revenge motive - Werner had no enemies, and it
is unthinkable that a child could incite such anger. If it
were revenge there might have been such provocation as
Pamela's rejection of previous suit. Vengeance would stop
short with the deed, for wild hatred has its quick descents
and rarely continues after the fatal blow. revenge may or
may not provoke sexual assault, but consider the conditions
of darkness, wind and temperature - nearly zero. Why,
in this theoretical case, would there be the systematic
disfigurement and the partial dismemberment? The theory
does not hang together. But former servants and associates
have been interrogated.

Trapped by a lunatic - Too much preparation is shown.
Lunatics do not go to a spot with a special purpose. Insane
he may have been, but not of the wild category. Would it
be reasonable to expect that a lunatic would combine in
his character the lustfulness and anatomical knowledge,

plus the theft impulse? It may be ruled out that wandering beggars early the next morning found the now missing articles alongside the corpse and carried them off. Chinese beggars have enough sense to flee the presence of a foreign body without stopping to take valuables which might lead to their arrest.

Killed in a House - This is the theory most generally held. Here is the process of reconstruction: At the rink, on the street afterwards, or by previous arrangement Pamela met someone she had known before, having considerable trust in him, certainly no fear, she accepted an invitation to drop into his house or some other place before going home. There she was assaulted. In the struggle Pamela may have been badly hurt; perhaps an arm broken, maybe knocked out altogether. If hurt the man feared exposure, as Pamela could identify him; he killed her to avoid this. Or the fatal blow already had been administered, although without any intent to commit murder. At any rate there was the man with a girl's body on his hands. What would he do?

He could not leave it in the house. A body is a difficult thing to transport, because of the tell-tale shape. He may have decided to dismember the body and carry away the parts. Or reduce it to a size for packing in a trunk. This might account for a start made on a disposal of the internal organs, so easy to make away with down a drain. The murderer quickly realized that the task was too much for him and the best thing to do was rush the corpse out and dispose of it in a remote place. Before doing so he had badly mutilated the body; he might have conceived the idea of making it wholly unrecognizable thinking that if she were found and identified he might be embroiled because someone knew of the friendship or had seen them together that night.

Here again we have an explanation for the missing property. Probably it is still where she took it. Certainly it is feasible that a crime of the kind, with its attendant operations, should have been undertaken indoors.

But how could he get the body to the lane? Had a rickshawman been used there would have been exposure ere this. What about an owner-driver of an automobile? He could have sent his servant on an errand, or, as it sometimes happens, a servant goes home in the evenings. The owner-driver could spirit the body from the house with another person knowing the search for an owner-driver whose servant goes back home at night, and who knows the particular neighbourhood — for who else would be aware of unless they were carrying a cadaver to the German cemetery a few yards away? Such a man would necessarily be young and strong and have known the girl. Here we limit the field still further.

Victim of a sex ritual - Some years ago there were reports of queer orgies in the west city somewhere near the Bell Tower where several men of perverted appetites gathered at exposure parties, and where young girls were taken. The case became known, possibly because one of the "guests" talked, as a foreigner is reported to have left the city in a hurry as a consequence. Perhaps the others remained and still are in Peking. The possibility of the girl having been taken to such a place by these insensates is not to be left out of police reckoning.

CHINESE WILL FIND TRUTH

There are one or two things to consider. One of importance is that the doctors are said to have found traces of a Chinese meal in the stomach, or in the cavity where the stomach was. This would bear out the theory of a visit to a house, as she had no Chinese food at the afternoon tea. Here is overwhelming testimony that the girl went somewhere after leaving the rink. The condition of the flesh was such as to discount the theory of attack by dogs. The disfigurement was confined to certain parts of the body. Animals would have no preferences. Some of her clothing had been removed. Her chemise was found underneath her body, the skirt alongside. Who would drag these off in the cold, dark and wind?

If murder will "out" anywhere in the world the conditions are all in favor of such a course in Peking. For nothing, absolutely nothing can be hidden from Chinese eyes. It is idiomatic that the Chinese servant knows the whole story of his master, his habits, his bank account, his every movement. Intense curiosity is coupled to analytical observation of a high degree in the Chinese servant, and all Chinese for that matter. Somebody knows something about the murder, apart from the murderer himself. If a Chinese has evidence, how can he be tapped? The Chinese hold strongly to the policy of "mind your own business." It is a ruling passion. Sometimes they can be lured or bribed from this position, but not always. Already a reward has been offered for information, but without success. Here is the way a servant or coolie class Chinese looks at the case:

"If I go the police I shall be examined. At any rate I shall be held a long time. My affairs may suffer. Better to say nothing. Then no trouble."

No amount of pressure will break down this wall of reserve. But the Chinese police have quiet ways of their own, even if it takes months of patience to reach an objective. The push and energy and scientific approach

24

may achieve results in the West, but the East applies its own slow and inscrutable way. Some Chinese may take a long time to ponder whatever he knows about the case, and then, impelled by that innate sense of justice, and remembering the helplessness of the girl victim, he will tell all. In this case, then, the thing to do is make furious haste in a slow Oriental way, trusting to the Chinese system to produce the right clue in its own conception of time.[4]

Gorman knew his readers extremely well. His article and writing style would have enthralled the large number of China's foreign community who had suddenly become avid armchair detectives. Gorman's comprehensive summary of the murder is important because it appeared so soon after the crime and was written by someone so close to the people and events. It transpires that the "home of friends" where Gorman said Pamela had left her bicycle the day before her death was in fact the Gorman family home, and the friend who called on Werner to offer him his hospitality on the evening after the body's discovery was almost certainly Gorman himself.

Gorman and his wife had two children, a girl and a boy, both teenagers and several years junior to Pamela. Pamela looked young for her age, and there appears to have been an element of social immaturity about her also, or that of a late-developer as, aged nearly twenty, her final examinations had been a long time in the completing.

Gorman was actually wrong about Pamela having attended Tientsin Grammar School for only two years: she had been a pupil there for at least the previous four,[5] during which time

4 "Peking Wall Mystery Baffles Foreign and Chinese Detectives", *Caravan* magazine, February 1937.
5 E.T.C. Werner, *Memorigrams*, (1940), p144.

she boarded with several missionary families, the last being the Mackenzies, a Canadian family.[6]

Hugh and Agnes Mackenzie were Canadian missionaries and members of the Union Church and had been in China for many years. Both were popular and respected local figures in Tientsin. They lived in the Mission House, an impressive ivy-clad dwelling in the British concession and within easy walking distance of the grammar school which their children attended. Set in an acre of garden, the residence could comfortably accommodate their seven children, up to seven servants, and a constant stream of guests.

The friendly open-house atmosphere of the Mackenzie home, along with the adventure playground garden and sense of family were all in stark contrast to Pamela's life with her reserved and older adopted father in Peking. The Mackenzie children remembered Pamela as a quiet, well-behaved young woman who was petite and attractive. Pamela fitted in well in the Mission House and was treated as one of the family. Provided with a room of her own, she otherwise shared most other aspects of the Mackenzies' home life, including walking the youngest daughter to the British-run Tientsin Grammar School, affectionately known as the "TGS".[7]

"Well behaved and charming" was how Mr. and Mrs. Mackenzie described Pamela.[8] Indeed, the whole Mackenzie family was fond of her, and also somewhat sorry for her. The children sensed that until coming to live with them, she had led a lonely existence and was somehow bravely coping with an inner sadness. They also had the impression that, although too polite to say, she did not get on well with her adoptive father, who they

6 "Werner Murder Unsolved", *Caravan* magazine, March 1937
7 Conversations by the author with Findlay Mackenzie and Louise McLean (children of Hugh & Agnes Mackenzie), 2014.
8 "British Consulate Holds Inquest on Pamela Werner", *Peiping Chronicle*, January 10, 1937.

understood to be difficult.[9] Pamela's adoptive mother died when she was a small child and E.T.C. Werner was her only remaining family.

Pamela appears never to have travelled outside China. Her adoption by the Werners from an orphanage as an infant might have been an informal one as there is no record or mention of how it came about. Details of her birth are also unknown, although it was probably local to

Hugh & Agnes Mackenzie.
(Courtesy of the Mackenzie family)

Peking. Her real parents may have been poor White Russian exiles and she may also have been illegitimate. If so, this last would have been an additional cause for silence on the subject. Pamela's given middle names were Greenhalgh Chalmers, after an uncle of her adoptive father.[10]

Life was very different for Pamela with the affable Mackenzies in Tientsin. The eldest daughter Florence had married

The Mission House in Tientsin where
Pamela boarded.
(Courtesy of the Mackenzie family)

the Scottish athlete Eric Liddell, who won gold in the 400-metre

---

9 Conversations by the author with Findlay Mackenzie and Louise McLean (children of Hugh & Agnes Mackenzie), 2014.
10 E.T.C. Werner, *Memorigrams*, (1940), p143.

race at the 1924 Paris Olympics. Liddell then became a mission-ary, working in China, and was for many an inspiring character. Living with the Mackenzies, Pamela would have known both the Liddells well.[11] And in Tientsin, Pamela, unsurprisingly, also had boyfriends, often a key subject in this kind of murder.

The value of Gorman's lengthy *Caravan* piece is increased all the more by the absence of surviving police records, either Brit-ish or Chinese. No exhibits or photographs appear to have sur-vived. Also missing are the case records of the British coroner's court held in Peking. All were possibly lost or destroyed during World War II, or later weeded by government clerks in accor-dance with a Whitehall policy of reducing old paperwork (only a minority of Foreign Office documents are preserved in the UK National Archives).

Caravan's version of events is corroborated by *The Peiping Chronicle* which published daily updates on the actions of the police and the coroner's court. The newspaper confirms that Pa-mela's body was found on the morning of Friday, January 8, with the British Consul for Peking, Nicholas Fitzmaurice, opening an inquest into the death the following day.

During the brief initial hearing on Saturday afternoon, the only witness to give evidence was the victim's father. Werner could only provide a partial identification, by recognising the victim's torn skirt, her wristwatch and an artificial flower she wore. No medical evidence was given.

Werner also reported to the court that Pamela had arrived from Tientsin on December 26. Tientsin served as a coastal port for Peking, the two cities being separated by a 120-kilometre train journey. According to Werner, Pamela had been a brilliant pupil and was the first at the grammar school to be awarded the

....

11 Conversations by the author with Findlay Mackenzie and Louise McLean (children of Hugh & Agnes Mackenzie), 2014.

Jubilee Scholarship for entrance to a British university.

Referring to possible routes home from the rink, Werner stated that Pamela did not use the *hutungs* – alleys – as she did not know them well. He also revealed that Pamela had only visited Peking once since his recent move to number 1, Kuei-chia-chang close to the Tartar Wall, and that she had only been on the road where her body was found twice before on her own. All of which suggests that Pamela was probably unfamiliar with the area.

Werner also explained that he was sure that Pamela had no boyfriends in Peking, and that two (un-named) ladies had been taking her out and introducing her to local society. Werner said that he had intended returning to England with Pamela at some stage that year after he had completed his research on the second volume of his book, *A Social History of China*.[12]

No boyfriends in Peking, perhaps. But what of elsewhere?

After the preliminary details on January 9, Fitzmaurice heard evidence from witnesses at several further public hearings at the British Embassy over the following weeks. *The Peiping Chronicle* and *The North-China Herald* (published in Shanghai) reported on them all.

The first court witness, the discoverer of the body, was an elderly unemployed Chinese called Chang Pao-hsien who had been out walking with his pet caged bird under the Wall just after 8am when he saw two unknown rickshaw coolies pointing to a man looking into the ditch. The three of them approached and saw the near-naked body of what appeared to be a foreign woman. He immediately reported the find to a policeman at the Number 19 police post nearby.

Police corporal Kao Tao-hung who had attended the scene gave evidence and described how he had directed another of-

---

12 "British Consulate Holds Inquest on Pamela Werner", *Peiping Chronicle*, January 10, 1937.

ficer to guard the body while he went for help. Kao said he saw a pair of shoes some five feet away, with a handkerchief inside one of them. He also noticed a belt and a foreign garment. He had not gone into the ditch with the body.

Werner was called again, briefly. On being asked if he knew of any suspects, he stated that he had "no suspicions".

Werner's cook, Keh Ying, forty-six years of age, said that on January 7, Mr Werner had macaroni for tiffin (lunch). Ying stated that he had left the home at 3 o'clock. On doing so he had asked Pamela if she wanted any food purchased, as she usually asked him to buy various Chinese sweetmeats. She said no as she was going out herself at 4 o'clock. She added that she would be back for dinner at 7.30 pm and requested meatballs and rice.

At half past ten that night, Keh Ying visited the rink on the instructions of a worried Werner. He found the rink closed and only sweepers cleaning the ice. A staff member had informed him that there had been more than two-hundred people skating there that evening. The cook returned and reported this to Werner. Keh Ying said he had not taken the wall road to and from the rink because it was unlit.

Werner's gatekeeper, Yen Ping, aged sixty-four, was next to give evidence. He reported that the Werners had eaten tiffin together at about 1pm. Pamela left home at about 3.30 - 4pm without speaking to him. Her father, who had left the house beforehand, returned from his walk at 5 o'clock. About an hour later, Werner asked Yen if Pamela had returned. She had not. The gatekeeper recalled his employer then becoming more and more anxious and at about 11 pm going out with a lamp to meet her. At midnight, Werner had returned alone stating that if his daughter had stayed at a friend's house then she ought to have sent him a note. Yen Ping had not left his post between noon and

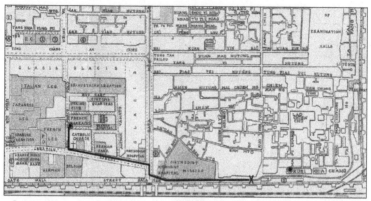

Contemporary map showing Pamela's route home. The rink was located, left, near the French Legation. Her home, in Kuei Chia Ch'ang, to the right. X marks where her body was found. (Poplar Island Press map of Peking)

midnight.[13]

Then, an enigma: Chao Hsi-meng, a thirty-four-year-old secretary at the Chinese YMCA on Hatamen Street was called to give evidence. On January 6 or 7, at about 3 or 4 o'clock in the afternoon, he remembered a foreign girl calling alone at the desk and making an enquiry about a room. She took with her a copy of the hotel regulations. Some ten days later, Colonel Han showed him a photograph of the girl, whom he recognised. When shown a group photograph in the court, the witness pointed to Pamela.

Constable T. Pearson of the British Embassy said that he learned of the murder at 2.15 pm. He then attended the scene with Fitzmaurice and Han and saw the body, which the Chinese police had covered with a mat held down by four stones. Pearson sent for a coffin and, with the help of some Chinese, placed the body inside, including the clothes found nearby. The coffin was then stored temporarily in a nearby temple before being transported to the Peking Union Medical College, known as the PUMC. Pearson later received all these items of property back from the PUMC, and

13 "Many Witnesses Called at Inquest on Miss Werner," *Peiping Chronicle*, January 30, 1937, and "Peiping Tragedy Investigated," *North-China Herald*, February 10, 1937.

Chinese newspaper Ta Kung Pao, *January 10 report: no Chinese involved*

additionally from Han, one pair of shoes, one pair of silk stockings, a comb, a handkerchief and a wristwatch. He did not know who had removed the wristwatch from the body.

The next witness, fifteen-year-old Ethel Gurevitch, had seen Pamela at the French rink on January 6. Old acquaintances, they skated together and Ethel invited Pamela to come for tea at her home the next day at 5pm. On January 7, Ethel arrived on time at the agreed location, a corner of the Wagon-Lits Hotel. She had to wait a few minutes for Pamela, who arrived saying that she had already been at the meeting point earlier, but she did not say where she had been in the intervening period.

The pair then had tea at Ethel's home – bread and butter and cake – but Pamela ate very little, stating that she was not hungry. During their conversation, Pamela mentioned that she had gone to the dentist that morning and had written letters in the afternoon. Pamela also said that her boyfriend was coming to Peking for a few days but did not say where he was going to stay. They went to the rink at about 6pm. They were together throughout except for a few minutes when Pamela spoke with another girl. At 7.30pm, having agreed to meet again the following day, Pamela left, saying that she was going home. When Ethel asked whether it was all right to go home on her bicycle in the dark,

Pamela replied: Yes, nothing can happen to me here in Peking. Ethel recalled seeing that she had her skates with her when she left, though she was unsure about the bicycle, which Pamela had parked earlier inside the rink compound. While skating, Pamela had complained of being lonely and having no friends.

Lilian Marinovski, age eighteen, skated a few circuits of the rink with Pamela, telling her of her own studies. Later, noticing Pamela, skates over her shoulder, leaving with her bicycle, Lilian stopped skating for a moment and asked her whether she was afraid of cycling home in the dark. Pamela replied that it did not matter, she always went by herself. Pamela left alone.

The photographer Fan Yun-chi gave evidence that the mat had been removed so that he could photograph the body at the scene. This statement is at variance with the Gorman article which complained that no photos of the body *in situ* had been taken.[14]

On February 1, Consul Fitzmaurice resumed the inquest to receive medical evidence from the autopsy. Initially, at least, this was held *in camera*, probably owing to the gruesome nature of the injuries, but this stipulation appears to have been soon dropped as *The Peiping Chronicle* reported the evidence in some detail on February 6:

Dr. Chang-hsiang Hu testifies

Dr. Chang-hsiang Hu, Professor of Pathology at the PUMC, who performed the autopsy, said that there was an injury to the left eye that was probably inflicted after death. Injuries to the left upper and lower right eyelids had caused haemorrhage, which indicated that they were inflicted before death. The head had been injured by some kind of blunt instrument. He could not say definitely what kind of instru-

14 "Many Witnesses Called at Inquest on Miss Werner", *Peiping Chronicle*, January 30, 1937.

ment but probably a blunt piece of wood or by a stone if the stone had a very smooth surface. The injury to the head could have been caused during a struggle.

In reply to a question witness said the injury was also consistent with a person falling on his head and sustaining an injury to the skull.

Body Mutilated

The body had been mutilated and these mutilations could have been done with a knife the blade of which was four inches long or longer. The nature of the wounds suggested that they were done with a pointed flat sharp instrument, probably with a double edge or at least one which was sharp on one side and the other thin but not a cutting edge.

There was an injury to the right shoulder, which had been done with one or possibly two instruments, one a knife, because the muscles were severed cleanly, and two, a blunt instrument because the fracture at the end of the humerus was done by a rather heavy instrument. This injury witness thought was inflicted after death, because there was no extensive haemorrhage round the wound in the tissue.

In reply to questions witness said that he thought it could not have been done by physical force alone: it must have been done with an instrument.

Referring to the mutilations on the front part of the body witness said the general nature of the cutting suggested that the flesh had been taken away in a single piece but he could not be positive. Six ribs on either side had been broken and all were broken outwards. To have done this pressure must have been applied from inside. He could make no suggestion as how this had been done.

These mutilations could have been effected by a surgeon's scalpel or by an amputation knife. The abdomen had two clean slits made through the diaphragm and the internal organs were missing. He believed that the missing organs had been removed through the slits. Dogs could not have done this. The clearness of the diaphragm and the abdominal cavity was not consistent with interference with by dogs. He thought it was done manually. There were no signs of animal teeth.

The stomach was found complete but not attached.

The nature of the wounds found on the face suggested that they were done by a flat instrument, possibly with a double edge.

Asked what injuries were received before death, witness replied that the haemorrhage of the brain occurred before death. There were also minor scratches which could have occurred before death. He could not say how long deceased lived after the blow on the head, which caused the haemorrhage of the brain but it was a blow which could have caused death within a few minutes.

Murderer Familiar with Use of Knife

Replying to questions witness said that the manner in which the body was mutilated suggested that it was done by someone more or less familiar with the use of a knife and more of less familiar with anatomy. All the mutilations could have been done by an experienced person in about half an hour, but by another person in from one to two hours.

Asked whether the mutilations could have been done in the open or must have been done inside a building with the aid of a light witness said he was afraid he could not answer that. Questioned further he said that he thought they could have been done on the spot where the body was found. If it was done outside in the dark witness thought it must have been done by a more or less expert person, a butcher or a hunter.

Questioned further about the possibility of dogs having interfered with the body, witness said that the chest wall and neck suggested that dogs might have devoured some parts but he admitted that it was possible that dogs had not touched the body.

Witness could not give an idea how long after death the mutilation took place, he said. He thought the chest was first mutilated, which would have drained off much blood from the abdomen, and then the abdomen was cut. This would account for the lack of blood in the abdominal cavity. There was no evidence of clotting of blood in the blood vessels, which he thought indicated that mutilation took place after death. He added that clotting sometimes did not take place for some hours.

He thought it must have been mutilated within five or six hours of death. He could not say how long before the finding of the body death had taken place as it had been left in a cold place and was in a good state of preservation. It was quite possible that mutilation had taken place immediately after death.

Witness found no trace of dental work on deceased's teeth. She had well-preserved clean teeth. There were 26 present, the usual number for a person of her age being 28 to 32. Three were missing. The gums had healed and he could not say when the extractions had taken place.

Struggle Before Death

Witness found on the body evidence of a struggle before death.

Recalled later, witness thought half a dozen blows were

struck on the head. This he judged from the distribution of the haemorrhage.

He expressed the opinion that the person responsible for the mutilations had first had the intention of dismembering the whole body but had changed his mind. His reasons for this opinion were the removal of the chest organs, the drainage of the blood from the abdomen and lower limbs, and the almost complete severance of the right arm.

The cause of death was a fractured skull and haemorrhage of the brain.

Dr. Maxwell gives evidence

Dr. J. Preston Maxwell, Professor of Gynecology and Obstetrics at the PUMC gave evidence and at the conclusion expressed the opinion that the death of deceased was not the work of an ordinary sexual sadist. It shows signs of being the work of a maniac but whether of a sexual maniac he could not say.

There was evidence to show that she had been interfered with, but it was not possible to state definitely whether this occurred before or after death.

Dr. H.B. Van Dyke, Professor of Pharmacology at the PUMC, gave evidence concerning the stomach of the deceased. It was the stomach of a healthy person. There was food in it and from the state of digestion he formed the opinion that the meal was eaten less than four hours before death. The minimum time it could have been eaten before was three-quarters of an hour. Witness found rice and meat in the stomach, date skins and something that might have been fig seeds.

It was the opinion of witness that, if death took place after 7.30 that evening, the contents of the stomach could not have been from what had been eaten at lunch.

He formed the opinion that the contents of the stomach represented an ordinary type of Chinese meal, neither
of the feast type nor of the coolie class but a middle class
meal. the presence of date skins and what appeared to be
fig seeds indicated this.

Witness looked for signs of poisoning but found none.
The girl had not been chloroformed.

The inquest has been adjourned and the verdict will be
given later. [15]

Although failing to state which organs were missing entirely,
this newspaper account of the autopsy allows a number of reasonable conclusions to be drawn:

• While still alive, Pamela was struck a number of times about
the head with a blunt instrument.
• At least one of the blows proved rapidly fatal.
• There were other minor wounds suggesting a struggle.
• Sexual intercourse had occurred either before or after death.
• Two or more instruments had been used in mutilating the
body.
• The perpetrator possessed some knowledge of anatomy.
• The mutilations could have occurred at the scene.
• The times of the death and mutilation were unclear.
• The motive for the mutilation was unclear.

The challenge for the police was now to translate facts into
results.

---

15 "Pamela Werner Fought For Her Life, Evidence Shows Head Blow Caused Death",
  Peiping Chronicle, February 6, 1937.

2

THE CHINA MESS

REGIMES, REVOLUTIONS & ENCLAVES

THE CHINA IN which Pamela Werner lived and died was a politically complex place. How was it in 1937 that armed Japanese soldiers patrolled parts of what was a supposedly independent sovereign state? And why were large slices of many Chinese ports and cities controlled by foreigners?

For many centuries, throughout many of its greatest periods of history, China was in effect a closed society, suspicious of foreigners, quite literally shut off to outsiders. Geographically separated by the natural barriers of oceans, deserts, mountains and sheer distance, China developed its own civilization in semi-isolation. For two and a half centuries up to 1911, China had been ruled by the Manchus, originally from Manchuria in the far northeast, and the collapse of their dynasty threw the country into a cauldron of confusion that lasted for more than a decade.

Unlike many other parts of the world, China was never fully colonized by Europeans, and then only in small yet strategic pockets of land, more by happenstance or misadventure than by deliberate or concerted desire for conquest. The goal of trade and meeting the requirements of the traders underpinned what amounted to partial colonization. But China was simply too large for it ever to be a serious target for European colonization, even by the British, who from the early nineteenth century through to the 1920s outnumbered any other foreign group in China (then to be outnumbered by the Japanese).

Britain's East India Company had been trading with China since the early eighteenth century, but in highly constrained terms. All European traders were confined to the port of Canton (Guangzhou), and were only allowed to live on one island in the river off the city for a part of the year. All trading had to be conducted through a dozen designated Chinese traders, the Hongs. In an effort to open up relations and allow for full trade, the British sent two missions, and in 1793, Lord Macartney succeeded in obtaining an audience with the Manchu emperor, Qian Long. His proposals for trade were rejected out of hand. Qian Long, in a message given to Macartney to pass on to George III, said:

"If I have commanded that the tribute offerings sent by you, O King, are to be accepted, this was solely in consideration for the spirit which prompted you to dispatch them from afar. Our dynasty's majestic virtue has penetrated unto every country under Heaven, and Kings of all nations have offered their costly tribute by land and sea. As your Ambassador can see for himself, we possess all things. I set no value on objects strange or ingenious, and have no use for your country's manufactures."

The main article of trade between Britain and China was tea. The English had become hooked on the brew in the 18th century, and the only source of the leaves at the time was China. In return for tea shipments, the Chinese merchants would basically only accept silver, which placed huge strains on the global finance system. The British were desperate to find some commodity that the Chinese would accept to balance the trade and they settled in the end on smuggled shipments of opium.

Opium had been smoked and used for medicinal purposes in China since time immemorial, but the main producer of the drug was India, now under British control. The high quality and cheap Indian variety quickly became popular, and the smoking of it a social problem that concerned officials at all levels of the imperial administration – at least, those who weren't partaking. In 1839 an imperial commissioner, Lin Zexu, was sent to Canton and had huge supplies of the drug stored in the foreigner trading post destroyed. The merchants protested to London and war ensued, a war that, due to a huge disparity in military technology, the Chinese were bound to lose. The war ended in 1842 with the signing of a treaty under which China was forced to pay a war indemnity, to cede the island of Hong Kong to Britain and to allow foreign traders and missionaries to reside in Treaty Ports along the coast – Canton, Foochow (Fuzhou), Amoy (Xiamen), Ningbo and Shanghai. British subjects were also granted extraterritorial rights, which meant that they were subject in China only to British law and were excluded from the jurisdiction of Chinese officials and courts.

The Opium War left China not only defeated but also humiliated. The pattern was set for the remainder of the century as further conflicts led to further concessions. The Manchus, China's last imperial dynasty originally from Manchuria in the far northeast, presided over a corrupt regime trying through virtually medieval means to govern a vast country. Foreign governments continued to expand their influence, and all the strategic ports of the country ended up with prime stretches of land under foreign control. Shanghai was by far the most important. It developed within a few decades from a minor Chinese fishing village into one of the world's great trading metropolises, and the heart of city was under foreigner control.

Most significant, and ominous, was the growing influence of Japan, a regional power which also won for itself rights and territory within a weak China. Like its enormous yet ineffective neighbor, Japan had also long been a closed society and had suffered similarly from a forceful insistence by foreigners on open trade. Japan, however, had adapted and recovered quickly, and its rulers were ambitious. Whereas the Western nations were primarily interested in securing safe and lucrative trade, Japan's ambitions went much further. Lacking coal and other natural resources of her own, Japan aspired to having an empire and dominating the whole of east Asia, and possibly much beyond. Further disaster and loss of face for China occurred in 1894 when she was badly beaten by the well-organized Japanese in a conflict over control of Korea. This was the First Sino-Japanese War.

Chinese humiliation and political discontent simmered and eventually boiled over in the form of the Boxer rebellion of 1900. The Boxers were a mixed and incoherent movement of proto-nationalists with followers bent on ridding China of all foreigners. Ruthless and brutal, the Boxers' main targets were the many Christian missions in northern China, often sited in vulnerable remote locations. The Boxers slaughtered hundreds of European missionaries and their families as well as tens of thousands of Chinese Christian converts. That summer, the rebellion culminated with the dramatic siege of the Legation Quarter in Peking. For nearly two months the desperate occupants, Peking's foreign community and some of the luckier Chinese Christians, held out against the Boxer hordes, assisted to some extent by the Manchu military. In August 1900, the siege was lifted by the arrival of a hastily-assembled multinational force of soldiers which fought its way to Peking from the coast.

The Boxers were destroyed and then, less heroically, much of Peking was looted by the victors. In the subsequent peace agreement signed by eleven countries in 1901, China was made to pay a heavy indemnity, and the existing unequal treaties were reinforced. In order to prevent a repetition of the siege, the Legation Quarter in Peking was enlarged, walled, gated and bordered by *glacis* (open spaces affording a line of defensive fire). In effect, the Legation Quarter became a sizeable foreign-ruled, walled compound in the middle of Peking. Notably, its legations – the Japanese among them – were also granted the right to keep their own garrisons of soldiers to guard their interests as well as the rail line to Tientsin and the sea. Foreign troops from many nations – marching, guarding, parading, training, drinking and socializing – became an everyday feature of life in the city. It was an ever-present reminder to the Chinese of their weakness.

The Manchu dynasty survived the Boxer rebellion, partly due to the strength of character of the aged Empress Dowager, Tz'u-hsi (also written Cixi), a formidable and resilient woman who ruled the Manchu Empire for nearly half a century. Following her death in 1908, the Manchu dynasty was eventually overthrown by a popular revolt in 1911 and was replaced by what amounted to anarchy.

"The era of civil wars in China lasted for twenty years, from 1911 to 1931," wrote Sir Eric Teichman, a British diplomat who had spent his entire career in China who initially retired in late 1936, a few months before Pamela's murder, although he returned to serve again in China during World War II. "It seemed as though the Chinese people, having overthrown their Manchu rulers, were incapable of governing themselves."[1]

The Kuomintang (Nationalist Party) led by Generalissimo Chiang K'ai-Shek re-unified the country in 1927 and placed its capital in Nanking to the west of Shanghai, spurning Peking to

....

1 Affairs of China, Sir Eric Teichman, Methuen Publishers (1938), pages 16-17.

the north. They were faced with a stupendous task. China was in a state of disintegration and decay and whole swathes of the country were controlled by warlords or were overrun by bandits. But huge progress was made by the national government between 1928 and 1937. As Teichman says, "Less than ten years later a measure of unity had been achieved, banditry had everywhere decreased, the finances and the currency had been straightened out, commerce and industry had been revived, new measures of public health and education had been initiated, thousands of miles of new motor roads had been constructed, and the foundations of a new China had been firmly laid. But at every step forward towards unity and reconstruction China and Kuomintang met with blows and obstruction from Japan."[2]

Such was the tumultuous political backdrop to Pamela Werner's birth and upbringing. The Kuomintang had made solid progress in bringing to an end the years of civil war and chaos that followed the fall of the Manchu dynasty, only then to be confronted with the growing menace of Imperial Japan. In 1931, the Japanese occupied Manchuria, now northeast China, and created the puppet state of Manchukuo. And in January 1932, emboldened by its success in Manchuria, Japan also attacked the Chinese-controlled parts of Shanghai, taking care to avoid the foreign settlements with their small garrisons of Western soldiers, mostly American and British. In Shanghai, Japan met with unexpectedly stiff opposition from Chinese troops resulting in a negotiated stalemate and the introduction of large de-militarized zones. This setback made the Japanese temporarily cautious about further military adventurism, but before long Japanese troops were patrolling these 'de-militarized zones', effectively handing them control of much of North China, Peking included.

....

2 *Affairs of China*, Sir Eric Teichman, Methuen (1938), page 17

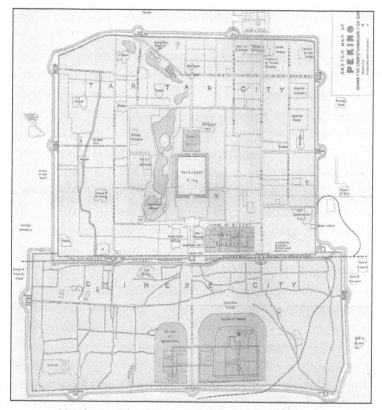

Map showing Peking's Tartar and Chinese cities and their walls.
The Legation Quarter is right centre. (Alamy)

The rising confidence and organization of the Chinese government under the Kuomintang and the insatiable ambition of the militarists in Japan placed the two forces on an inevitable collision course. Matters came to a head in August 1937, when the Japanese engineered another spurious incident, this time at the Marco Polo Bridge outside Peking. It was the beginning of the Second Sino-Japanese War and of years of killing on a colossal scale.

Peking, China's traditional capital, and home to Pamela, was neither a trade port nor an industrial centre. Situated in the north of the country and over a hundred miles from the sea, the city owed its existence to its proximity to the passes leading north to Mongolia – the city was established as the capital in the era of Mongol rule in the thirteenth and fourteenth centuries. In the 1930s, still relatively untouched by modern development, Peking retained an air of a place where, as one foreigner described it, "the past seemed to live on unchallenged,"[3] Its unchanging aspect made it hugely attractive to foreigners, one of whom said Beijing was "the most attractive town in the world and no one should be allowed to die before seeing it."[4]

Peking was a city dominated by its historical features: ancient monuments, gates, towers, temples and palaces. But of all these great features, the most imposing were the city walls. Largely destroyed in the late 1960s and early 1970s by the communist rulers, the Peking of the 1930s was dominated by them. The wall surrounded the whole city, was about twenty-five miles in length and in places as much as sixty feet high.[5] It was wide enough to run a broad road or march an army along its top, completely dwarfing the medieval fortifications of European cities. Pierced with gated entrances and graced with lofty defensive towers, this colossal feat of construction formed two city-sized rectangles hard against one another, together forming a shape like a squat figure-of-eight. Of these two great squares, the northernmost was known as the Tartar City (the Inner City in Chinese), and the southernmost as the Chinese City (or the Outer City in Chinese). The latter was so-called because the Manchu rulers had once forced the Chinese to live only there. In the middle of the Tartar City was the Forbidden City, the 180-acre home of the emperors,

....

3 *Diplomat in Peace and War*, Sir Hughe Knatchbull-Hugessen, John Murray publisher (1949), page 101
4 *Fish, Fowl and Foreign Lands*, J.D. Greenway, Faber & Faber Ltd (1950), page 54
5 *In Search of Old Peking*, by Lewis Charles Arlington and William Lewisohn, published by Henri Vetch (1935).

Postcard showing the east gate entrance to Legation Street, through which Pamela would have passed on her way home

until the last, Puyi, was finally expelled in 1924.

Not far from the Forbidden City, to the east and slightly south, was the square mile of the Legation Quarter, the diplomatic enclave of which the broad Tartar wall protectively formed the southern side — protective only if the foreign occupiers had control, a close-run thing back in 1900. The majority of Peking's foreign community lived and worked within the Legation Quarter's guarded gates. It consisted of European-style hotels, hospitals, embassies, apartments, shops, schools and gardens. It was for its occupants both clean and safe, and given the poverty, and the alien sights and smells of the city beyond, it is not surprising that many foreigners rarely ventured outside the Quarter's gates except to travel. The Chinese, unless they numbered among the thousands of employed servants, gardeners and coolies, were excluded from the Legation Quarter entirely. Tradesmen, teachers and night soil coolies collecting the contents of the latrines, were given special passes. Such was the legacy of the Boxer Rebellion, an event still within living memory for many.

Entrance Gate to the British Embassy, Peking

As to Peking beyond the Legation Quarter, it was another world. Gertrude Bell wrote in 1903: "Your rickshaw dashes in and out, bumps over boulders, subsides into ditches, runs over dogs and toes and the outlying parts of booths and shops, upsets an occasional wheelbarrow, locks itself with rickshaws coming in the opposite direction and at a hard gallop conveys you breathless, through dust and noise and smells unspeakable to where you would be."

Julia Boyd in her excellent book, *A Dance with the Dragon*, described the city: "The colorful chaos of Peking's streets belied the formality of the city plan, laid out in the fifteenth century on strict *feng-shui* principles. Wide avenues ran in straight lines from north to south, east to west, wall to wall. But in their interstices lay a network of muddy lanes or *hutungs* filled with endless crowds of ragged Chinese in butcher blue, the interiors of their ramshackle shops overflowing with pigs, rickshaws, garbage and overpowering smells. While the mediaeval exoticism of Peking's streets was for many foreigners thrilling, the ubiquitous beggars and excrement, the corpses chewed by stray dogs, cruel public punishments and an all-pervading stench were also a powerful deterrent." The top of the city wall, crumbling and beset with weeds in many places, was considered a refuge along which foreigners could walk for miles, enjoying the scenes of the city below. "Seen from this elevated point, Peking was surprisingly green and tranquil. Looking north, the foreigners could gaze across the sweeping roofs of the Forbidden City to Coal Hill, where the last Ming emperor hanged himself. To the south lay the Chinese City, where the victorious Manchus forced their new subjects to live and which over the centuries had retained its distinctive character."[6]

Most of the thoroughfares of the city were the narrow and unpaved alleyways lined with grey blank walls interspersed with doorways. What lay inside the doorways was completely hidden, but was usually courtyard houses, built to the same set model, single-storey buildings facing the courtyard square, often featuring flowering shrubs and songbirds in bamboo cages.

Edward Theodore Chalmers Werner was one of a number of Peking's foreigners who chose to live outside the Legation Quarter in just such a courtyard house, at Number 1, Kuei-chiach'ang, a lane of similar courtyard residences.

---

6 *A Dance with the Dragon*, Julia Boyd, I.B. Taurus (2012), prologue.

3

THE LONER

MR PINFOLD

THE INVESTIGATION into the murder of Pamela Werner was led by Colonel Han Shih-ching, magistrate and chief officer of the Chinese police in Peking. Gorman, writing in *Caravan*, described Han as having twenty years' experience, and elsewhere he is referred to as being celebrated[1] and even famous, with a long record of successes.[2] Evidently Han was a well-known figure in Peking. Gorman was circumspect in his portrayal of the general Chinese character, possibly mindful of not offending the sensitivities of his hosts, and even more careful not to suggest criticism of the Chinese police, praising Han and his officers in Peking for their professionalism. For however competent Han and his junior colleagues, the standards of policing and detective work in the Peking of 1937 could not have been ideal. In its attempt to forge a modern state, the ruling Nationalist Government of Chiang Kai-shek was keen to form an effective national police force to replace the traditional local militias. Policing had

....

1 Murder-related articles, *Caravan* magazine, February & March 1937 editions.
2 "Blow Caused Death of English Girl", *Gloucester Echo*, January 9, 1937.

become a national priority,[3] but the Nationalists had only come to control Peking in the late 1920s, and for many years prior, much of northern China had been run by various local warlords. A modern and efficient Chinese police force was still in the making. The world over, standards in policing tend to reflect the state of the government and society in which they exist; and medieval was how many outsiders described China at this time.

Gorman's other interesting claim, that Peking was the safest city in the world, was perhaps racially selective, as a scan through reports in *The Peiping Chronicle* during the opening months of 1937 illustrates: police raids on drug dens involving scores or even hundreds of arrests; over a dozen public executions of heroin dealers; 500 inmates escaping a prison during a fire; robbery involving a firearm at the home of a senior civil servant; 28 kilograms of heroin seized at a railway station. These accounts of local crime may have been simply the tip of an iceberg as the newspaper reflected the interests of its English-speaking foreign readership, not those of the local Chinese. While the Werner case, for example, received a good deal of day-by-day attention in the English-language publications, entirely Chinese stories were brief and generally contained a sensational aspect to them such as: a photograph of a notorious murderess being transferred to jail; a report of part of a lip being bitten off during a domestic incident; the execution of a man who murdered his parents; a blindfolded murder victim killed by sword.[4]

But Gorman was probably correct in the sense that most foreigners in Peking, with their associated status and privilege, were indeed safe from violent crime, especially within the guarded Legation Quarter where many of them lived and worked, and from whence many of them rarely strayed. But the Werners did

....

3 Frederic Wakeman (Jr.), *Policing Shanghai*, pages xv-xvi.
4 Articles from *Peiping Chronicle*, January-May 1937.

not live in the Legation Quarter, and Pamela's body was discovered outside its confines.

In 1937, the Chinese police calculated Peking's population to be a little over one and a half million,[5] probably a conservative figure that may only have included those registered and living within certain walls. Whatever the true figure, it can come as no surprise that Peking's population generated its share of crime. But to what extent? What was the context and nature of crime in the city where Pamela was murdered?

The experience of Ernest Peters may provide some insight. A former artillery soldier from Kent in southeast England, Peters served for six years as a junior police officer in the Shanghai Municipal Police, only leaving China in 1935, a year or so before Pamela's murder. Shanghai, China's most important port and already one of the largest cities in the world, possessed a population at least as big as Peking's. Shanghai was also far more cosmopolitan than Peking with huge slices of the city literally controlled by foreigners in settlements or concessions. The Shanghai Municipal Council, an elected body of foreign nationals independent of any country or government, though largely British-led, existed primarily for the benefit of the many thousands of foreigners living and trading in the International Settlement. Wealthy and powerful, the council even had its own police force, employing over 5,000 officers who were as diverse as Shanghai itself. And like the city, the force was racially divided with separate sections for British, Japanese, Russians, Sikhs and Chinese recruits. Rank and seniority were also largely organized on a racial basis.

On his return to the UK, Peters candidly described his time in the force in his 1936 book, *Shanghai Policeman*, giving read-

---

5 *Peiping Chronicle*, October 20, 1937.

ers refreshingly clear insights into the role of police at that time,
using terms and descriptions that would never be published today. Peters described Shanghai as a city rife with violent crime.
Murder and sudden death were frequent occurrences, whether
as the result of violent family arguments, suicides, shoot-outs
during armed robberies, petty face-saving and jealousies, and
even feuds between police officers. Peters's strong opinions were
forged by his street policing experiences. He was unsparing toward everyone and described things as he saw them. To Peters,
the Chinese were an enigma. Whilst they were resilient, apparently inured to pain and discomfort, cheerful in appalling adver-
sity and frequently physically courageous, he also found them
cunning, idle, fatalistic and possessed of a ruinous propensity
for drug abuse and gambling. Such were Peters's dealings with
the common folk of Shanghai. Through his line of work, he witnessed a side of life which few Shanghai foreigners would have
been aware. He was of the opinion that he learnt more about the
city and its people in six months as a policeman than the Settlement's foreign businessmen did in ten or twenty years.[6]

Life was cheap in China, and Peters was far from being alone
in making the observation.[7] Other foreign observers in Peking
complained of the callous indifference to the bodies of beggars
left lying for days on paths which were regarded as an incon-
venience, to be shifted overnight from outside one doorway to
another.[8] In Tientsin around this time, there was a mystery over
a score of floating corpses dragged from the river, some bearing suspicious wounds.[9] For the estimated four to five hundred
million poor in China,[10] the vast majority of the population, life

6   E.W. Peters, *Shanghai Policeman*, chapter 1.
7   Sir Eric Teichman, *Affairs of China*, (1938), p157.
8   "Dead Bodies on the Streets", *Peiping Chronicle*, letter to editor, January 15, 1937.
9   "Bodies in River Puzzle Tientsin Chinese Police", *Peiping Chronicle*, April 25, 1937.
10 Sir Hughe Knatchbull-Hugessen, *Diplomat in Peace and War*, (1949), p96.

Chief Inspector Richard Dennis.
(Courtesy of Diana Dennis)

could be very cheap indeed.

If Shanghai was China's version of the Wild West, the port of Tientsin, situated much closer to Peking, was smaller and tamer. Tientsin also had its own foreign-controlled areas, albeit much smaller than those in Shanghai. Among these was a British concession with its own police force for which worked the officers Richard Dennis and Richard Botham, both later assigned to the Werner case.

In the Tientsin force's annual report for 1940, a few years later, Dennis, as chief of police, listed the following violent crimes occurring in the less than half-a-square-mile concession area alone: two murders (shootings); two attempted murders (one with an axe, one with a kitchen chopper); and eight armed robberies. All these incidents involved Chinese suspects and Chinese victims alone. Foreigners had not been directly involved and therefore may not even have been aware of them. Dennis also mentioned 532 theft reports, but went on to make favorable comparisons with the crime figures for previous years, especially considering various extraneous factors that were beyond his force's control.[11]

It is worth pointing out that crime figures the world-over have always tended to be a political football; there is no body of data subject to greater manipulation and selective presentation. Indeed, the statistics of criminality tend to say more about the compilers and their audience than the offences themselves. It matters little, then, that the records of offences committed during

....

11 Tientsin British Municipal Council, annual police report, 1940.

the same period in Chinese-controlled Peking have disappeared. The reality for many of Peking's people living outside the safe Legation Quarter was that crime, whether petty, violent or serious, was almost certainly a feature of everyday life.

Inspector Richard Botham arrived in Peking on Saturday morning, January 9, the day after the body's discovery. He had made the long journey in order to play hockey that afternoon, representing Tientsin in an inter-port match against a local team.[12] His stay in the city was to prove longer than planned. Following instructions from his superior, Dennis, in Tientsin, Botham's sporting plans were put aside and that morning he called upon Consul Fitzmaurice to offer assistance. Keenly aware of the fears and outrage among members of Peking's foreign community, a grateful Fitzmaurice immediately accepted; the aid of experienced British police officers would be most welcome.[13]

As Pamela's body was found outside the Legation Quarter, on Chinese territory, the Chinese police were formally in charge of the murder investigation. This was an important stipulation and it meant that the British police could only assist, policing being subject to the geography of boundaries. Had the crime occurred within the Legation Quarter it would have been up to its own small police unit to investigate. Headed by the elderly legation secretary, W.P. Thomas, the Legation police role chiefly involved staffing guard posts and reporting minor crimes and traffic accidents. Murder was beyond its limited experience, but not that of Botham and Dennis, both ex-Scotland Yard. While Pamela's murder may not have been on "their patch", there was no lawful reason why they could not offer to *assist* Han and the Chinese police.

Botham and Dennis were recruited by the foreigner-controlled

12 *Peiping Chronicle*, social column, January 10, 1937.
13 UK National Archives, FO 371/21004 China. Code 10 Files 2047 - 2396, consular report.

Tientsin Municipal Council directly from London's Metropolitan Police, where both had served as detectives in CID departments, though it would appear not together. Born in Nottinghamshire and the son of a train driver,[14] Richard Botham joined the Met aged about twenty in 1925 and was allocated the warrant number 114448. Ten years later, he was a detective constable on N district (Islington) in North London and sufficiently well thought-of to be offered a post in Tientsin.[15] The offer brought with it promotion, a jump in two ranks to inspector, something that would have taken him many years to achieve in London. Resigning from the Met, Botham and his wife sailed for China in July 1935.[16] Eighteen months later in Peking, by then in his early thirties, confident and 'finely built', Botham was said to cut an impressive figure.[17] It was Botham, rather than his superior Dennis, who was to be the principal British police officer on the case, spending many months based in Peking. Dennis, while overseeing Botham's work, remained largely at his desk back in Tientsin. He had, after all, a police force to run. Nonetheless it was the name of Dennis which featured heavily in the world's press reports on the Werner murder, even above that of Han.

Botham did not work alone in Peking. He was supported by Sergeant George Binetsky who was also on loan from the Tientsin force. Binetsky appears to have beaten Botham to Peking by a good twelve hours, and was present during the search of Pamela's bedroom on Friday evening. Twenty-nine years of age, short and powerfully built, Binetsky was one of a number of stateless White Russians employed by the Tientsin Municipal Council. By

---

14 National Archives, 1911 UK census (Netherfield, Nottinghamshire, schedule 268).
15 UK National Archives, MEPO 4/349/185 Register of leavers from the Metropolitan Police.
16 SS Potsdam passenger list, leaving Southampton for Yokohama, July 9, 1935.
17 E.T.C. Werner, *Memorigrams*, (1940), p148.

1937, he had been a police officer for four years.[18] He was born in 1907 to a Russian father and a stateless mother in Harbin in the far northeast of China,[19] a busy railway town with a large Russian population that was to increase dramatically a decade later with refugees fleeing the Bolshevik revolution. Many desperate Russians crossed the border into China after the defeat of the White Army in the 1920s. Some came from wealthy or even aristocratic backgrounds but arrived destitute; they were poor white immigrants within a poor country, and employment as a police officer with the British in Tientsin was a good position to hold. As the junior officer to Botham in Peking, Binetsky would have done much of the legwork for the British investigation.

Given the frequent mention of Scotland Yard in contemporary newspaper articles, it would be easy to overestimate the role played by the British police officers in the Werner murder case. It was Han who had ultimate responsibility for the investigation, and importantly, it was Han's Chinese officers who were first on the scene and conducted the initial enquiries in the first hours and days, a crucial period in any investigation. What Han felt privately about the professional help or interference of foreign police officers with whom he may not have worked before is not recorded. He may have been grateful for the assistance offered, but if he wasn't, he probably had enough experience to realise that if the investigation failed to achieve a result, it would better having them involved from the very beginning rather than later be accused of failing because of their absence.

Whatever the reality, *Caravan* described the Chinese and British police as fully cooperating, with Botham operating from both

18 UK National Archives, FO 366/2930 Payment of pensions to former employees of the British Municipal Council at Tientsin on account of their claims against the Chinese Government for service benefits.
19 UK National Archives, HO 334/200 Naturalisation Certificate: George Nicolas Binetsky. Of no Nationality. Resident in Tientsin, North China. Certificate AZ37396 issued January 10, 1948.

the Chinese police station in Morrison Street well outside the Legation Quarter, and from the British Embassy itself. A working arrangement appears to have been made in which the British police dealt with enquiries relating to the foreign community, leaving the Chinese free to deal with their own people. This would have made practical sense as Botham and Dennis, both recent arrivals in China, spoke little or no Chinese but held an obvious advantage when it came to dealing with the foreign community.

Botham, for instance, was probably the "Scotland Yard detective" who called on the American journalist Helen Foster Snow (1907-1997) at her courtyard home only two doors away from that of the Werners. Snow recorded the visit as occurring one evening soon after the murder. Botham commented on how dark and remote the location was and wondered what possessed the Snows to want to live there. He clearly displayed an open mind as to the crime's motive, doing nothing to disabuse the twenty-nine-year-old American of the possibility that she may have been the target herself. Snow and her journalist husband Edgar possessed communist sympathies which made them unpopular with many in the foreign community. In the event, Botham appears to have gained little of note from the interview; on the night of the murder, the Snows had returned home late from a party in a motor car and may therefore have driven past the body, but had seen and heard nothing.[20]

Another of Botham's early moves was to post an entry in *the Peiping Chronicle:*

Inspector Botham's Appeal to Public
"Inspector R. Botham of the British Municipal Police in Tientsin, who has come to Peiping to assist in solving the

....

20 Helen Foster Snow, *My China Years,* (1984), p218.

the Pamela Werner murder mystery, makes an appeal for
assistance from the general public, that is from all people
who saw Miss Werner on the night she disappeared or at
anytime between December 27, when she arrived here from
Tientsin, and the time of her disappearance.

He would be grateful if any person who saw Miss Werner that night, January 7, any person who spoke to her, any
person who saw her speaking with someone else, at the
French skating rink or elsewhere, or saw her without other
people, especially men, between December 27 and January
7 would go to see him at the Morrison Street police station
between 5 and 7.30 p.m."[21]

A $1,000 reward (during this period the Chinese used Mexican
dollars) had already been offered for information leading to the
apprehension and conviction of the suspect or suspects[22] (a small
fortune for the average Chinese person).

Appeals were made in English-language and Chinese newspapers as well as on the local radio.[23] Gorman also reported enquiries being made at the French rink as to the victim's possible
routes around Peking and with everyone who knew her. All this
would have been standard in a murder investigation and, giv-
en the public interest in the case, it's hard to conceive that such
ground would have gone uncovered.

The police were busy on the streets also. Newspapers reported word of the detention of a rickshaw coolie. The man had allegedly been found washing a possibly bloodstained cushion.[24]

21 *Peiping Chronicle*, January 12, 1937.
22 "$1,000 reward will be paid for information leading to the arrest and conviction of ..."
   Peiping Chronicle, January 10, 1937.
23 "The Pamela Werner Case", *Caravan* magazine, February 1937.
24 "Arrest For Foochow Murder", The Daily News (Perth), January 13, 1937. The headline
   was an editorial error based on the fact that Werner had once been British Consul in the
   port city of Foochow (Fuzhou).

The story, however, appears not to have progressed further and was soon supplanted by developing events. For, suddenly, an arrest that sounded far more promising was confirmed.

Peiping Chronicle, January 14:
Suspect Held in Werner Murder Case Believed to be
Foreigner Reuter
The most important development so far in the Werner murder mystery occurred late last night when Captain Han of the Chinese police and Inspector R. Botham of the British police in Tientsin, acting together, detained a man on suspicion.

The arrest was made on Tuesday, January 12. Newspapers across the world reported that a foreign male had been arrested and that, on searching his house in the city, police found a pair of bloodstained shoes, a bloodstained dagger and sheath, and a handkerchief similarly marked. It was said that "these objects the man could not or would not explain."[25]

A day later, the unidentified male was still in custody. With an excited tone, the local press reported the scraps they had gleaned: the man lived in a single room in an inn in the north of the city;[26] he was described as an Englishman; the items seized were being analyzed for blood type, and that the blood was indeed human.[27] The victim's father, E.T.C. Werner, later wrote that the man had been seen a day or two after the murder "scraping the ground with his foot on the spot where the body had been found."[28]

25 "Suspect Held in Werner Murder Case Believed to be Foreigner", *Peiping Chronicle*, January 14, 1937.
26 "Murder Mystery Still Unsolved", *Peiping Chronicle*, January 15, 1937.
27 "Suspect in Werner Case Released", *North-China Herald*, January 20, 1937.
28 National Archive, Kew, FO 371/23513, Letter from E.T.C. Werner to the British Ambassador to China, October 3, 1938.

None of the local English-language newspapers were bold enough to name the man in custody. This reticence was not mirrored by the American news correspondents on the scene. This news item was published by an Indiana newspaper:

Suspect is Held in British Murder Case

A British "remittance man" named Pinfold is held by police in connection with the rape-murder of pretty, blonde Pamela Werner... Chinese police said today.

The man is held on a technical charge of vagrancy.[29]

Held in custody in a Morrison Street cell, but not yet charged with any offence, Pinfold's name ought not to have been released by the Chinese police. Nor should it to have been published in a newspaper. But Indiana is a long way from China, and a "remittance man", or pensioner, arrested in China for some form of vagrancy was unlikely to engage a lawyer with a reach long enough to extend to the United States. In any event, Pinfold was thus partially identified; no newspaper gave his first name, but other speculative reports had him aged fifty, born in Canada, having a Chicago police record, and, very strangely, involved in one of China's "periodic revolutionary movements."[30]

One Chinese newspaper published in Peking on January 14 gave new details regarding Pinfold with the headline: "Major Suspect, Briton Pinfold Arrested Yesterday Morning - Bloodstained Clothes and Knife Found in His Accommodation". The report said that the Chinese police were initially reluctant to investigate the case, but finally decided to "capture the murderer for the sake of the safety and security of city and people." A rickshaw puller had been detained, it said, who had told the police

29 "Suspect is Held in British Murder Case", *Logansport Pharos-Tribune*, January 16, 1937.
30 *The Times* (Hammond Indiana), January 15, 1937.

he had taken a foreigner to the Jinghua Apartments [sited in the Tartar city about a mile north of the Legation Quarter].

> "With this clue, the District Police Chief Han Shih-ch'ing, together with several policemen went at about 8am yesterday morning to Jinghua Apartment and detained the foreigner, and found bloodstained clothing and a bloodstained knife. At the district police station, the man claimed to be Ping Fude, British, about 60 years old. He had once served in the Fuchow Customs under the charge of the Consul-General Werner. With regard to Pamela's death, Ping Fude has not yet admitted to murdering her, but it is assumed that, as he said he was fired by Werner for misconduct, he killed Werner's daughter out of revenge. The district police station, together with Inspector Botham, examined the evidence and interrogated the suspect, and it is believed the case will be solved in two or three days."[31]

Pinfold, a foreigner in China, uncooperative with the police, arrested for vagrancy, a detainee without a first name. He was a mysterious character, seemingly impossible to identify. But a close examination of the Peking consular registers preserved at the National Archives in Kew helps to illuminate this shadowy figure. Amongst the lines and columns of numbered correspondence documented in the leather-bound volumes are thousands of references referring to routine miscellany such as applications for visas, insurance claims, lost passports, registrations of overseas births. In June 1937, five months after the murder and Pinfold's arrest, a Mr Collet was recorded as enquiring after the whereabouts of Mr Fred Pinfold.[32] Who Collet was or why

....

31 Yih Shih Pao (益世报) January 14, 1937
32 UK National Archives, FO 692/7, Consular Correspondence 1929-1938.

he wanted to find Fred Pinfold remains unknown, as the register en-
tries were very brief and the correspondence they related to long ago
destroyed. It is not even clear if the
Embassy was able to assist Collet
with an address, but this singular
1937 enquiry helped point the way
to identifying the man behind the
name in the newspapers. And once
found, it is easy to understand why
Mr Pinfold was so elusive.

Frederick Samuel Pinfold was
baptized at Saint Giles church,

Pamela as a young child

Reading, Berkshire in the south of England on December 13,
1874, having been born in October in the same parish. He was
the first, and seemingly only, child of young parents Frederick
and Ann Pinfold, whose marriage may not have been a happy
or successful one. In any event, Frederick senior, described as
a manufacturer's foreman, died less than four years later of tuberculosis.[33] What then became of Frederick's mother is unclear,
as she seems to have disappeared from her son's life. In the 1891
census, a sixteen-year-old Frederick Pinfold, now an engineer's
apprentice, was recorded as living with his widowed aunt and
her teenage daughter in Saint Giles' parish.

Leaving aside the loss of his parents, Fred Pinfold's family
background appears to have been modest if not actually impoverished, living amidst ordinary working people in Reading,
a town that expanded considerably throughout the nineteenth
century owing to its flourishing manufacturing industries. Cru-

....

33 National Archives, death certificate of Frederick Pinfold GRO 1879 Vol 02c page 253.

cial to the young man's future was his trade apprenticeship. By the time of the next census in 1901, Pinfold, then an electrical engineer in his mid-twenties, had moved away from Reading to lodgings near London's Covent Garden (then the capital's fruit and vegetable market) where he almost certainly worked for Verity & Sons of King Street, a well-established firm of electrical manufacturers and the only one in the Covent Garden area in that era. The introduction to this employment was probably through a man already employed by the electrical firm, one the unmarried Pinfold later rather curiously described as his godfather and next of kin. Something of the loner was beginning to show itself in Pinfold.

At some stage, probably during the early 1900s, Pinfold travelled to China. If the Chinese newspaper was correct, he was in Foochow around the same time as Werner (consul 1910-1913). However, Shanghai may have proved a more attractive option; a rapidly growing city and the greatest centre of commerce in the region, it would have presented good employment opportunities to an electrical engineer. Pinfold was certainly there at some point, joining the Shanghai Volunteer Corps,[34] an armed militia of foreigners created to protect the city's huge International Settlement. Dating back to 1853, the Corps was regarded as a wise deterrent in a turbulent country. It was run by the Shanghai Municipal Council and was in effect a private army run by a private body of foreigners. It was a force to be reckoned with. The Corps included individual companies based on volunteers' nationality (British, American, Chinese, German, Portuguese, Japanese), and cavalry, artillery and support units. Pinfold enrolled in an engineer unit.

Throughout the first three years of World War One, a politi-

34 Library and Archives of Canada, Attestation records of Frederick Samuel Pinfold, record of previous military service, Canadian Expeditionary Force, service number 1263391.

cally chaotic China, though sympathetic to the Allied cause, remained neutral. This left the diverse members of the Shanghai Volunteer Corps, many of whom in any case had divided loyalties, with little to do other than continue to guard a foreign enclave in a country far away from the European conflict. Despite its neutrality, however, the British and French governments were determined to somehow exploit China's resources in the war in Europe. One result, after much diplomatic delay, was the formation in 1916 of the Chinese Labour Corps, an organization which brought together more than 100,000 Chinese peasants and workers. It was supervised by a similarly improvised group of foreign officers, mostly British subjects but also including Americans and Russians. Large companies of labourers were formed for transportation to Europe where they were to be used for general digging, building, shifting, loading – indeed, any work requiring large numbers of men. Men in the Labour Corps would not be used on the front itself, but behind the lines, though not necessarily out of danger (as many of them would discover). They were not soldiers and were unarmed, but were sufficiently schooled and disciplined so as to form a cohesive and reliable group. Time was pressing; the Allies required its presence in the field urgently.

On arrival at the barracks, recruits were given a medical examination and had their heads shaved (including cutting off any remaining traditional long-plaited ponytails, or "queues"). They were then attached to a company commanded by a foreign officer, known among them as their "father", often with some affection. These officer fathers consisted of men such as Pinfold. Ideally they possessed some previous military experience, but it appears that almost any reliable foreign male with a measure of life experience of China was suitable material: missionaries, journalists and merchants were all employed as officers of the

Chinese Labour Corps.[35] Pinfold went too, in some capacity.

The lack of transport ships available to Europe was a major problem. The fathers had plenty of time drilling their companies into shape while waiting for a ship. When finally on board a transport, the voyage was both long and dangerous. In February 1917, the French passenger ship SS *Athos* was torpedoed off Malta with the loss of over 700 lives, most of them Chinese, and thereafter most transports were forced to sail a much longer eastern route across both the Pacific and Atlantic oceans via Canada and the Panama canal. A month or so after the *Athos* disaster, however, the SS *Phemius*, including Quartermaster Sergeant Pinfold and the other men of the 2nd Battalion Chinese Labour Corps, sailed from Shanghai via the Cape of Good Hope and Sierra Leone, so avoiding the Mediterranean, and arrived safely at the port of London in May 1917.[36] Good fortune had thus far accompanied Pinfold and his colleagues, but not so the *Phemius*; she was sunk by a U-boat a month later in the Atlantic on her return journey to the Far East.[37]

The London port list of the arriving China Labour Corps contains only eight European names. They include seven officers traveling first class, and Pinfold traveling second class. The Chinese labourers, over eleven hundred of them, were listed only by number. As a quartermaster in charge of provisions and the only ranked sergeant, Pinfold appears therefore not to have been an officer or father to the Chinese labourers. He may or may not have gone with the battalion to France and the front. He may have been present only for the voyage from China. It's impossible to say, for Pinfold then disappears from record again for a whole year.

....

35 Daryl Klein, *With the Chinks*, (1919) p5.
36 Port of London passenger list, arrivals, *SS Phemius*, May 2, 1917.
37 Miramar ship index, *SS Phemius*, June 4, 1917.

In May of 1918, he reappeared at a Canadian barracks at Seaford on the south coast of England where he enlisted with the Canadian Expeditionary Force as a sapper in the Canadian Engineer Reserve Battalion. The Canadian army enlisting a non-Canadian far from its own shores was not unusual; such was the pressure to recruit large numbers of men that a great percentage of the Canadian expeditionary troops were foreign-born and many had never so much as set foot in Canada. As an electrical engineer, Pinfold would have been a useful addition.[38]

Pinfold's enlistment papers into the Canadian Army are revealing. Aged forty-three, he already possessed iron-grey hair. He was also recorded as weighing 149 pounds, with hazel eyes, a ruddy complexion, and standing 5 foot 7 inches tall. He appeared to be healthy with his only period of previous illness being an episode of food poisoning in China nine years previously. He was single, had never been married and had no children. There appeared to be some confusion over the status of his mother, with the scribe completing the recruitment process paperwork first writing and then crossing out the word "widowed." And then to the question whether his mother was alive, Pinfold answered that he "could not say" one way or the other. He gave his address as the Overseas Club in Aldwych, London which was either a receiving address for letters or at best a temporary lodging. He gave his next of kin as his godfather, a Mr Evans of Verity's Limited, the company that had likely employed him in Covent Garden many years before.[39]

Why Pinfold chose to volunteer for the War at this late stage is unknown; he may have only just been released by the Chinese Labour Corps. Why he chose the Canadian rather than British

---

38 Library & Archives of Canada, Attestation records of Frederick Samuel Pinfold, record of previous military service, Canadian Expeditionary Force, service number 1263391.
39 ibid.

Army is also unknown. He may have been rejected by the British, or have been too old, although the British Army service age was increased to fifty at around this time. The War of course would be over in six months, but that was not in the least bit obvious to anyone at the time. Again, what service Pinfold subsequently saw on the front in Europe is unclear.

In December 1918, he was promoted to Lance-Corporal and remained with the Canadian Army until the following summer of 1919[40] when he appears to have taken advantage of military transport from Liverpool to Quebec where he was demobilized in August. On leaving the Canadian army, he was once again described as healthy. Then, rather typically, Pinfold disappears from the records again until he resurfaces fully eighteen years later in Peking in January 1937 in connection with the Werner

Pamela, a studio photograph taken shortly before her death

murder. Where he went after his demobilisation in 1919 is not known. He gave a forwarding address for army payments as the post office in Vancouver, Canada, from which port he may have travelled back to China. However, his much-abbreviated military record also makes an ambiguous mention of Chicago, which may also have been his destination.[41]

And that is all, to date, that can be found about the man taken into custody in Peking, as solitary and shadowy a figure

40 ibid.
41 ibid.

now as he would have appeared to the police back in 1937. In one sense, the newspapers of the time were correct in stating that Pinfold was "from Canada", as he had served in their armed forces, and that he had "lived for a time in Chicago", as well he may. Living some distance from the Legation Quarter in diminished circumstances, Pinfold was aged sixty-three at the time of the murder.

But if the press and Peking's foreign community thought they now had their murderer, they were to be disappointed. After several days in a Chinese police cell, Pinfold was released without charge. "Werner Murder Suspect Freed" was the headline in the *Peiping Chronicle*. There was, many newspapers reported – with far less gusto than at his arrest – insufficient evidence to link him with the murder.[42]

In the absence of any existing police notes, what can be deduced from the Pinfold arrest? Just how serious a suspect was he? The answer is probably not very serious. The pressure to make arrests in a murder investigation is something of a crime-film cliché, but it is one based on a degree of truth. The likes of a lowly rickshaw coolie washing suspicious stains off a cushion in the street and an ageing foreign vagrant with blood on his clothing make for easy arrests. They also have the desired effect of showing to the media and the public that the police are active in their work. That is not to say that the arrests were necessarily unlawful or unwarranted; the grounds for arresting someone are generally much lower than those required for a charge. An uncommunicative or obstructive vagrant with blood stains would have been fair game in a high-profile case like the Werner murder. Pinfold was detained in a Chinese police cell, but the law concerning extraterritoriality and British subjects meant that it

---

42 "Werner Murder Suspect Freed", *Peiping Chronicle*, January 17, 1937.

was for the British authorities to control and direct Pinfold's custody: the interviews with Pinfold appear to have been conducted by Botham; the case assessment and outcome - the decision-
making - was firmly in British hands. Ultimately, however, the
detention of both the rickshaw coolie and Pinfold appear to have
led the police nowhere. That strongly suggests that during the
interviews Pinfold denied wrongdoing and provided plausible
explanations for movements and conduct. That coupled with insufficient evidence of involvement probably led Botham to a decision to instruct Police Chief Han to release the suspect. Neither
Pinfold nor the rickshawman are mentioned again in connection
with police investigations. In a case of this kind the desire of police officers involved to achieve a result - and swiftly - would
have been considerable; had the police considered Pinfold to be
a serious candidate then all manner of time and resources would
have been invested in the pursuit of a case against him. There is
nothing thereafter to suggest such action. And any subsequent
police interest in an already publicly-known suspect would have
been difficult to disguise or keep secret.

And that, in effect, is all that is known today of the police
murder investigation, by both the Chinese and the British. During the months after the murder, the newspapers ran sporadic
reports of rumors of new developments or imminent police action. *The Peiping Chronicle*, January 26:

Report Denied

A local Chinese newspaper reported yesterday morning
that an Italian had been arrested by the Chinese authorities
on Sunday in connexion with the murder. The Royal Italian
Embassy made inquiries from the Morrison Street Police
Station yesterday and was told that the report was abso-

lutely without foundation."[43]

Sometimes such stories coincided with the departure or arrival in Peking of the British police:

Captain Botham in Peiping Again

The arrival in Peiping last evening of Inspector R. Botham of the British Police in Tientsin revived rumours that an arrest had been made by the local Chinese authorities in connexion with the Werner murder case, but inquiry in authoritative Chinese quarters elicited an emphatic denial. It is however generally believed that important developments in the case are pending.[44]

But the stories came to nothing. There were no further arrests. No named suspects. No appeals for knowledge of any particular person's whereabouts. Of course, neither the Chinese nor British police had any of the technological advantages available to murder teams today. No CCTV, no DNA analysis, no credit/debit card tracking. No mobile phone records, criminal intelligence database, or offender-profiling. Fingerprinting *was* available, but their recovery from different types of surfaces was greatly limited compared to today. Exposed to the elements of a Peking winter's night, there were probably none to be had from the scene. Without these evidential tools, the police detectives of 1937 Peking had to rely on the physical evidence before them, seeking witnesses, and divining intelligence from mere rumor.

On Saturday, June 26, after a five-month adjournment, Consul Fitzmaurice resumed the inquest at the British Embassy. He found the evidence inconclusive and announced a verdict of

43 *Peiping Chronicle*, January 26, 1937.
44 *Peiping Chronicle*, February 25, 1937.

British Embassy entrance hall, Peking. The coroner's hearing would have been held in this or a similar room

"murder by person or persons unknown." *The Peiping Chronicle* reported that "although the Chinese and British police have worked feverishly on the case the mystery of the girl's death has not been solved." It also spoke of Botham examining scores of persons of many nationalities. A British subject had been detained in connection with the case, it added, but was subsequently released.[45]

Some ten days later, Japanese and Chinese soldiers clashed during night exercises near the Marco Polo Bridge not far from Peking. It was the catalyst for eight years of war between the two nations.

---

45 "Coroner Pronounces Verdict of Murder in Werner Mystery", *Peiping Chronicle*, June 27, 1937.

4

THE FATHER

E.T.C. WERNER

DESPITE CLAIMS TO a healthy income,[1] Werner may have chosen his home at Number 1, Kuei-chiach'ang, due to the area's cheap rent,[2] although the decision may also have been influenced by the thought that his stay there could be a short one owing to his intention to return to Britain with Pamela within a year or so. By foreign standards, the area was not a desirable one; half a mile or so east of the Legation Quarter, Kuei-chia-ch'ang was situated in a previously scenic but by then run-down and remote corner of the Tartar City, one served by little more than dirt tracks and hutungs. Scattered with rubbish dumps, the area was also home to an old German cemetery, a place to which the Chinese traditionally had a strong aversion.[3]

It would have been at this courtyard address that Werner typed his letter of complaint to the MP Harry Day on July 12, 1937, a few weeks after the final coroner's hearing, and only a few days after the shooting incident between Japanese and Chi-

....

1 Werner Case Unsolved", Caravan magazine, March 1937.
2 Hoover Institution Library & Archives, Nym Wales papers 1931-1998 (Helen Foster Snow), page 156 box 17.
3 Lewis Charles Arlington and William Lewisohn, In Search of Old Peking, (1935).

A view of part of the walls of Peking

nese soldiers at the Marco Polo Bridge. In his letter, Werner berated Anthony Eden for his ignorance of Pamela's murder:

Dear Sir,

According to a report in the local press, Mr. Anthony Eden, Secretary of State for Foreign Affairs, at question time in the House of Commons on the 16th June 1937, stated in reply to a question put by you, that "no British subjects had been kidnapped or murdered in China in the last 12 months."

That statement is erroneous. On the night of January 7, 1937, my only child, Pamela, was murdered in a most brutal and dastardly manner and her body horribly mutilated. In a few days time she would have been 20 years of age. She had returned to my home in Peking only twelve days before, having completed a brilliant five years educational career at the Grammar school in Tientsin, where she gained not only the two Cambridge certificates but also the first Silver Jubilee Scholarship instituted there.

It was a foul sadist [sic] crime, committed in all probability at one of those sexual orgies which are such a crying disgrace to the foreign community in Peking. She was waylaid on returning from skating from the French rink at 7.30 p.m. on that night, and her body, after mutilation, thrown at the foot of the city wall.

The case has been grossly mismanaged. The "gravest suspicion" rests on a destitute British ex-soldier, an American ex-marine, and another American, all close friends and known to indulge in the grossest sexual excesses. On the first of the three a dagger, handkerchief, and the dagger-sheath, all stained, as well as his shoes, with human blood, were found. Yet no arrest has been made, though six months have elapsed since the occurrence of the most ghastly tragedy in the history of the foreign community at Peking.

A fatal mistake – and not the only one – was made by the detectives in neglecting to take finger-prints from the girl's shoes found near the corpse when it was first discovered.

As it is, the murderers are still at large, and parents now are afraid to let their children go out in Peking unless adequately safeguarded.

It is high time that the murderous devils were arrested and brought to justice. Yours in the name of law and civilisation,

Edward Chalmers Werner.

H.B.M. Consul, Foochow (retired).[4]

Werner appeared to be suggesting he had come by intelligence relating to the crime that the police and authorities had missed.

4   UK National Archives, FO 371/21004 China Code 10 Files 2047 - 2396, July 1937 letter from E.T.C. Werner to Harry Day MP.

He charged gross incompetence on the part of the investigators. Werner, the murder victim's elderly father, frustrated by the police's inability to apprehend the murderer, had been forced to turn detective.

Despite the intense media interest, it appears the story and the murder itself did not stir much attention in the British Foreign Office in Whitehall. It was a turbulent time for international relations. After years of military skirmishing and political feuding, 1937 saw the commencement of the long-anticipated war between China and Japan, a conflict that eventually resulted in the deaths of over twenty million people. Closer to home, at least from a British point of view, was the Spanish Civil War, already in its second year. As if to signal future intent, the expanding armed forces of Nazi Germany and Fascist Italy were both sending military aid to the Spanish nationalists. For much of the world, war, or the threat of war, loomed large. After a few months, the murder, while still very much the talk of Peking, appears to have slipped off the Foreign Office radar entirely.

Question time in the House of Commons, Westminster, June 16, 1937 found Anthony Eden, later prime minister but at that time Secretary of State for Foreign Affairs in Neville Chamberlain's government, fielding questions from members of parliament.

Anthony Eden, British Foreign Secretary in 1937

Most of those posed that Wednesday afternoon concerned the pressing subject of the civil war in Spain but one question was related to more distant international troubles. Harry Day, the Labour MP for Southwark Central, rose from the green bench to address Eden about instability in China and asked to what extent the lives and property of British subjects had been adversely affected during the previous twelve months, and what steps had been taken to safeguard them.[5]

Ministers were given notice of tabled questions, giving their support staff time to gather facts and prepare meaningful answers. Rising to reply, Eden stated reassuringly that no British subjects had been kidnapped or murdered, and that all possible efforts were being made to safeguard their lives and property. And with that, Eden and the House moved swiftly on to the subject of the war in Spain.

Many MPs were well-known for asking ministerial questions as doing so kept their names in the newspapers. Harry Day was one of them. Coming as it did only a few weeks before the event that triggered full Sino-Japanese conflict, Day's China question received only limited press attention. But a month or so later, Eden had to apologize; he had got his facts wrong and had unwittingly misled the House.

Harry Day had since received a strongly-worded letter from a man living in Peking, the retired British consul, E.T.C. Werner, whose daughter had been murdered in that city on January 7. The father, it transpired, had read a British newspaper report of Day's question and Eden's reply stating there having been no murders in China and was outraged.

As Eden was then absent from London, it was left to an aide to write and make amends: it was explained to Day that Eden had requested the Embassy in Peking to inform Mr Werner how deeply he regretted what had appeared to be a misleading reply, and to pass on his sympathies for the father's sad loss. It was made clear that Eden was greatly concerned that he should have unwittingly caused Werner further distress.[6]

....

5 Hansard, House of Commons debate, vol 325 c 339, June 16, 1937.
6 UK National Archives, FO 371/21004 China. Code 10 Files 2047 - 2396. Includes letters to, from and on behalf of Eden, Werner and Day.

In Parliament, both Day and Eden had been referring to the effects on British citizens of the growing political conflict in northern China between the Chinese Nationalist Government and the Empire of Japan which would soon develop into full war. In the circumstances, the oversight was perhaps understandable, and the exchange generated virtually no press attention in London.

As a retired British consul and a successful and published writer with over fifty years' experience of living and working in China, Werner knew Peking and both its foreign and Chinese societies a good deal better than most. Importantly, he also knew the internal structure of the British Government establishment and he used this knowledge to full advantage in pushing the case of his murdered daughter. Dissatisfied with one tier of authority, he simply went straight over their heads. Over the ensuing years, he wrote many letters targeting men including the British Ambassador to China and Foreign Office officials in Whitehall. These communications stirred up a great deal of trouble and proved difficult to ignore, properly formed and addressed as they were. As a result, Werner's reports that survived the chaos of the coming war were minuted, logged, filed. Many of them still exist and are preserved in the UK National Archives, filled as they are with the writer's assertions and the names of those allegedly involved in the crime.

Aged seventy-two at the time of Pamela's death, Werner was one of seven children of British parents, Joseph and Harriet Werner.[7] He was born in Dunedin, New Zealand in November 1864.[8] Possessing some form of inheritance, Werner's father was described by his son as having a wanderlust. New Zealand was just one of many stops made by the growing family during years

....

7   E.T.C. Werner, *Memorigrams*, (1940), p3.
8   E.T.C. Werner, *Autumn Leaves*, (1928), p465.

of frequent if unexplained travel. While still an infant, Werner accompanied his parents to Peru, Panama, Jamaica and Mexico, and then on to Havana and New York before traveling throughout much of Europe.

Serious schooling for Werner started with the family's return to England and the subsequent death of his father. For nine years, the young Edward Werner attended Tonbridge, an old and distinguished public school for boys in Kent. Despite possessing a sharp intelligence, and perhaps partly because of his already spiky character, the young Werner left Tonbridge early: "I preferred to leave school before reaching the top of the pyramid," he later said.[9] He then attended a 'crammer' school in the City of London where he studied for two years for a Foreign Office examination, working hard and revising late into the night while commuting daily from the family home in Richmond-upon-Thames.[10]

After passing the student interpreter examination, and having read a book on the country, Werner was keen to work in Japan. But the vacancies in that popular posting went to the two top scoring candidates, so Werner was despatched with four other students to China instead. Fate had dealt him the better deal, he wrote in his 1928 book *Autumn Leaves*, an autobiographical-come-anecdotal account of his life.

All new staff to the British China Service (as the Foreign Office staff assigned to China fondly referred to themselves) were first posted to Peking for training and study. Werner's long journey from London to Peking in 1884 was by a series of ships and boats, with the last leg of ten miles completed inelegantly astride an ass, upon which humble form of transport the nineteen-year-old Werner arrived outside the great city walls on the afternoon

9 ibid.
10 ibid.

E.T.C. Werner, age 45

of July 4. He later wrote: "Every thing and being around us was Oriental, as yet untouched by Western "civilisation": the people, languages, costumes, buildings, architecture, conveyances; we were the only bits of incongruity in an all-pervading, calm, dignified, mediaeval East."[11]

Entering Legation Street, the main road through the undefended and pre-Boxer Legation Quarter, as yet "unpaved and deep in dust," a travel-weary Werner and his colleagues eventually reached the entrance of the British Legation, a huge gate surmounted by a tower and the Union Flag. Inside the compound—some twenty acres in area—was a "bit of England",[12] shaded by trees and featuring closely-clipped lawns. It was little changed a decade later when another new consular recruit arrived:

> The main building was the Minister's residence, a beautiful Chinese building with an imposing entrance by a raised pathway passing under two stately porticoes. All these were covered with the official green tiles permitted to (Chinese) officials of high rank... the students and chancery assistants were housed in three sets of buildings... there was also the chapel, a theatre and a bowling alley... we were allowed an extraordinary amount of freedom and were always relied on to play the game.[13]

....

11 ibid.
12 ibid.
13 Sir Meyrick Hewlett, *Forty Years in China*, (1943) pp4-5.

As with all the new students, Werner was allocated his own bedroom, study and bathroom. He was also provided with a personal servant or 'boy' and his very own Chinese tutor for two years of study of the native language. According to Werner, the standards of attainment in Chinese varied hugely from student to student. Success not only depended on the diligence or otherwise of the individual, but also on the scarcity of all-too inadequate textbooks, coupled with the idiosyncrasies of the allocated native teacher. Learning the Chinese language, however, was something in which Werner appears to have been successful.

Life in Peking for consular recruits was a healthy one, at least compared with many other far-flung parts of China. The climate was dry and frequently windy with Peking's temperature ranging from stiflingly hot to well below freezing. For foreigners with time on their hands, days could be spent at the local racecourse or on excursions to temples in the nearby Western Hills. There were also opportunities for pony-riding, polo, tennis, hockey, football, skating, bowling and athletics. And, notably, there was "generous hospitality from all" — the foreign community in Peking were great social entertainers.[14] In fact, largely ignoring international squabbles back home, "the whole Legation Quarter... was a happy hunting-ground with doors thrown open for all who chose to enter them, and a welcome for any who did enter."[15] Even Werner, who in his twenties was already of a stiff disposition, occasionally entered into this heady social scene, writing of "days of youthful gaiety and indiscretion."[16]

Werner enjoyed his early years in China and the time spent in "dear old Peking",[17] for he had by this time developed a deep

14 ibid.
15 ibid.
16 E.T.C. Werner, *Autumn Leaves*, (1928), p499.
17 ibid. p528.

fascination for the country and its culture, one that was to remain with him for the rest of his life.

Werner's first and, as it turned out, only spell of consular work in Peking proved shorter than he probably hoped for. For several years after his study period, he remained at the Legation tasked with junior administrative work. From 1890 onwards, he was posted 'south' to serve at the British Consulate of one Chinese port and concession after another: Canton, Tientsin, Macao, Hangchow, Kiungchow and others. Typically, such postings were for several years at a time, usually with a six-month home-leave furlough granted every three or so years. Werner found all of these postings disappointingly dull compared with Peking, a city unparalleled in China for its history and culture. Worse still was the tropical climate of many of the southern ports which Werner described:

> ...everything was continually being mildewed for three-quarters of the year, when the walls of one's rooms dripped with moisture, when one's skin did ditto, the pores seeming never to close, when one was constantly stung by mosquitos and sandflies, when ladies sitting at dinner had to put their feet and ankles into paper bags to prevent them being bitten... white ants ate through the floors of rooms and pillars of the houses, when the atmosphere seemed almost too solid to breathe and prevented sleep at night, when one yearned for a 'bite of frost' – these tortures combined with generally insipid routine work and the mercenary ideals of the community in general, who were there of course to make as much money as they could and took no interest in any literary pursuits, was most depressing.[18]

18 ibid. p556.

Promotion was almost invariably slow in the China Service, but particularly so for Werner. It wasn't until 1900, after over fifteen years in China with spells as first assistant, pro-consul and vice-consul, that Werner gained promotion to the rank of consul at Kiungchow. He was never promoted again. Nor was he ever posted again to Peking.[19] Ordinarily a time-serving man in the China Service, after completing stints in comparative backwaters, might expect to be given roles of increasing responsibility in the major cities of Shanghai, Nanking and Peking and eventually achieve the rank of consul-general, with its increase in pay and pension. But over the years Werner had succeeded in making a bad name for himself in many circles. He himself realized that he was too abrasive, too abstinent, too unwavering and too independent of mind to get on with many of his fellow foreigners and consular colleagues. He did not fit in with the in-crowd of "jolly good fellows" and deplored the club-bar drinking culture enjoyed by so many. Realizing that his career was not taking him to higher office, Werner devoted his spare time to his "supreme pleasure", the study of Chinese culture, creating a library for himself in one of the rooms at each consulate in which he worked.[20]

Frustrated by what he saw as the "secret reports, impediments, lies and injustices of his superiors", Werner wrote: "Consular officials may be said to be (1) those who aim at reaching the highest posts, and if possible becoming ministers; (2) those who aim at retiring at the earliest opportunity... and who occupy their leisure in some special study."[21]

Werner did occasionally receive praise from his superiors. In

19 UK National Archives, annual Foreign Office list.
20 E.T.C. Werner, *Autumn Leaves*, (1928) p535-539.
21 ibid. p530.

February 1906 he was sent on an urgent mission to the city of Nanchang in the southeastern province of Kiangsi, sailing in a British gunship on the 150-mile river journey from his post at the river town of Kiukiang. There, his grim task was to ensure the effective investigation of the murder by a Chinese mob of the Kingham family, a British missionary couple with two young daughters. The "Nanchang massacre", as it became known, was a particularly brutal one in which six French Jesuits also lost their lives.

From survivors' accounts it transpired that the head of the French Catholic mission had invited a local Chinese magistrate to dinner and afterward asked him to sign a document that would bring to an end a long-standing dispute over some trivial damage to a signpost. Probably feeling under duress, the magistrate at first refused, but then eventually assented and signed. Then, seemingly in some fit of shame and remorse, he found an isolated room in the mission in which to cut his own throat, a wound from which he died some days later. Outside, it was assumed to be murder and an enraged mob converged on the mission. Outbuildings were set ablaze and the head of mission, Père Lacruche, was chased through the streets, first into and then out of a friend's house, before he was overcome and beaten to death. Five young freres, only recently arrived from France, too slow or unsure of where to turn, induced a boatman to take them across a river to safety. But threatened by the mob, the boatman turned back. Another foot-pursuit ended with all five being stoned to death in a lake.

Not content with this slaughter, and determined to find and deal with more "foreign devils", a mob broke through the gates of the nearby compound occupied by the Kinghams, who were holding a church service at the time. Reverend H. Kingham, unaware of what had transpired, went out to speak with the crowd, only to be assaulted, and had several teeth knocked out. Similar to the Jesuits' plight, the unfortunate Kingham family also made a hopeless dash for shelter, seeking refuge in a nearby empty house. Despite the improvised barricades, the mob made a hole in a wall, broke their way in, and bludgeoned the Kinghams and their eldest daughter, Gracie, to death. Dragged by his heels and dumped into a nearby muddy pool, the Reverend Kingham still displayed small signs of life. On seeing this, one of the mob waded in and finished him off with a wooden pole. The youngest daughter, Vera, age five, only escaped violent death thanks to her Chinese amah hiding her under her clothing.

On hearing of this atrocity, Werner's unenviable task was to arrive safely at the scene, avoid a similar fate to the Kinghams (hence the gunboat), refuse the many conciliatory bribes offered by the local officials, and insist that justice be served. In the event, rather than further violence, Werner met with a great deal of official fawning regret and was afforded an escorted entrance into the city, the route lined with fearful and silent crowds displaying suitably sombre and contrite faces. Then the gunboat left, leaving Werner alone and, in his words, the only foreigner "in a city of 800,000 anti-foreign Chinese all anxious to propitiate me."[22] Some weeks later, ten Chinese men were found guilty of murder and beheaded, an event Werner chose not to stay to witness. Culpable Chinese officials were dismissed and financial arrangements made to support the Kinghams' surviving orphan. For his endeavours in Nanchang, Werner reported receiving the approval of the British Minister in Peking.[23] Coming six years after the Boxer Rebellion, the Nanchang Massacre illustrated the dangers foreigners continued to face in China and went a long way to explain their continued insistence on protective enclaves,

....

22 ibid. p589.
23 ibid. pp581-593.

gates, walls and soldiers.

Five years later, Werner witnessed more killing as a result of the Chinese revolution and the final overthrow of the Manchu dynasty following an uprising in October 1911. By this time he was posted to the port of Foochow.

> We had three days and nights of real war, during which I got practically no sleep or rest. Having urgent requests for gunboats from nearly every port of China, the (British) Admiral naturally could not comply with them all, but he sent me a torpedo-boat destroyer, from which thirty men were landed, fifteen of whom had to remain on the shore near the vessel, the other fifteen being placed at my disposal for the protection of foreign residents, whose habitations were spread over six square miles of territory.
>
> Gunfire, shooting at sight, and looting were going on all around. The Chinese barricaded the streets and started hunting the Manchus as if they were so many hares. One could see a mob of twenty or thirty Chinese chasing at full speed a solitary Manchu, who, running down a street and reaching the barricade, would attempt to jump or scale it, but, falling back, was invariably mortally wounded, shot dead, or cut to pieces.
>
> Old men as well as boys still in their teens were hustled along, kicked, buffeted, struck, spat upon, jeered and sworn at by the crowd, and after being rudely knocked off their feet, shot through the heart by young student cadets ... As each victim was thrown onto his back and shot, the crowd bent over, staring at him during his dying spasms.[24]

24 ibid. pp640-642.

Werner described being repelled by the Chinese attitude toward captured prisoners, and he was equally ashamed of the voyeurism displayed by some foreign merchants. But the end of Manchu rule in Foochow coincided with changes for Werner too.

> With the defeat of the Manchus, the suicide of the Viceroy, and the precipitous flight of the Provincial Judge … things gradually resumed their normal state. Things having settled down, I applied for a fortnight's leave and went to Hong Kong to meet my fiancee, who arrived from England two days later.[25]

Long-term bachelor Werner must have raised a few of his colleagues' eyebrows by his decision to marry. Whilst on furlough in the summer of 1910 and holidaying in Aldburgh on the Suffolk coast, Werner met Gladys Ravenshaw, the second daughter of a retired colonel and diplomat who had served in India. A year later, after a suitable correspondence, Gladys sailed out to meet Werner in Hong Kong, where the pair were married in the Anglican cathedral on December 12, 1911. He was 47; she was 24.[26]

Judging from the wedding photograph, Gladys Ravenshaw appears to have been tall, certainly taller than her husband. She was also dark and slender, and something of a beauty. She was a fine dancer and enjoyed outdoor sports.[27] Why it was necessary for her to enter what appears to have been an arranged marriage with a man so much older than herself and to take up a life so far from home is unclear, but prejudice may have played a part. A consular colleague of Werner's later described Gladys as "a very attractive young woman, possibly with some Indian

....

25 ibid.
26 "Men in the East", *Caravan* magazine, January 1937.
27 E.T.C. Werner, *Autumn Leaves*, (1928) p682.

blood."[28] Born in Sussex, Gladys was one of four sisters, two of whom were born in India; the claim of Indian blood may or may not have been true.[29] But at the time, such things mattered. In China, like elsewhere, marriage between different races was widely frowned upon by both foreigners and Chinese, as were the children of such unions.[30] No one subscribed more to this attitude than Werner himself, who wrote disparagingly of a British official's son taking a Tibetan wife and providing him with "half-baked grandchildren."[31] Werner's later sensitivity over his wife's parentage, together with a severe bout of marital insecurity—"he became madly jealous of all his vice-consuls"[32]—soon led him into a great deal of professional trouble. And dramatically so.

A few years later in September 1913, the Werners were woken just past midnight by a drunk and hostile British customs official. The man had taken it upon himself to climb the Foochow Consulate's iron entrance gates in order to smash the ornate lamp that graced the top. Werner and his wife, incensed by this latest example of the foreign drinking-club culture, dressed quickly and ran downstairs, Werner arming himself with a whip on the way. The pair angrily pursued the miscreant into the club bar which was situated next door to the Consulate.

An ugly altercation ensued. Mrs Werner's parentage was insulted, and the customs officer was struck several times about the head before the parties were forced apart by various club members, including the French Consul.

With few allies in Foochow to support his version of events, Werner was accused of badly over-reacting. He vehemently de-

28 School of Oriental & African Studies archive library, P.D. Coates collection (PP MS 52) letter from Sir Alwyne Ogden, October 3, 1973.
29 National Archives, UK census for Worth, East Sussex, 1891 & 1901.
30 P.D. Coates, *The China Consuls*, (1988) p421.
31 E.T.C. Werner, Autumn Leaves, (1928) p664.
32 School of Oriental & African Studies archive library, P.D. Coates collection (PP MS 52) letter from Sir Alwyne Ogden, October 3, 1973.

The Werners' wedding, Hong Kong, 1911

nied any wrongdoing whatsoever. Telegrams were transmitted, reports were written to and by superiors, and apologies were demanded. The upshot was that the Werners were sent home to England on furlough where he was offered a face-saving early medical retirement. This, Werner obstinately refused, producing a doctor's report declaring him medically fit, only to have retirement forced upon him nonetheless by an equally adamant Foreign Office.[33]

Foochow therefore turned out to be Werner's final consular posting, one he left precipitously in late 1913. In the spring of 1914, his retirement was finally confirmed; he was only 49. But life in the China Service was recognized in Whitehall to be so remote, so harsh and so hazardous to a man's health that a year in China counted for far more in service than the same period in many other parts of the world.[34] Werner qualified for a full, long-service consular pension.

Werner's had been an eventful career. He was raised and schooled in Victorian England, of which his character was very much a product. He had experienced the last years of old Imperial China under the ruthless hand of the Empress Dowager and he had survived the Boxer Rebellion, during which he was posted in Kiungchow on the southern island of Hainan. He had then witnessed the revolution of 1911, the end of the Manchu dynasty, and the beginning of China's further descent into political anarchy.

Along the way, Werner had also gained a law degree. During an extended two-year furlough in 1905, he studied at the Middle Temple in London and succeeded in qualifying as a barrister-at-law. Such personal development was encouraged by the Foreign Office owing to the peculiar legal duties of consuls in China of

33 UK National Archives, files T 1/12110, FO 369/683 & FO 228/1861.
34 School of Oriental & African Studies archive library, P.D. Coates collection (PP MS 52) letter from G.V. Kitson, March 28, 1974.

officiating over British court cases. But in the long run, the exercise appears to have gained Werner little credit with his employers. He later bemoaned the few opportunities his minor postings afforded him to make use of his hard study and newly-acquired legal knowledge.[35]

On receiving Foreign Office confirmation of his retirement, the Werners returned to China, where they would live on a pension. Held

Gladys Ravenshaw

up by the war in Europe, they eventually arrived in Peking in the summer of 1915,[36] a city Werner called the "intellectual centre of Asia."

How well the young Gladys Werner took to life and society in Peking remains unknown, but like many others in her position she would probably have enjoyed the advantages of being a foreigner in China, where the exchange rates and cost of living differential meant that even a relatively modest income afforded a lifestyle of grand houses and servants that could never be achieved back home. In addition to this, she took on the role of mother, albeit an adoptive one.

Werner later described his wife's health as delicate and said she suffered from a heart condition,[37] which may or may not account for the Werners having no children of their own. Whatever the case, after some childless years of marriage, the Werners adopted Pamela.[38] The child's given birth date of January 26, 1917 may or may not have been a notional one, or perhaps was related to the

35 E.T.C. Werner, *Autumn Leaves*, (1928) p548.
36 ibid. p681.
37 ibid. pp667 & 687.
38 "Werner Case Unsolved", *Caravan* magazine, March 1937.

P.W.

Pamela when a small child

date of her adoption. It is unclear.

Gladys was not able to enjoy the arrival of Pamela for very long. In 1921, she travelled alone to New York where she stayed with one of her married sisters while receiving specialist treatment for a heart condition.[39] She returned to China after some months, her health apparently improved. But she soon developed influenza, followed by meningitis and died in Peking on February 6, 1922. Her husband described her as being buried in "a peaceful grave in the beautiful British cemetery beneath the trees and flowers... When she passed it seemed like the ceasing of exquisite music... Death had laid his hand upon my heart as a harper lays his open palm upon his harp, to deaden its vibrations."[40] With his wife gone, Werner, then in his late fifties, was alone again, save for five-year-old Pamela and a Peking home run by a small number of Chinese servants.

Werner now devoted himself full-time to study and writing. Though his career may have been, as he saw it, unfairly thwarted by his superiors, at no stage had he permitted himself to be idle. Over the years he wrote extensively, with books and scholarly articles published on all manner of Chinese subjects, including the country's history, sociology and culture. The best-known of his books was *Myths and Legends of China*, published in 1922. At the time, *Myths and Legends* met with some acclaim, but many modern readers have criticized it for being inaccurate and hav-

39 E.T.C. Werner, *Autumn Leaves*, (1928) p687.
40 ibid. p688.

ing an irritating and condescending
tone. Werner possessed a love/hate
relationship with China; while he
was fascinated by Chinese culture
and admired it greatly, he was also
unsparing in his candid observations and criticism of the national
character, and wrote unashamedly
in the same fashion. Perhaps in his
defence it may be said that Werner
was at least open in his rudeness.

"Emotionally the Chinese are
sober, industrious, of remarkable

E.T.C. Werner, age 60

endurance, grateful, courteous, and ceremonious, with a high
sense of mercantile honour, but timorous, cruel, unsympathet-
ic, mendacious, and libidinous," he wrote. "Intellectually they
were, and to a large extent still are, non-progressive, in bondage
to uniformity and mechanism in culture, imitative, unimagina-
tive, torpid, indirect, suspicious, and superstitious."[41]

As well as books, the industrious Werner wrote numerous
articles for newspapers and journals, completed translations of
Chinese studies by other writers, gave lectures to local university
students and enjoyed the membership of various local historical
and sociological societies. He explained: "The pleasure in acquir-
ing knowledge consists, for me, not in the possibilities of reward,
pecuniary or other… but in its acquisition, simply and solely…
when one piece of work is finished, I put it out of my mind, in
order fully to concentrate on the subject in hand."[42]

Werner's *Myths and Legends of China* was published in the same
year as his wife's death. Another book, *Autumn Leaves*, followed

41 E.T.C. Werner, *Myths and Legends of China*, (1922), p22.
42 E.T.C. Werner, *Autumn Leaves*, (1928) p687.

six years later in 1928. To use Werner's own description, *Autumn Leaves* was a gallimaufry of his collected ideas and articles. It provides a useful account of Werner's life and his time in China, but nowhere within its autobiographical pages is there mention of Pamela. Werner describes his parents and his marriage to Gladys and her tragic death, his studies, his publications, his relations with a wide number of named people. But of Pamela, he included not a single word, not even an allusion to her. Nothing.

Ten years later, Werner was to make up for this silence. Never once referring to Pamela while she was alive, Werner had plenty to write and say concerning her in death. From 1937 onwards, the remainder of Werner's life was dedicated with great tenacity to the task of seeking justice for her murder.

The key piece of evidence Werner reported uncovering was provided by a nineteen-year-old rickshaw coolie, a witness who, according to Werner, had been discounted or ignored by the Chinese and British police through either incompetence or corruption. This Chinese youth had been working on the streets of Peking the night of Pamela's murder and said he had witnessed a small group of men enter a well-known brothel at Number 28, Ch'uan-pan hutung with a wounded yet conscious young woman. A few hours later, he said he was forced by the same men to carry the semi-conscious victim in his rickshaw the short distance to the foot of the wall where Pamela was found the next morning. Leaving the men as soon as he could, the coolie had not seen what happened to the victim, but, given the nature of events, he had been fortu-

Wentworth Prentice in 1917. (US National Archives & Records Administration)

94

nate to escape with his own life. Crucially, the witness said he knew the men involved. He had carried them in his rickshaw on other occasions before that night. All of them were foreigners.[43]

Werner's principal murder suspects were two Americans and an Italian: Wentworth Prentice and Fred Knauf, a dentist and a former marine respectively, and Ugo Cappuzzo, a medical doctor attached to the Italian Embassy. All three were still in Peking. What was more, Werner believed others were also involved: Werner's information was that Pinfold, the man the police arrested but later released, had also played a part in the crime.[44]

The motive for the murder, Werner concluded with certainty, was sexual. Pamela had simply been the latest victim of a foreign-run sex-ring operating in Peking, the members of which were all respectable men. Police corruption and judicial incompetence had meant that their crimes had gone undetected, something Werner was determined to bring to an end.[45]

43 E.T.C. Werner, *More Memorigrams*, (1948), p191.
44 UK National Archives, FO 371/23513/1510 Murder of Pamela Werner. Code 10 file 1510, letter from E.T.C. Werner to the British Ambassador to China, October 1938.
45 UK National Archives, repeat allegations of police corruption by E.T.C. Werner within letters to the British Ambassador to China, 1938-1941, within files FO 371/23513 and FO 371/35815

5

THE INVESTIGATION

SUSPECTS IN THE OPEN

Werner began his one-man investigation into Pamela's murder in September 1937 just as the police were bringing their own to a close.[1] His work was not conducted entirely alone: where Werner didn't or couldn't look into leads himself, he employed unnamed Chinese agents to act for him,[2] but in essence it was very much his own enterprise. His investigation soon developed into an obsession, taking up the greater part of his time and remaining energy. It was a quest in which he persisted over the coming years despite the mounting difficulties and restrictions caused by the escalating Sino-Japanese war, the advent of the wider World War, and later, by his eventual detention in a Japanese internment camp. Werner even continued with his task post-war, back in England after departing China shortly before its fall to the communists in 1949.

Commencing in April 1938, Werner wrote twenty-three

....

1 UK National Archives, FO 371/25315/1510 Murder of Pamela Werner Code 10 file 1510, letters from E.T.C. Werner to the British Ambassador to China, October 1938 and June 1939.
2 ibid.

lengthy investigative reports to the Foreign Office.[3] The last of these was dated just six days before Pearl Harbour in December 1941, but most are from 1938 and 1939, the first few years after the murder when Werner's investigative efforts were in full flow. Not all of the reports appear to have made it through war zones and reached their destination, but those that did reveal the twists and turns, and the results, of his enquiries. Werner did not pull any punches. He named the murderers. He criticized the incompetent. And he identified the corrupt.

In 1948, after the war's end, having been largely ignored by officialdom, Werner made a final summary of the circumstances of the murder as he believed it had occurred and had been missed by the police. He included this summary, outlined in the following paragraphs, in his final book, *More Memorigrams*. As previously with *Autumn Leaves*, this strangely-titled publication also included many of his cultural observations on China, but it then altered direction entirely to include a long and bold chapter describing Pamela's murder. In his earlier reports to the Foreign Office, Werner put names to each suspect, but the book's cautious publisher must have drawn a line at allowing them in print. So Werner had to be content with merely referring to *Man A* and *Man B* etc.

"The names of the two men responsible for the murder are known beyond any reasonable doubt, and, as stated, will be made public at the trial," Werner wrote. "For the time being, I distinguish them in order in which they come on the scene."[4]

Man A, Werner's chief suspect, was Wentworth Prentice, an American dentist in his forties and a long-term resident of Peking. With his wife and children long since returned to the USA, Prentice lived alone in a rented upstairs flat at Number 3 Legation Street in the heart of the Legation Quarter and close to the

3 E.T.C. Werner, *More Memorigrams* (1948), p208.
4 ibid. p188.

French ice rink. From this flat, he also ran his private dental practice.

This, in summary, is Werner's view on what happened:

The semi-destitute Pinfold acted as a pimp and a supplier of young women to the outwardly respectable Prentice.[5] On the January evening that Pamela failed to return home, Prentice, having heard from Pinfold of her recent return from Tientsin, sent a Chinese coolie to intercept her at the rink and deliver her a note. The ruse Prentice employed was that a former school-friend of Pamela was waiting to greet her at Prentice's flat.

Werner: "Inveigled by this deception, Pamela went to the flat, which is situated at the top of a narrow winding stairway. Expecting to meet her girl friend (and intending, as she must have, to stay only a few minutes, since she had to be home by 7.30), she found only the man B."[6]

Werner's alleged Man B that night was not Pinfold but Ugo Cappuzzo, a young Italian doctor attached to the Italian Embassy. Cappuzzo also possessed a successful private practice and, like Prentice, lived near the French ice rink with his wife and several young children. (His address was usually given as number 1 Nan-chia-tao, though this may refer to a place of work either inside or outside the Legation Quarter).[7]

Werner held that Prentice and Cappuzzo had operated this way with young women before. He didn't explain why Pamela herself was selected, but for some reason the two men thought that she was the type of girl who would meekly submit to their

....

5 UK National Archives, FO 371/25315/1510 Murder of Pamela Werner Code 10 file 1510, letters from E.T.C. Werner to the British Ambassador to China, October 1938 and June 1939.
6 E.T.C. Werner, *More Memorigrams* (1948), p189.
7 a) School of Oriental & African Studies library archive, MS 380730 Lionel Henry Lamb collection, October 1947 Peiping Address Book for the Foreign Correspondents Club of Peiping, & b) Archivio Storico Diplomatico, Rome, archive "Le Rappresentanze Diplomatiche e Consolari Italiane a Pechino 1870-1952, folder 186, file 9043 "Cappuzzo".

sexual requirements. And the production of a knife usually ensured that they got their way. They made an error of judgement
in assessing Pamela. She put up a spirited fight. And as a result,
she received a severe beating.

After these initial assaults the two men realized they were
in trouble. Ordinarily, shame could be relied upon to ensure the
silence of a rape victim, but on this occasion, there was no hiding
Pamela's injuries. They had gone too far, even by their own standards. A panicked telephone call was made from the flat in order
to summon a motor car (by now telephone lines were common
among foreigners in Peking, and Prentice certainly possessed
one).[8] A motor car soon arrived. And with it brought the involvement of another American, a former marine named Knauf.[9] The
semi-conscious Pamela was then carried out of the flat, down
the stairway, bundled into the waiting motor car and taken on a
short three-minute drive out of the Legation Quarter to a notorious bar-come-brothel in the Tarter City.

It was while waiting for a fare at this Russian-owned venue,
Number 28 Ch'uan-pan hutong, that Werner's young rickshaw
coolie, named Sun Te-hsing, witnessed the motor car's arrival at
the narrow-doored entrance to its compound. He saw three men
leave the vehicle with a woman, with two of the men supporting
the woman under each arm. The motor car left after money was
given to the driver and the small group entered the courtyard of
Number 28, closing the door behind them.[10]

Some hours later, around midnight, Sun Te-hsing was again
at the same spot when the lamp above the door to Number 28
was suddenly turned off making the lane even darker, "and the

8 US National Archives, consular report on the death of Wentworth Prentice 393.113.
9 UK National Archives, FO 371/25315/1510 Murder of Pamela Werner Code 10 file 1510,
   letters from E.T.C. Werner to the British Ambassador to China, February 1939, June 1939,
   October 1939.
10 ibid.

fat woman and houseboy of the place accompany the same men out, and then go back, shutting the door behind them... two of the men were supporting the girl, then dressed only in a long thin undergarment, with cloth covering her head."[11]

At this stage Pamela was apparently still alive; the witness heard her breathing and sobbing. He thought she may be drunk, like the men with her. After loading the victim onto Sun Te-hsing's rickshaw, one of the men joined her on its seat while the other two stayed on foot. The men aggressively demanded the frightened coolie to take them the short distance to the Wall Road, whereupon on reaching a remote spot, he was chased off with the flourish of a knife.

"The shorter man (Cappuzzo) got out and said to me: "*Ni ch'u pu ch'u?*" ("Will you go away or not?") The same man then struck at me with a dagger, cutting my sheepskin coat at the left shoulder. This so frightened me that I ran away with my rickshaw along the Wall Road.[12]

Pamela was then bludgeoned to death by the wall with a brick. Using a lamp in the black of night, Prentice and Cappuzzo began a desperate attempt to dispose of the body by firstly dismembering it before giving up on the task and burying the remains in the ditch. But, either disturbed or simply panicked, they abandoned this also and ran off after they caught sight of the lights of a motor car driving along the wall road toward them. Fortunately for the criminal pair, the motor car's occupants, a Doctor Kurotchkin and friends on their way home from a Russian Christmas party, drove past the scene without noticing anything (something, Werner reported, they later confirmed to police).[13] Pamela's body was discovered the next morning still

....

11 E.T.C. Werner, *More Memorigrams* (1948), p192.
12 ibid.
13 ibid. p223.

lying in the shallow depression where it had been abandoned.

According to Werner, the identities of those who killed Pamela were virtually common knowledge among Peking's Chinese residents. As were their deranged habits: "They are an open secret," he wrote.[14] And word of the identity of the killers had also reached the ears of many foreigners, some of them outside China. A friend of Werner in America wrote in sympathy to him: "I believe I could name one of the murderers and even send you his photograph".[15]

And the Chinese police also knew, said Werner. He wrote: "It is generally, and rightly, said in Peking that in most cases of murder the Chinese police know who the murderer is, though it is quite a different matter from their being willing to arrest and charge him."[16]

Colonel Han, Werner alleged, had reached the same conclusion as himself as to the identity of the murderers. To Werner's disgust and frustration, he also learned that Han was entirely compromised by his own corruption, having received regular bribes from the brothel keepers of Number 28, the first inkling of which had come early in Werner's investigation when he noticed Han start and become alarmed when the old man first made mention of the venue.[17]

In effect, according to Werner, the corrupt Han had become the murderers' protector. Han was the most senior Chinese official connected with the case. No Chinese police action would take place without his agreement. So no action was taken. The British police from Tientsin, speaking little or no Chinese, were reliant on being supplied with accurate information by their Chinese counterparts. But they hadn't received any.

· ·

14 ibid. p198.
15 ibid.
16 UK National Archives, FO 371/25315/1510 Murder of Pamela Werner Code 10 file 1510, letter from E.T.C. Werner to the British Ambassador to China, October 1938.
17 ibid.

In any event, the former Scotland Yard men did not impress Werner. Though acknowledging Dennis as a man of integrity,[18] Werner thought the chief inspector was slow and his murder theories entirely wide of the mark which resulted in him "going on wild goose chases."[19] Most importantly, he rated Dennis's professional judgement as poor having allowed himself to be taken in by the Chinese police.[20] As for Inspector Botham, the man drank too much, "quaffing flagons of beer while airing to all and sundry his theories of how and by whom the murder was committed."[21] Botham also displayed a crass rudeness in front of his Chinese hosts, boasting of his infallibility and arrogantly wagging his finger at them, an act akin in Chinese culture to an assault.[22] Consul Fitzmaurice, meanwhile, had shown himself to be simply incompetent.[23] Unlike Werner, Fitzmaurice did not possess a law degree and was ignorant of evidence and judicial procedure.

For Werner, the entire case had been grossly mismanaged by both the Chinese and British officials. The whole investigation had been one long abject failure. As a result, the rapists and murderers of Pamela were still free to walk the streets of Peking. Justice went unserved.

Werner described the case to the Foreign Office as "an astonishing example of British official incompetence,"[24] and he was

....

18 E.T.C. Werner, *Memorigrams* (1940), p148.
19 UK National Archives, FO 371/25315/1510 Murder of Pamela Werner Code 10 file 1510, letter from E.T.C. Werner to the British Ambassador to China, October 1938.
20 ibid, postscript to letter from E.T.C. Werner to the British Ambassador to China, December 1938.
21 UK National Archives, FO 371/25315/1510 Murder of Pamela Werner Code 10 file 1510, letter from E.T.C. Werner to the British Ambassador to China, February 1939.
22 a) UK National Archives, FO 371/25315/1510 Murder of Pamela Werner Code 10 file 1510, letter from E.T.C. Werner to the British Ambassador to China, June 1939, & b) E.T.C. Werner, *Memorigrams* (1940), p148.
23 UK National Archives, FO 371/25315/1510 Murder of Pamela Werner Code 10 file 1510, letter from E.T.C. Werner to the British Ambassador to China, December 1938.
24 E.T.C. Werner, *More Memorigrams* (1948), p212.

scathing of Peking Consul Nicholas Fitzmaurice and of Allan Archer, who succeeded Fitzmaurice in the post in July 1937.[25] And
yet, though let down, as he saw it, on all sides, Werner never quite
lost faith with the wider British establishment. He never gave up
writing to their superiors in London appealing for the delivery of
justice. He continued despite receiving what can only be described
as repeated diplomatic brush-offs, polite and carefully worded replies that were nonetheless devoid of any meaningful action. Werner, having had a lifetime's experience of the Foreign Office, must
have recognized these responses for what they were. Nonetheless,
he seems to have kept with the belief that he would eventually
galvanise someone of sufficient rank into seeing that justice was
served, and that in time he would live to see some form of trial.

It ought to have occurred to Werner that Foreign Office staff of
all ranks, were: 1) preoccupied with the effects of war across much
of the globe, and 2) possessed of little influence over a murder
investigation on Chinese territory in a largely lawless country being fought over by Nationalist, Communist and Japanese forces.
In August 1937, no less than the British Ambassador to China
was shot, his vehicle strafed by a Japanese aircraft. But none of
this stopped Werner from persisting in his efforts to trigger some
form of action from the British authorities. Short of Werner taking
the law into his own hands, which despite his occasional losses
of temper would have been out of character, there were few op-
tions available to him. The British establishment remained his best
hope. While he criticised a whole number of his compatriots for
their incompetence and inactivity, he never once impugned their
honesty or integrity. Still less did he ever suggest that one of their
number was directly involved in the crime. That allegation would
come from elsewhere. Had Werner known of that allegation, he

25 UK National Archives, annual Foreign Office list.

would have doubtless been both surprised and deeply shocked.

Werner had identified the killers to his own satisfaction, succeeding in his investigation where the police had failed, or perhaps where some had *chosen* not to succeed. He had found Chinese witnesses of the events around Prentice's flat, he had found the all-important rickshaw coolie present at Number 28 and the Wall Road, and he had also amassed a wealth of intelligence on the characters and habits of the suspects. He achieved all this largely through the use of what he described as agents – local Chinese with local knowledge. These men were both paid by and reported to Werner, and, importantly, to no one else.[26] Through this practical means, coupled with his dogged perseverance, Werner revealed that Peking harboured what he had already suspected, a circle of foreigners linked by their nefarious sexual habits and free to commit murder.

Eventually, Werner, in his mid-seventies and, by his own account, no longer in rude health[27] and frustrated and disappointed with the lack of any official response to his reports, summoned up the courage to door-stop the suspects himself. This wasn't so much to challenge them, he later explained, but rather to gather evidence and test their reactions.[28]

Two of his suspects weren't hard to find. Werner knew well the narrow stairs that led to Prentice's dental practice. The dentist himself was no stranger either: years before, in 1930, Prentice had straightened Pamela's erupting teeth.[29] Then, not long after the murder, Werner had briefly bumped into him in the street. But their paths did not cross again in Peking. Perhaps Prentice wisely

26 UK National Archives, FO 371/25315/1510 Murder of Pamela Werner Code 10 file 1510, letters from E.T.C. Werner to the British Ambassador to China, October 1938 et al
27 ibid.
28 UK National Archives, FO 371/25315/1510 Murder of Pamela Werner Code 10 file 1510, letter from E.T.C. Werner to the British Ambassador to China, July 1939.
29 UK National Archives, FO 371/25315/1510 Murder of Pamela Werner Code 10 file 1510, letter from E.T.C. Werner to the British Ambassador to China, February 1939.

kept his distance from the old man. Or simply ignored him.[30]

Doctor Cappuzzo was also easily tracked down. Werner devised a ruse in order to meet him at his place of work, as he explained in a letter to the Ambassador:

> His private house is in the Legation Quarter, very near to Prentice's flat. He and Prentice are, or at least were, close friends. He is Doctor to the Italian Embassy Marine Guard.
>
> Not having met him and wishing to get some idea as to what kind of man he was, I called at the small Italian hospital near the Peking Hotel.
>
> When he entered the waiting room I said: "You are Dr. Cappuzzo?"
>
> He said: "Yes."
>
> I said I would like to ask if the Varaldas were returning to Peking.
>
> He said he believed they were still in Rome.
>
> He asked who I was, and when I told him, he started, and said: "When your daughter was killed I was in Hong Kong."
>
> Not wishing to arouse his suspicions, I left, but on going out of the gate, I asked the gateman if Dr. Cappuzzo had been to Hong Kong, and he replied: "No, he has not been away for many years."
>
> A few days later, Mrs Skiotis of Skiotis & Co, confirmed this with emphasis and others have repeated the same statement. Nor can I get any evidence of his having left Peking from either the British or American travel agencies.[31]

---

30 UK National Archives, FO 371/25315/1510 Murder of Pamela Werner Code 10 file 1510, letter from E.T.C. Werner to the British Ambassador to China, October 1938.
31 UK National Archives, FO 371/25315/1510 Murder of Pamela Werner Code 10 file 1510, letter from E.T.C. Werner to the British Ambassador to China, July 1939.

This peculiar little meeting probably occurred in the first half of 1939, two years after the murder. Brief as it was, Werner, normally so combative, may have been caught off-guard, suddenly confronted as he was by the polite and outgoing Cappuzzo on his own turf. Though the hospital gateman was scarcely Cappuzzo's personal secretary and diary-keeper, and the doctor may not have needed travel agents, it transpires that Werner was nonetheless correct about Cappuzzo's whereabouts at the time of the murder. On 17 January 1937 (just after Pamela's burial and Pinfold's release from custody) *The Peiping Chronicle* listed Cappuzzo as one of several foreign doctors who attended a ceremony in honour of a medical colleague at the French Embassy. It was not until several weeks later, on February 4, that the society column of the same newspaper mentioned Cappuzzo leaving Peking for south China in connection with research into tropical diseases. This was almost certainly the same visit to Hong Kong that Cappuzzo later mentioned to Werner. Contrary to his claim in the waiting-room, Cappuzzo appears to have indeed been in Peking when Pamela was murdered.

Werner was in better form when he called upon Knauf, an ex-marine in his forties, who Werner knew went hunting with Cappuzzo.[32] Cappuzzo and Prentice may have possessed respectable fronts to show the world, but Werner knew Knauf to be a heroin dealer and someone frequently in trouble with the American Consulate.[33] Consulate staff provided Werner with an address where Knauf could be found in the Tartar City and he went to the address on Monday, July 17, 1939. Knauf was not in, but Werner returned that same afternoon, an oppressively hot day. The letter continued:

....

32 ibid.
33 ibid.

As I went toward the Chinese house on the north side of
the small courtyard, he looked out over the top of the paper
window, and my first impression was that I was looking
at an animal instead of a human being. He has a long face,
very large eyes, a pronounced Roman nose (this was noticed by the rickshaw coolie on the night of the murder),
and a body (only partly covered with a kimono, as is his
custom) evidently thickly covered with dark hair. It struck
me at once how repulsive he must appear to any refined
girl, and how scared she would be at such a sight.

His manner of speaking, however, was pleasanter...
though after the first few sentences he apparently got the
impression that I had come to accuse or have a row with
him and adopting a loud tone and hostile attitude he was
obviously prepared to resort to violence.

To put him off his guard, I said I had not come to accuse him, but only to seek information. He then assumed a
milder attitude, and asked who I was (though he certainly
knew already, as I had told the gateman in the morning).
He said his trouble with the American consul was nothing,
and that he never lost his temper except with Chinese...
He said that he had never seen Pamela, had only been in
number 28 Ch'uan-pan Hutung once and that a year before
the murder. Also he said he knew of the murder only from
what had appeared in the local English paper. Generally, he
denied everything point blank, but admitted knowing Cappuzzo... and often gone hunting ... He emphasized his very
close friendship with Prentice.[34]

This tense exchange continued further, until Werner struck a

....

34 ibid.

nerve by reminding Knauf of the latter's association with a woman of ill-repute and of the fact they had jointly run a bawdy establishment. With this, Knauf's face grew pale with anger and the interview fast drew to an end. Knauf was conveniently called away from the room by his houseboy, and his parting words to Werner on the subject of the killers were that "he would bring them to me" (i.e. to Werner).[35]

With that chilling promise from Knauf, Werner left. He reported sensing a curious atmosphere in the house, of which Knauf appeared to occupy only a small part. Doors were locked from room to room. People moved about furtively. The place was sparsely furnished. Knauf gave Werner the impression of someone whose belongings could fit into one bag. Typing out a record of the encounter later, Werner was more convinced than ever that he had just called on one of the killers. Slowly but surely, he felt certain he was uncovering the truth.[36]

35 ibid.
36 ibid.

6

THE US MARINE

FRED KNAUF

FRED KNAUF was born in the USA on 5 June 1893 in the small town of Mosinee, Wisconsin, to the west of the Great Lakes.[1] According to the census of 1900, he was the youngest of five siblings that survived their childhood years. Born in Calumet, Michigan, his widowed father Frank Knauf was a labourer of German descent. Frank Knauf appears to have moved his family to Mosinee in the decade preceding Fred's birth. Others like the Knaufs may have done the same as the 1900 census shows a number of other families of German and Scandinavian origin all living in the same street.[2]

Situated on the Wisconsin River, Mosinee owed its rapid growth to its saw-mills and extensive logging industry. The surrounding hardwood and coniferous forests provided the bulk of the town's employment. Aged twenty-one, Fred Knauf escaped Mosinee and what he may have seen as the limited way of life it offered. A month after the start of the War in Europe in 1914, Knauf, in a spirit of adventure, made an abortive attempt to enlist

1   US National Archives, Knauf passport application 16 September 1920.
2   Twelfth Census of the United States (1900), Mosinee, Marathon, Wisconsin.

Fred Knauf in 1920.
(US National Archives &
Records Administration)

with the Canadian army[3] before traveling to the city of Saint Paul in neighboring Minnesota, and signed on as probationer in the United States Marine Corps.[4] The word *escaped* seems apt as Knauf rarely returned to his hometown. His siblings on the other hand appear to have remained locally.

As it turned out, Knauf never fought in Europe. American public and political opinion in 1914 was very much against any involvement, and it would be another three years before America joined the Allies, by which time Knauf was posted to quite the other side of the globe: China.

Initially, probationer Knauf undertook recruit training at the great naval yard of Mare Island, California. On successfully completing the course, he enlisted formally with the US Marine Corps in January 1915. He gave his former occupation as farmer, but later altered this to "ball-player" which may have contained some truth as he had featured as a star baseball pitcher in Mosinee.[5] In fact it was Knauf's sporting prowess that soon proved to be the major influence on his career in the Marine Corps. The versatile Private Fred Knauf, 5' 9" tall and 153 pounds,[6] excelled at baseball, basketball, ice hockey, cross-country running and athletics.[7] He could even turn his hand to soccer.[8] Knauf's sporting skills soon gained him special privileges in the Marine Corps. Then

3 "Knauf Tells of Far East", *Mosinee Times*, March 1, 1944.
4 United States Marine Corps muster rolls, Mare Island, California, 1914.
5 University of Wisconsin Digital Collection Center, Madison, Wisconsin; "Baseball" (team of 1912), *Mosinee Centennial, 1857-1957*.
6 National Personnel Records Center, St Louis, Missouri; official military personnel file for Fred Knauf.
7 "Colorful Character", *Leatherneck* magazine (USMC), volume 14 issue 12, December 1931.
8 "Winter Sports", *Leatherneck* magazine (USMC), volume 10 issue 1, January 1927.

as now, armed forces throughout the world take great pride in their representative sports teams, with team members frequently sheltered and generally looked after in a way they could not hope to be otherwise, especially when a lowly private like Knauf. Throughout his many years of service Knauf appears to have taken full advantage of this special treatment.

From California, Knauf was transported by troopship to Cavite in the Philippines before arriving in China in late 1915 for what was to be his first of many postings with the 38th Company in Peking.[9]

In common with other nations, the United States stationed troops at strategic ports and cities in China, as had been its right ever since the Boxer rebellion of 1900 and the resulting Protocol of the following year. The troops' role was to safeguard American interests by protecting the thousands of American citizens and their property in China. They were also there in order to be a force for good by promoting stable government in a chaotic country. In fulfilling these roles, the American commanders were required to tread a difficult path, displaying a military presence and a readiness for combat while doing their utmost to avoid involvement in any of the numerous conflicts. The US Government had no desire to become embroiled in Chinese internal strife.

The number of American troops in China varied in direct response to the threats posed by changing political and revolutionary instability. During the worst turmoil of the civil wars in 1927 there were some 7,000 American servicemen stationed in the China, over 500 of them at the legation barracks in Peking.[10] The US Marine Corps maintained a continuous presence in the country for several decades right up until 8 December 1941. It

9 National Personnel Records Center, St Louis, Missouri; official military personnel file for Fred Knauf.
10 Chester M. Biggs Jr, *The United States Marines in North China 1894-1942* (2003), p157.

*USMC Legation baseball team, circa 1916, with Fred Knauf front row, left.
(Chinamarine.org)*

was a strange and often difficult foreign posting, and it was with
some pride that those involved referred to themselves as "the
China-Marines."

The Peking Marine barracks were located close to the American Legation in a large corner of the Legation Quarter. Facilities
in the compound were excellent. Describing life for marines in
the Far East, the Corps' magazine *The Leatherneck* listed the Peking barracks as possessing tennis and handball courts, swimming pool and a gymnasium.[11] Additionally, on the adjacent glacis, there was room for baseball, football, track athletics, and ice
hockey. Knauf starred in the Peking or all-China Marine Corps
team for nearly all these sports, even captaining the basketball
team in his first year in China.[12] These were winning teams which
achieved sporting glory for the Marines by competing against
the United States Army (with which the Marines had a special ri-
valry), and also local civilian teams. Not only was this beneficial

11 "Living with the Marines in Peking, China", *Leatherneck* magazine (USMC), volume 7
issue 1, January 1924.
12 "Winter Sports," *Leatherneck* magazine (USMC), volume 10 issue 1, January 1927.

for morale, but it also fostered a good image for the Corps. As a result, sportsman Knauf was highly valued by his commanders and with their support he achieved the rare privilege of posting after posting to China, always to Peking, some of them back to back.

Peking in particular was a plum two-year tour for a young marine. During times of major military conflict elsewhere in the country in the 1920s and 1930s, Peking itself saw relatively little unrest. Life was comfortable for the marines fortunate enough to be there and their pay went a very long way. The men hired room-boys to clean and tidy their quarters, to press their uniforms, to wash their laundry, to cook their meals, in short, to complete all a man's routine chores save for maintaining a weapon. That, a marine had to do for himself.

Apart from the various sport and games activities, there were also the many other attractions Peking had to offer—public bars, cabarets, restaurants, dancers, prostitutes, cheap wine and beer, and inexpensive steaks. Nowhere Stateside could a marine private paid $21 a month find a rickshaw waiting to haul him to all this entertainment and back again for the equivalent of a few American cents. Life in the city for a China-Marine was as good as it got.[13]

Fred Knauf was far from shy when it came to advancing himself. In April 1925, while briefly back at Mare Island, he took it upon himself to write directly to the newly-announced United States Minister to China, John Van Antwerp MacMurray (1881-1960), then Assistant Secretary of State in Washington:

My Dear Mr. MacMurray,
The usual order of things may not call for congratula-

....

13 Chester M. Biggs Jr, *The United States Marines in North China 1894-1942* (2003), p171.

tions from a Private of Marines, yet I wish to offer my own humble well wishes along with others of more important stations in life.

I too am returning to Peking and was packing my trunks when I ran across a picture of your family taken in Peking sometime in 1917, and the very next day I read of your name as the probable nomination for the Peking post. I am going out via commercial liner as I have made two trips that way and like it much better than the transports. I still remain a Private although I now have ten years of service. Athletics form sort of a barrier to promotion and it seems that until I cease to play in the various teams I will no doubt retain my present rank.

I always look back with pleasant memories to the days when I was orderly in the Chancery and I hope I may be so fortunate again. It seems that I can still taste the cake which you and Mrs. MacMurray sent over to me Christmas day 1917.

Hoping that you may enjoy a pleasant and successful tour in Peking, I am,

Sincerely and respectfully yours,

Fred Knauf

Private, U.S.M.C.[14]

For a mere private first class in the 1920s to write to a United States Minister to China (the equivalent of ambassador), effectively making a bid in advance for the coveted role of orderly, shows enormous nerve on Knauf's part, not to say brazenness. But it paid off. Knauf returned to Peking and within a very short

....

14 Mudd Manuscript Library, Princeton University; MacMurray papers, letter from Knauf to Hon, J.V.A. MacMurray, Assistant Secretary of State, Washington, D.C., April 6, 1925.

time became Minister MacMurray's orderly.[15] Sporting talent and the recommendation of his commanding officer alone were unlikely to have proved enough to have secured the position; Knauf would have needed something more to offer. MacMurray evidently knew him already, and would not have chosen or agreed to accept Knauf as a personal attendant unless he was organized, reliable, discreet and also immaculately turned-out, i.e., a sharp looking marine. Throughout his career in the regulars, Knauf's service record repeatedly described him as of "excellent character," and he received a good-conduct medal despite a couple of fines for early minor disciplinary offences. As Knauf observed in his letter, promotion could be slow in the peacetime Marine Corps, but he made corporal at last in 1927.[16]

Knauf also held onto the role of orderly to the Minister in 1929 when, frustrated by Washington's China policy, MacMurray resigned and was replaced by Nelson T. Johnson (1887-1954). This change in minister most likely required some deft adaptability on Knauf's part, as MacMurray and Johnson were very different characters. The urbane, slim and dapper MacMurray was scholarly, dryly witty, but short on small talk and carried "the coiled alertness of a jockey."[17] Johnson, on the other hand, was possessed of a rounder figure and was both approachable and amiable. He was open and direct with people, possessing what was described as an infectious smile and a great sense of humour.[18]

John Van Antwerp MacMurray is now best known for his

....

15 United States Marine Corps muster rolls, Peking, 1925 (October).
16 National Personnel Records Center, St Louis, Missouri; official military personnel file for Fred Knauf (1927 promotion to corporal).
17 *How the peace was lost; the 1935 memorandum, Developments affecting American policy in the Far East: prepared for the State Department by John Van Antwerp MacMurray;* edited by Arthur Waldron, Hoover Institution Press (1992)
18 Buhite, Russell D., *Nelson T Johnson and American Policy Toward China 1929-1941,* (1968), p2.

Memorandum of 1935, written at the behest of the US Government to comment on the political situation in China. This he did, explaining that in his opinion both US and Chinese government policies had mistakenly frustrated legitimate Japanese expectations and therefore increased the chances of war, i.e. that the Empire of Japan was not solely to blame for the growing tensions in the Far East. The memorandum was not well-received in Washington and was quietly shelved. It was only rediscovered among the archives and subsequently published in 1992, long after MacMurray's death.

Nelson T. Johnson, a man popular among the foreign diplomats of Peking,[19] remained posted in China for many years until being appointed Ambassador to Australia in May 1941. MacMurray and Johnson were both capable men and unlikely to have suffered fools; Knauf would have had to maintain high standards to retain his position. And retain it he did, until his retirement from the regulars after sixteen years of service. Knauf then joined the reserves in 1931. Just before this, however, in late 1930, he was involved in a frightening reminder of China's continued lawlessness and instability, in an incident reported by newspapers in the Far East:

U.S. Marines Attacked - Men Fired Upon Then Robbed

The latest foreigners to suffer attack by bandits are two American marines, namely Corporal Fred Knauf and Quartermaster Sergeant Wandt.

Six bandits, five of whom were in uniform, opened heavy fire on the marines' automobile yesterday afternoon, seventeen miles northward of Peking when the Americans were returning from Tangshan.

....

19 ibid. p1.

The Americans stopped the car, but the bandits continued to fire, even while they were getting out. Some of the
shots came perilously near, but the marines were not hit.
One bandit then held up the marines, while five searched
them, securing $130, a gold watch and chain and a flash-
lamp.[20]

Fortunately, both marines survived the ordeal. A year later, under the headline "Colorful Character", the official US Marines
magazine *Leatherneck* reported on Knauf's career:

On November 5, 1931, at Mare Island, California, Corporal
Fred Knauf was transferred to the Fleet Marine Corps Reserve after over sixteen years of excellent service. Knauf,
one-time known as "Waffles" owing to his unlimited capacity for stowing away the hot-bread, was one of the best all-
round athletes in the Marine Corps for many years. Freddie
also holds several other records. First, I believe, in order of
importance is the number of trips to and from Peking he
has made via commercial liner for the writer can remember
four occasions when Freddie crossed the Pacific at his own
expense. And it is believed that he also has spent more time
with the Peiping Legation Guard than any other Marine
as he has been out there off and on for over twelve years.
Moreover, to show that his liking for the one-time capital
of Old Cathay has not waned, Freddie is embarking on the
Shiyo Maru at San Francisco the 14th of November en route
to his old stomping ground in Peiping, where he will become affiliated with one of the foreign business concerns.[21]

----

20 "US Marines Attacked", *The Singapore Free Press and Mercantile Advertiser*, November 13,
1930.
21 "Colorful Character", *Leatherneck* magazine (USMC), volume 14 issue 12, December 1931.

And with that fond send-off Knauf, age thirty-eight, went straight back to Peking. This time as a reservist, but effectively a civilian. The "foreign business concern" was almost certainly one of the number of bars that catered for his former comrades in the Marines. His retainer pay of $22.20,[22] and perhaps years of careful saving, in all likelihood made this financially possible, though quite how he managed to afford repeated expensive commercial liner cruises across the Pacific is a mystery, as they ought to have been beyond his purse.

Corporal Knauf was indeed "a colorful character." And in a sense a successful one also. He had discovered his ideal posting, managed to remain there, and spent much of his career being paid to play ball-games. And now he could make a living catering to the wants of serving marines and other like-minded men in the city he knew so well. In the year 1931, the retired Fred "Waffles" Knauf was an experienced reservist, a fine athlete, and a popular former marine all round, but the image was not to last. Knauf's reputation was to suffer a distinct transformation for the worse. And it wasn't only Edward Werner who felt ill-will toward him.

Soldiers' off-duty drinking and its associated bad behaviour has always been an annoyance for their commanding officers. And like most other postings, Peking had its night-time attractions. Several of the city's bars were run by former marines specifically for the benefit of former colleagues. However well-run and correctly licensed, such establishments were bound to be associated with men coming to grief: drunkenness, absenteeism, assaults, petty crime, debt, girlfriends, venereal disease, embarrassing incidents with the Chinese police. None of which would

22 National Personnel Records Center, St Louis, Missouri; official military personnel file for Fred Knauf.

have endeared the proprietors to the local commanding officer.

As a reservist, such perennial problems with bars would have left Knauf in an awkward position. Knauf's reserve unit was nominally based in California, requiring him to obtain permission from the Marine Corps to live outside the USA. This privilege had to be renewed annually through the local commanding officer in Peking. By the close of 1937, the then commanding officer in Peking, Colonel John Marston, had developed a poor opinion of him. Commenting on Knauf's latest application to remain in China, Marston wrote to Marine headquarters in Washington:

> Corporal Knauf is a resident of Peiping, and possesses a questionable reputation. He has no obvious means of support other than his retirement pay, and his associates are not of a reputable class. Distinctly he is not a credit to his Marine Corps affiliations nor to his nationality. It should be stated, however, that there are very few discreditable things on his record susceptible of legal proof. He had several incidents with the Chinese police in the past, though during the current year it is my understanding that he has been free from entanglements with the police. In brief, he is a man who has an unsavory reputation due to his association with certain unsavory elements in Peiping.[23]

Knauf's reputation appears to have sunk a long way. Realising his lack of hard evidence to support his allegations, Marston recommended that Knauf's application be turned down on account of the US policy of discouraging its citizens from living in a then unstable China. Headquarters agreed, and Knauf's application was refused. But this decision was surprisingly overturned

23 ibid., (letter from Commanding Officer Peiping to Commanding General, Department of the Pacific, December 15, 1937).

when Knauf subsequently submitted a written appeal, citing how he stood to lose his entire savings, wrapped up as they were in investments and loans in China.

A few months later, Knauf was in trouble with the US authorities again. The US Embassy in Peking received a letter from two local Chinese complaining that Knauf was habitually violent toward them and others. The letter, written in comically poor English, involving phrases like "makes very bad show" and "had much trouble," went on to describe how a verbally abusive Knauf used to live in a whorehouse, how he cheated Chinese out of money and threatened to kill them, and that people were afraid of him.[24]

This time, US Marine Corps headquarters were willing to recall Knauf to the United States immediately. But before doing so, and in a display of fairness, they asked staff at the Embassy in Peking to investigate. It transpired that the letter-writers could not be traced and the boarding house address they provided could not be identified. The report concluded that the correct address may have been lost in translation, but embassy staff conceded that the letter could equally be a fake "sent by persons who, although desirous of making trouble for Corporal Knauf, prefer to keep their identity hidden."[25] Knauf remained in Peking.

Just what was Knauf up to in Peking that caused such bad opinion of him? After leaving the regular Marines in 1931, Knauf became consistently vague about his official means of income, referring to "one of the foreign business concerns," then later describing himself as a "real-estate and automobile broker." He was not employed by any other person, he explained loosely, but "I have sufficient funds to enable me to reside here for about four years, not counting my retainer, and prospects for me to estab-

24 Ibid., (document relating to complaint, July 30, 1938).
25 Ibid., (document relating to complaint, Sept 24, 1938).

lish myself in some respectable business here in China are very encouraging."[26]

If Knauf was running a bar-brothel, legal or otherwise, it is possible that simple competition from others may have caused problems of their own. But would this alone have caused so much official invective from Colonel Marston? Significantly, Marston could not substantiate his bad opinion of Knauf with evidence, something that ought not to have been that difficult to obtain if it related to something as fixed and easily located as a disreputable bar or brothel.

Edward Werner's information was that Knauf was a heroin dealer.[27] China certainly possessed a long history of opioid abuse in all forms. The advent of heroin in the late nineteenth century as a concentrated and injectable form of opium was well received amongst many addicts in China as it was elsewhere. There was thus a need for heroin dealers. But as the Chinese had plenty of their own, it's unlikely that they would have required the services of Fred Knauf. It is possible that heroin was supplied or used at a bar or brothel linked to Knauf and that the customers were US Marines, which would undoubtedly have made him an enemy of Marston. Though this theory is plausible, the effects of heroin abuse are generally so corrosive that it would be difficult for a marine or the Corps to conceal it for long. Knauf himself appears to have shown no signs of drug abuse. He remained extremely fit, as his annual reservist medical examinations showed. Indeed, the veteran ball-player just kept going, joining civilian teams comprised of members much younger than himself. "One of the oldest players in North China," as he

---

26 Ibid., (document, December 29, 1940).
27 UK National Archives, FO 371/25315/1510 Murder of Pamela Werner Code 10 file 1510, letter from E.T.C. Werner to the British Ambassador to China, July 1939.

was described,[28] Knauf played defence for the Peking ice hockey team for many years, and throughout the key month of January 1937. Some of the games were played at the French rink in the Legation Quarter,[29] the same rink where Pamela was last seen alive.

USMC temporary ice rink, Peking, similar to the one where Pamela skated. (Chinamarine.org)

Interior of a USMC temporary ice rink, Peking. (Chinamarine.org)

....

28 "Tientsin Defeats Peiping 3-2 in Thrilling Ice Hockey Game", *Peiping Chronicle*, February 6, 1937.
29 *Peiping Chronicle*, society/sports column, January 9 and 23, 1937.

7

THE DENTIST

WENTWORTH PRENTICE

THE MAN WERNER suspected of inflicting the blows that killed Pamela was Wentworth Baldwin Prentice. Like his fellow American Fred Knauf, he too was a long-standing resident of Peking. By January 1937, aged forty-three, Prentice had been living and working in the city for almost twenty years, ever since his arrival from the USA as a newly-qualified dentist. Assisted by a few Chinese staff, he ran a private practice from an upstairs apartment at Number 3, Legation Street, the main road running through the centre of the Legation Quarter.

Prentice's background was very different from that of the former US Marine. A year younger than Knauf, Prentice was born on June 6, 1894 in Norwich, Connecticut, a pleasant harbour town some 140 miles north of New York City.[1] His Methodist parents, Myron and Alice, had three sons, Wentworth being the eldest. Myron Prentice was a successful retail grocer with his own store, and was prosperous enough to live in a large, detached, timber

---

1   US National Archives, Wentworth Prentice passport application, August 29, 1917.

house in a leafy Norwich street.[2] He also ensured that his sons achieved a good education. From the age of fourteen, Wentworth attended Norwich Free Academy, a local school where entrance was by examination only. Both he and his younger brother were bright and excelled, scoring particularly highly in mathematics. Wentworth was president of the school's music club and vice-president of his class.[3] In his last year at the academy, he was given the following leg-pulling in a farewell valedictory:

> "Went" is a popular son of a prominent grocer. Great lover
> of music and some musician. He is also a great acrobat.
> Some romance attached to this promising young man.
> They say he has lost his heart to a pretty cornet player. He
> is often seen in the vicinity of Warren Street. Never mind
> "Went," we all fall.[4]

On leaving Norwich Academy both brothers entered Harvard University, a hundred miles further north in Boston, Massachu-

setts. From 1913, Prentice studied at the Harvard Dental School. It is not known why he chose dentistry, but the previous century had seen great advances in this area as it evolved from a trade into a serious and respectable medical science. Dentists in the United States could also take the title of doctor.

During his time at Harvard, Prentice continued his religious observances, attending the nearby Epworth Methodist

Wentworth Prentice at Harvard University. (Harvard School of Dental Medicine)

2   Thirteenth and fourteenth US National census, 1910 & 1920, Norwich, New London, Connecticut.
3   1912 Norwich Free Academy Mirror (yearbook), Norwich, Connecticut.
4   ibid.

church where he led services, gave sermons with such titles as "Are you a follower of the crowd or of Jesus?"[5] and, more improbably, "Amusements".[6] His brother did similarly. Wentworth played violin at the same church, both solo[7] and in ensemble pieces.[8] Methodism ran deep. Described by the University as "quiet, likeable, good humor, and consistent hard worker,"[9] there was nothing to suggest a sinister streak in Wentworth Prentice's character.

Prentice graduated from Harvard in 1916 and for a short time worked at the nearby Forsyth Infirmary.[10] The following year, he made firm plans to become a Christian missionary, and in May 1917, aged only twenty-two, he married a young woman a couple of years his junior, whom he appears to have met through the Methodist church in nearby Cambridge.[11] A few months later, they made for a handsome couple in their joint passport photograph: she pretty and petite, he dark and slim with brown hair, brown eyes, sporting a moustache, and smartly dressed in a well-fitting suit, tie and stiff collar.

The Prentices booked to leave the United States that September for Peking under the auspices of the Methodist Episcopal Church. Prentice had been engaged to work as a missionary-dentist in the Methodist Hopkins Memorial Hospital. In the midst of these life-changing events, however, Prentice found himself inconveniently subject to the June 1917 national draft. The United States had entered the war in the spring of that year, and, fearing it would not receive sufficient volunteers (as was the case), the government of President Woodrow Wilson introduced

....

5 "Epworth Methodist,", *Cambridge Tribune*, March 14, 1914.
6 "Epworth Methodist,", *Cambridge Tribune*, October 23, 1915.
7 "Epworth M. E. Church", *Cambridge Chronicle*, October 23, 1915.
8 "Epworth Methodist,", *Cambridge Tribune*, December 19, 1914.
9 Harvard Medical School archives, Boston, Massachusetts
10 ibid.
11 *Cambridge Tribune*, Church Notices, October 23, 1915.

conscription for all men aged between 21 and 31. With his heart already set on China, this could not have been welcome news for Prentice. Nor was it for the Methodist Board of Foreign Missions in New York, who wrote urgent letters of support to the local Cambridge Exemption Board in the hope that their man might be excused military service in order "to fill an important position in missionary work in North China."[12] Time passed, and the date the Prentices were due to sail drew ever closer. But while the war was in full flow, the Exemption Board were sympathetic toward Prentice's position, describing his application as "meritorious."[13] Also, on examination, Prentice was found to be physically unfit and was discharged due to his defective eyesight.[14] Though Prentice certainly appears to have worn glasses, this arrangement may have judiciously suited all parties.

The newlywed couple sailed from Vancouver to China on the steamship *Empress of Russia*, departing on September 27, 1917.[15]

The change of life from student to missionary-dentist in China must have been something of a baptism of fire for the young and inexperienced Prentice, but overall he appears to have adjusted well and fitted in with the foreign society in Peking, joining the city's International Lodge of Freemasons.[16] In 1921, four years after his arrival, he wrote the following letter describing his role to prospective colleagues back in the US:

Each dentist will spend at least six months in the language

....

12 United Methodist Archive & History Center, Drew University, New Jersey: employment file of W.B. Prentice, letter July 20, 1917 from the missionary board to the exemption board.
13 US National Archives, Wentworth Prentice passport application, August 29, 1917, attached district exemption board report, August 27, 1917.
14 ibid.
15 ibid.
16 Massachusetts, Mason membership cards, 1733-1990; Wentworth Baldwin Prentice, International Lodge Peking, initiated January 7, 1920.

school and will be given opportunity to continue his language study on part time throughout the first two years. As none of the various fields of dentistry have been seriously developed, if the new-comer has a desire to specialise in certain fields, he can do so to very great extent.

Although an important feature of our work is the extending of work to the other missionaries and community, no dentist will be expected to perform this regular office work more than half time. The remainder of his time will be given to: 1) Lecturing, 2) Teaching in clinics and special departments, 3) Research work, 4) School administration, 5) Visiting school clinics. Homes and heavy furniture will be provided in the mission compound. Salaries and furlough (after five years) will be arranged by the mission.

The missionary call has never been given to the dental profession as a whole. I am certain that there are many Christian dentists who would seek to enter the missionary ranks if the fact of the great need became known to them. The great feature of the work in Peking is just this opportunity, the giving of one-self to a life of service to the Master.[17]

Clearly, after four years in China, Prentice still professed his faith strongly and wholeheartedly supported his missionary vocation. A joint dental programme in Peking was agreed between the Methodist Hopkins Hospital and the Peking Union Medical College (funded by the Rockefeller Foundation), involving three dentists at the hospital and one oral surgeon at the medical college.[18] Unfortunately, this humanitarian plan was beset by staffing problems. There simply weren't enough qualified dentists

17 United Methodist Archive & History Center, Drew University, New Jersey: employment file of W.B. Prentice, letter from Prentice to a Doctor Ward, May 27, 1921.
18 United Methodist Archive & History Center, Drew University, New Jersey: employment file of W.B. Prentice.

who were willing to exchange a comfortable and lucrative career back home for the meagre pay of a missionary amid the squalor of China, a situation that placed all the more pressure on those already there.

The Prentices soon became parents to three children, two girls and a boy, all born in Peking between 1918 and 1921. In May 1922, after nearly five years in China, the young family of five returned on furlough to the United States to stay, initially, at Prentice's parents' home in Norwich.[19] They then received the welcome news of an extended stay in the US as Prentice had been awarded a student fellowship at Harvard with a stipend of one thousand dollars to further develop his dental skills.[20] It was not until the autumn of 1923 that the Prentice family set off again for Peking, upon which event the Cambridge Tribune newspaper ran a feature describing Prentice's work there, and the great variety of his patients "... some of whom come a thousand miles to avail themselves of this service, for the Chinese who wish to pay, and clinics for those unable to pay."[21] The article painted a glowing picture of missionary life. But it was not to last for Prentice; a schism soon appeared in his marriage.

The return to Peking proved disastrous for Prentice. Mrs Prentice made it obvious that she hated China. She felt no commitment to the missionary calling, she was observed smoking in public, and even seen dancing with men who were not her husband. This was all too much for the Methodist authorities to accept, in their small and conservative missionary community of the 1920s. The Mission Board called upon the couple to re-dedicate themselves wholeheartedly to the missionary calling. Pren-

....

19 List of United States citizens arriving at the Port of San Francisco from Shanghai on the SS *Golden Gate*, May 6, 1922.
20 United Methodist Archive & History Center, Drew University, New Jersey: employment file of W.B. Prentice.
21 "Dr. Prentice Sailed Recently for China", *Cambridge Tribune*, October 6, 1923.

tice was willing to do this, but his wife refused to even discuss it. Prentice tried for a compromise, pleading his wife's poor health and suggesting she return home to recover. But the Board would not have it. It was all or nothing. They would not sanction what they saw as the break-up of the marriage. They wanted Prentice to stay on at the hospital, but not without his wife.[22]

In the event, Mrs Prentice returned to the United States with the three children, sailing home in June 1926. On board the ship with her was a US "China-Marine" who she would later marry.[23] The whole experience was no doubt an emotionally painful time for all involved.

Prentice never saw his children again. Nor did he ever return to the United States. Picking up the pieces of his life, he remained in China. Forced to leave the Methodist hospital, the compound and the missionary life, he established his private dental practice at a prime location in the heart of the Legation Quarter. He treated many of the foreign community of Peking, and as a result became a well-known figure. Aside from letting his masonic membership lapse in 1935,[24] there is little on record relating to him over the following decade, except to record that he was still living and working at Legation Street in January 1937 when Pamela was murdered.

Prentice had experienced his share of personal misfortune, but outwardly at least he had led an apparently blameless life as a respectable professional dentist and former missionary. There was nothing to suggest otherwise. Werner, however, saw things differently. Prentice's dental practice was just a short walk from the French ice rink, and the narrow staircase leading to his at-

22 "In Search of W.B. Prentice", unpublished work in progress, by Eric Politzer, from records of the United Methodist Archive & History Center, Drew University, New Jersey.
23 List of United States citizens arriving at the Port of San Francisco from Shanghai on the SS President Lincoln, June 10, 1926.
24 Massachusetts, Mason membership cards, 1733-1990; Wentworth Baldwin Prentice, International Lodge Peking, membership ceased, July 8, 1935.

tached apartment was on Pamela's likely route home on the night she was murdered.[25]

25 E.T.C Werner, *More Memorigrams*, (1948), p189.

8

THE DOCTOR

UGO CAPPUZZO

THIRTY YEARS' OLD at the time of the murder, the Italian Doctor, Ugo Cappuzzo, was a good deal younger than Werner's two American suspects. Unlike Knauf and Prentice, Cappuzzo was a comparative newcomer to China.

He first arrived in China in 1933; a newly-qualified medical doctor from Legnaro, near Padua in northeast Italy, aged twenty-six.[1] Short and slim, with thick black hair combed straight back in the style of the time, the young Cappuzzo was photographed a few years later alongside Italian diplomatic staff as they celebrated King Victor Emmanuel's birthday, walking a little to the rear of the senior men of the group as they inspected a parade of Italian soldiers and sailors in the Legation Quarter.[2]

Doctor Ugo Cappuzzo, 1948.
(Archivio Storico, Rome)

1 Archivio Storico Diplomatico, Rome, archive "Le Rappresentanze Diplomatiche e Consolari Italiane a Pechino 1870-1952, folder 186, file 9043 "Cappuzzo".
2 "Italian King's Birthday Celebrated in Peiping", *North-China Herald*, November 27, 1935.

King Victor Emmanuel's birthday, Legation Quarter, 1935; Cappuzzo on the right

By this time, November 1935, Cappuzzo had been appointed doctor to the Italian Embassy. The old King's birthday parade was caught on camera for the Shanghai-based newspaper *North-China Herald*. Cappuzzo also took a place on the parade review stand itself, immaculately dressed with cravat tie, top hat and tails. The flags, emblems and uniforms were fascist ones. Back in Italy, Mussolini and his National Fascist Party were firmly in control. Though he could not then have known it, this close association with the Fascist government would later cost Cappuzzo dearly.

In order to get a picture of the man, it is necessary to fast-forward a dozen years to 1947 when Cappuzzo, still living and working in Peking, was featured in an American newspaper, *The Bee*, in an article written by an adventurous American reporter, under the headline:

Poor Chinese Villagers Pay Tribute to "Miracle Man"
- Italian Physician ended honeymoon to accept post.

The humble, hard-working peasants living in six villages forming part of a "no man's land" about twenty miles south-west of Peiping have reason to be thankful for a circumstance which twelve years ago interrupted the round-the-world honeymoon of a young Italian physician.

The doctor at the Italian embassy here had quit after a quarrel, a replacement was urgently needed and the nearest man qualified for the post was Dr. Ugo Cappuzzo of Padua, Italy, then passing through Shanghai with his bride.

Dr. Cappuzzo accepted the job, ending his honeymoon to come to Peiping where for the next eleven years he served as embassy doctor. For the last year Cappuzzo, who is now 39 years old, has been in private practice here.

For the last ten years he has gone every weekend to territory southwest of Marco Polo Bridge, starting point of the Sino-Japanese war, to minister to the inhabitants of his six "adopted" villages.

Since shortly after V-J Day these villages have been in a No Man's Land between the Nationalists and the Communists and the inhabitants lead an uneasy existence. For eight years previously they lived an equally uneasy life under Japanese control.

The doctor of No Man's Land has little material reward for his services. He never has asked for fees from his patients in the six villages but, so that they may not lose face, accepts the pathetic gifts they offer. During my visit to No Man's land with him, I saw grateful families bring their gifts - a pound or two of rice, a bag of peanuts, and sometimes a well worn, crinkled Chinese banknote equivalent in value to a nickel or a dime.

But one thing the doctor has and always will have

among the peasants to whom he has ministered these ten years is their respect. To some of them, who have watched him save their kin from seemingly certain death, he is a miracle man.

Many times he has performed an operation with an unhinged door placed on sawhorses as his operating table and the open sky as his lamp.

The simple country women forbidden by custom from seeing a man, even a doctor, for a month after childbirth, he must prescribe by hearing a description of their ailments. But the Chinese know that any doctor must feel a patient's pulse and so they tie a thread to the wrist of the ailing woman and give one end to it to the doctor, outside the room. He holds it gravely and the peasants think it communicates the pulse beats to him.

The weekend I spent with the doctor in No Man's Land. patients came from near and far. One of them rode thirty miles in a mule cart from Communist territory to be examined. the doctor found he had TB in an advanced stage.

Another man with heart trouble had to have paracentesis of the abdomen performed without anaesthetics. I could hardly eat when the same bowls were used when our dinner was served. Afterwards Cappuzzo told me it would have impolite if I had not eaten as our host would have lost face.

At night we slept in a peasant's home, outside, villagers were on the lookout, ready to awaken us and speed us back to Peiping if Communists came, as sometimes they do.

A commotion at 3 a.m. awakened us. A wolf was on the prowl and every dog for miles around was barking. We could not sleep after that. Instead we smoked until dawn. For breakfast we were given chow-dz (meat dumplings), boiled peanuts, and bygar, a potent white wine made of Kaoliang, a Chinese variety of sorghum. It goes down the throat like a flame and leaves a bouquet which makes no friends.

The peasants in No Man's Land which the doctor visits live a hazardous life. At any time a clash may flare up in their territory. Then they become refugees, fleeing in the direction of Peiping and returning when all is quiet. They grow hardly enough food to keep themselves alive, yet they must pay taxes to the government - and to the Communists. Some of the nocturnal visits of the Reds are to collect these taxes, which usually are paid in kind.

I saw the doctor perform an operation within one mile of the Communist outposts and I breathed a lot easier when we left the place.

Doctor Cappuzzo makes his weekend trips on an Italian army motorcycle presented to an Italian priest by the late Benito Mussolini.

It's a long, hard ride to the doctor's territory, I know because I travelled with him on the back seat - only there was no back seat, just a metal frame. The doctor carries a hunting gun with him, and ostensibly he is after water fowl, not microbes. As we left the hotel several persons wished him "happy hunting".

Doctor Cappuzzo is married and has four sons. Last year he sent them back to his homeland with his wife to continue their education. They are now living at Venice.

The doctor's original goal was five sons. Mussolini had promised that if any couple had five male children the offspring would get the best education Italy could provide - and free. Doctor Cappuzzo and his wife were still hoping for another son when Mussolini was beyond honoring his promise.[3]

The newspaper article painted something of a glowing image of the man. Of course, there was more to Ugo Cappuzzo than could be found within that one flattering report. He appears to have had several interesting sides to him.

The Partito Nazionale Fascista (National Fascist Party) under Benito Mussolini held power in Italy from 1922 and by the 1930s its grip on Italy was absolute. As in Nazi Germany, party membership gradually became a must for anyone wishing to advance their career. The young Doctor Cappuzzo was no exception. Either from conviction or simple expediency, it is impossible to tell, he joined the P.N.F. in 1929. Further to this, in his hometown of Padua he joined a unit of the Milizia Volontaria per la Sicurezza Nazionale, the MVSN - the paramilitary Blackshirts - later rising in China to the rank of *capomanipolo*, the equivalent of lieutenant.[4]

Why Cappuzzo chose Shanghai for his honeymoon in 1933 is unclear. Also unclear was the nature of his relationship with the influential Count Gian Galeazzo Ciano, a young Italian diplomat based in Shanghai who was also, importantly, Mussolini's son-in-law, and was soon to return to Rome to become Foreign Minister. But it was Ciano who recommended Cappuzzo for the vacant role of embassy doctor in Peking, a position he held for the next fifteen years[5] (Count Ciano, having later betrayed Mussolini in his hour of need, was executed by his own side in 1944).

For at least the early part of his tenure, during the 1930s, the position of embassy doctor was an ideal one for Cappuzzo. The role was actually an honorary one and while it provided free

....

3   "Poor Chinese Pay Tribute to 'Miracle' Man", *The Bee*, Danville, Virginia, December 19, 1947.
4   Archivio Storico Diplomatico, Rome, archive "Le Rappresentanze Diplomatiche e Consolari Italiane a Pechino 1870-1952, folder 186, file 9043 "Cappuzzo".
5   ibid.

embassy accommodation in the Legation Quarter, Cappuzzo received no salary. He attended to the Ambassador, the Embassy staff, and the Embassy guard—no small number of people and no small task. The role did, however, bring with it a degree of prestige and provided the opportunity for an evidently talented young doctor like Cappuzzo to take on other more interesting and lucrative medical work in Peking.

In addition to his role at the Embassy, Cappuzzo worked in the bacteriology department of the PUMC. He had a special interest in parasitic diseases.[6] He also performed surgery at the same hospital, where the impoverished Chinese population provided plenty of scope for honing his skill with the scalpel.[7] At times the only Italian doctor in Peking, he also worked from a small Italian hospital in the Legation Quarter where he appears to have run a private practice.

The most notable aspect of Cappuzzo's medical work was probably the trips he made away from Peking, all of which were voluntary. The 1947 newspaper article described the weekend motorbike trips he made to six of his adopted local villages in spite of the dangers and rudimentary conditions. But earlier, in the 1930s, Cappuzzo had made even greater expeditions, often for weeks and months at a time, to remote provinces far from Peking. These were impressive medical accomplishments for which Cappuzzo deservedly received a good deal of praise from both Chinese and foreign sources. Two of these journeys fell just either side of the murder of Pamela Werner. Cappuzzo spent about a month in Shansi province from From November 20, 1936, then at the beginning of February 1937, he travelled to the island of Hainan in the far south of the country, 2.700 kilometers from Peking.[8]

6 ibid.
7 Luke Anthony, *Chang-fu (Self-criticism)*, (edition 1997), chapter one.
8 Archivio Storico Diplomatico, Rome, archive "Le Rappresentanze Diplomatiche e Consolari Italiane a Pechino 1870-1952, folder 186, file 9043 "Cappuzzo".

Far more so than Peking, Shansi Province, several hundred kilometers to the west, was annually plagued with typhus, a deadly bacterial disease carried and spread between humans by body lice. The disease's fever-like symptoms also include a tell-tale rash, photophobia and delirium. Each spring, typhus flared in Shansi killing Chinese peasants in droves. Mortality rates among sufferers could be as high as sixty percent. Persuaded by the pleas of one of his private patients, a wealthy local Chinese artist, Cappuzzo and his equally gallant Chinese assistant first visited the province in 1935. The journey took several days and the two men arrived with supplies of anti-lice powder, cages of guinea-pigs and some basic lab equipment.[9]

Having first been greeted by the project's wealthy benefactor at his home in Taiyuan, the provincial capital, Cappuzzo and his assistant journeyed by mule-cart to an ancient village where the peasants lived in rudimentary cave houses carved out of the loess hillsides, sometimes fifteen to a room. Making a base in an abandoned temple, Cappuzzo was at once beset by problems. The village elders were receptive and welcoming, but they could not be persuaded that something so small as a louse could bring so deadly a disease. They laughed at the strange man from Peking; he made no sense. Instead, the villagers believed that typhus came with bad spirits and the northwest winds. Added to this, Cappuzzo soon realised that his supplies of anti-lice powder were wholly inadequate for the task. But the alternative — boiling every scrap of clothing in order to kill the lice and their eggs — was met with derision; the peasants only possessed one set of winter clothes and boiling them would ruin the padding.[10]

Discouraged by these setbacks, Cappuzzo set about concentrating on his main goal – creating a vaccine. In the mornings,

9 Luke Anthony, *Chang-fu (Self-criticism)*, (edition 1997), chapter three.
10 ibid.

he carefully collected individual lice from typhus sufferers, placing them in a glass tube while his assistant watched closely to ensure that no other bugs crawled unseen onto either of them. Cappuzzo collected 156 lice from one victim alone. Back at the temple-laboratory, the pair spent afternoons and evenings crushing the lice and injecting the resulting mash into the bellies of the guinea-pigs. The guinea-pigs were then monitored for signs of the disease before being killed at the optimum time and an emulsion made of their infected brains. The resulting samples were then transferred to further healthy guinea-pigs in order to preserve and stabilize the typhus in the animals before returning with them to Peking.[11]

Cappuzzo also needed to take back at least two hundred live infected lice. Collecting the lice was easy, the problem was how to feed them in order to keep them alive. A solution was to secure the services of local volunteers who had survived typhus and had therefore developed an immunity. Eight little wooden boxes were then constructed in order to house the lice, the bases of which consisted of a fine gauze. The boxes were then periodically strapped to the thigh of a volunteer, gauze to flesh, enabling the lice to feed on their blood.[12]

Taking care to regularly powder themselves throughout their stay in Shansi, both Cappuzzo and his Chinese assistant slept overnight next to their equipment in their makeshift laboratory. As did the guinea-pigs, for safe-keeping, and the live typhus-infected lice in their boxes ready for the journey back to Peking. One morning, Cappuzzo was awoken by a shrill cry of panic from his assistant. During the night, the gauze on one of the lice boxes had been gnawed through by a rodent and the box was now empty and its twenty-five live lice had escaped into the

11 ibid.
12 ibid.

room where they were sleeping. Somehow retaining his calm, Cappuzzo ordered the assistant to strip naked and hand him his clothes for inspection. Despite the anti-lice powder both men had dusted themselves with, Cappuzzo found two live lice in the seam of the assistant's underwear. He placed the lice in a glass tube and then examined the man's skin, finding two recent bite marks on his hip. With his heart in his mouth, Cappuzzo then repeated the procedure on himself and found three live lice and at least one bite mark. He fired the entire room with kerosene and tested the lice found in their clothes for typhus. All but one of them was positive. Cappuzzo did not need to tell his silent and tight-lipped assistant just how much trouble they were in.[13]

The men had the disease's eight-day incubation period to get themselves back to the relative safety of Peking. They did this accompanied by their samples, live lice, guinea-pigs, and one cheerful local with typhus immunity acting as lice-feeder.[14]

On their return to the Legation Quarter, the Chinese assistant developed a fever, followed soon by the other symptoms of typhus. Cappuzzo somehow escaped the disease. Using all his knowledge and the medical facilities available to him in Peking, far more than in a village in Shansi, Cappuzzo nursed his loyal assistant through the crisis and back to health.[15]

Cappuzzo then spent several months developing a vaccine, working against time in the hope of having one ready for the inevitable typhus epidemic the following year. His gathering and production technique does not appear to have been original, and probably replicated the pioneering typhus vaccine research of the Polish biologist, Rudolf Weigl, described only a few years before. Nonetheless it was bold and dangerous work by Cappuzzo.

....

13 ibid.
14 ibid.
15 ibid.

He initially found that the vaccine he produced in his laboratory worked on fresh guinea-pigs. He then took the huge risk of injecting himself with the same. How well he slept over the next week or so, wondering if he would develop the disease, is anyone's guess. But Cappuzzo's vaccine proved a success. After a series of tests on volunteers, he returned to Shansi to vaccinate groups of students, missionaries, local militia and the villagers from whom he had originally collected the lice. Trustingly, the people bared their arms to the doctor's needle.[16]

Cappuzzo's work with typhus in Shansi was a brave and daring achievement. This, and his other work on infectious diseases from 1935 to 1938, brought him deserved recognition in both medical and diplomatic circles across many parts of China.[17] But not everyone was enamoured of Cappuzzo.

Early in his tenure as embassy doctor, one staff member—it is not clear who—went to the trouble of writing a lengthy letter to his superior, presumably in Rome, complaining of how Cappuzzo was not worthy of the position. The Doctor, he complained, was rude to embassy staff and abused his powers. He was overbearing and self-important, manipulative and money-grasping. He was liked by no one. He had refused to surrender his Black Shirt identity card, to which he was not entitled having not served the full qualifying period. The letter contained a good deal of venom. Its author clearly wanted the youthful and bumptious Cappuzzo cut down to size.[18]

How much trouble the letter caused Cappuzzo is difficult to say, but he kept the role of embassy doctor. In part at least, the letter may have been the result of a personality clash between Cappuzzo and the letter's author. But over the years, the sub-

....

16 ibid.
17 Archivio Storico Diplomatico, Rome, archive "Le Rappresentanze Diplomatiche e Consolari Italiane a Pechino 1870-1952, folder 186, file 9043 "Cappuzzo".
18 ibid.

ject of money appears to have been a constant cause of dispute between Cappuzzo and his Italian superiors. There were long battles over expenses and the return of embassy funds. Having provided him with the honorary embassy role and rent-free accommodation, Cappuzzo's superiors thought him ungrateful of such generosity; he ought to be thanking them rather than moaning. Cappuzzo, for his part, thought many officials failed to appreciate the standard of the "free" service he provided the inconsiderate embassy guards and staff, and failed to recognise the true value of his research and philanthropic work and the cost it brought to himself (he suffered from a month of malaria during his 1937 visit to Hainan). It was at times a fractious relationship.[19]

Cappuzzo seems to have been an outgoing character, and he and his wife were mentioned regularly in *the Peiping Chronicle's* social column attending medical gatherings and Legation parties. But bird shooting appears to have been his favourite pastime. There was plenty of wildfowl to shoot in China and Cappuzzo indulged himself both in Peking and when away on his distant travels. He always took his guns with him. Geese appear to have been his most frequent victims.[20] Shooting birds was both a socially acceptable and common pursuit at the time.

Knauf, Prentice and Cappuzzo. Three very different men from very different backgrounds who may not ordinarily have been expected to have met with one another or to have much in common. But the small world of the Legation Quarter had a tendency to throw people into perhaps unlikely associations. Werner believed bird-shooting was a link between the three, and he may well have been right in that. He also believed they had formed a sex-ring.

....

19 ibid.
20 Luke Anthony, *Chang-fu (Self-criticism)*, (edition 1997), chapter five.

9

THE INVESTIGATOR

A FATHER DISTRAUGHT

EDWARD WERNER'S character was unquestionably volatile and always had been, and his argumentative nature revealed itself again in a second confrontation with one of his American suspects, Fred Knauf, on September 12, 1939.

Werner had called at the Peking home of another former US Marine, and an associate of Knauf's, who went by the name of Jack.[1] Werner was showing this man photographs of Pamela and her bicycle in the hope of provoking a reaction, when Knauf suddenly walked in on them. Werner described this unexpected collision in a letter to the British Ambassador a few days later:

> He said, in a loud tone of voice "you called at my house," snatched at the photos, and, before he had looked at them, added "I never saw the girl in my life," then, when he had looked at them, said "she's pretty." Neither he nor Jack made any remark about the bicycle in the second photograph.
> When I said "I was just going to your house to ask what

1 UK National Archives, FO 371/25315/1510 Murder of Pamela Werner Code 10 file 1510, letter from E.T.C. Werner to the British Ambassador to China, October 1939.

you intended when you said 'I will bring them to you,'" he began shouting violently, denied that he had made that statement, became extremely abusive, and finally shouted "I'll go to the Consul." So I said "come along," and we proceeded to the British Consulate, where a verbal battle took place before Mr. Garner,[2] Knauf continually saying "all I want is to be left alone and nobody to go to my house." He kept emphasizing that he was a very good friend of Prentice.[3]

At last, Knauf said to the consul, "may I speak to you privately?" The Consul agreed, and he and Knauf proceeded to the landing. After Knauf had left, the Consul returned to his office and said "he merely repeated what he had said here".[4]

To anyone appraised of the facts, the encounter would have provided a most unlikely spectacle; Werner and Knauf, the murder victim's father and his suspect, walking purposely together through the streets of Peking to the British Embassy. It

was a distance of at least half a mile, made in order that the two could argue about Knauf's alleged involvement in the crime before a most likely bemused British vice-consul. In fact, more than unlikely, the incident seems ridiculous. It is not credible that a man who was complicit and involved in rape and murder would voluntarily accompany the victim's father to a meeting with a government official, one with a judicial

Arthur Ringwalt, US diplomat role, albeit of a different nationality.

2 then vice-consul.
3 Werner's principal suspect.
4 UK National Archives, FO 371/25315/1510 Murder of Pamela Werner Code 10 file 1510, letter from E.T.C. Werner to the British Ambassador to China, October 1939.

The circumstances require explanation.

Werner had learned of where to find Knauf through the US Embassy, where his contact-informant was Arthur Rumney Ringwalt (1899-1981), a career diplomat who later held a number of senior overseas positions, but at that point was a lowly third secretary.[5]

In June 1939, Ringwalt had met with Werner, probably after a previous contact, and informed him that his suspect, Knauf, "had again got into trouble of the same kind as that in which he had frequently been embroiled, by swearing at and violently assaulting Chinese. Ringwalt went on to say that he even contemplated having him sent away from Peking."[6] If true, this disclosure was at best indiscreet of Ringwalt.

Later that month, Werner left for his annual holiday at the coastal resort of Peitaiho, as did many of Peking's foreign community, to escape the worst of the summer heat. Not long after, Ringwalt wrote to Werner at his Peking address, asking him to call again at the Embassy as he had information that might be of interest. The letter was forwarded to Werner, who immediately made the long train ride back to Peking and went to see Ringwalt. The latter then informed Werner, without giving away details, that the latest Knauf dispute had in fact been settled. But he also gave Werner the private addresses of both Knauf and his friend Jack.[7]

This was an act of pure mischief-making on Ringwalt's part. And a reprehensible one at that, which was probably why he asked Werner to call on him rather than risking supplying the information to him in written form. Whatever his perceived iniq-

5   Harry S. Truman Library, oral interview with Arthur R. Ringwalt by Richard D. McKenzie, June 5, 1974.
6   UK National Archives, FO 371/25315/1510 Murder of Pamela Werner Code 10 file 1510, letter from E.T.C. Werner to the British Ambassador to China, July 1939.
7   ibid.

uities, Knauf was after all an American citizen who was entitled to reasonable protection from Ringwalt. Werner, on the other hand, was *not* entitled to help from the US Embassy, nor should he have been provided with the private addresses of American citizens without their permission. Ringwalt knew that Werner suspected Knauf of being involved in a brutal murder, and yet he provided the vulnerable old man with the address of his daughter's murder suspect knowing full well that he would probably go there and confront him, something Werner duly did. Ringwalt might have been sending Knauf his next victim. He would certainly have been culpable had the visit resulted in violence.

But Ringwalt was presumably confident that there was no such risk, did not believe that Knauf was guilty of the murder, and did not take Werner's crime theories seriously. The only credible explanation for Ringwalt's improper conduct was that he was using Werner to deliberately create problems for an errant American citizen who in turn had created problems for the Embassy. And given Knauf's subsequent exasperation, Ringwalt certainly succeeded.

As part of Peking's Legation community, Ringwalt probably already knew of Werner's peculiar nature, a character no better exemplified than by that ugly Foochow Club lamp-breaking incident in September 1913, during Werner's final year as a British consul. The fracas generated all manner of telegrams, reports and statements, including many between Werner's superiors in Peking and those of his adversary, Mr. Lyons, a junior official of the Chinese Maritime Service (a Chinese national customs service run by foreigners, mostly British, on behalf of the Chinese Government). The archived papers do not paint a flattering picture of Werner.[8]

8 UK National Archives, FO 228/1861 To and From Miscellaneous.

There were several independent witnesses to the scene inside the Club, and the Chinese gateman and watchman had seen the events at the Consulate entrance. Contrary to what Werner alleged the following morning and later recounted in his book *Autumn Leaves* published in 1928, he and his wife had *not* caught up with Lyons at the Consulate gate, still less were they assaulted by him. By the time the Werners had dressed, run downstairs and arrived at the gate with its broken lamp, Lyons had already returned to the club bar next door. Werner entered brandishing a whip with his wife bearing a stick of some kind. Incensed and out of control, Werner struck Lyons several times about the head using the butt of the whip, continuing to do so even whilst Lyons was effectively pinioned by the French Consul, who tried to help by intervening. Mrs Werner, close behind her husband and wearing her dressing gown, also struck Lyons with her weapon. There was a good deal of colourful language. Eventually the onlookers managed to persuade Werner that the scene was no place for a lady, and he retreated to the Consulate with his wife.[9]

No one gained any credit from the incident. Lyons, it transpired, had dined at the Club and had stayed on afterwards at the bar. He admitted to an act of stupidity in climbing the Consulate gate and smashing the ornamental lamp above it. He then returned to the club bar. He categorically denied assaulting the Werners when they suddenly appeared, pointing out that he was being held back by others. But Lyons also admitted to insulting Mrs. Werner by making an unworthy reference to her parentage though it is unclear whether this was before or after the blows she delivered.[10]

Had Werner not inflamed the situation, the whole matter might just have blown over. Lyons had been drunk and disor-

9 ibid.
10 ibid.

derly but Werner had lost his temper and badly overreacted. Werner, the Consul for Foochow and in a position of authority, might have realized he had erred badly and should have seen the wisdom to bringing the embarrassing incident to a swift end. He didn't. Instead, over the next few weeks, he compounded his initial folly by adding to it with a series of further poor judgements.[11]

Rather than explaining his actions on the night as being down to a regrettable loss of temper, Werner set about justifying the striking of a pinioned man by resorting to embellishment and plain dishonesty. Insisting that Lyons had assaulted him and Mrs Werner at the Consulate (presumably thereby justifying his arming himself with a whip), Werner described Lyons inexplicably returning and climbing the gate on three separate occasions, thereby presumably affording the Werners sufficient time to dress, descend the stairs and arrive on the scene. Unfortunately for Werner, however, both the Consulate gateman and the watchman saw Lyons scale the gate only once, and saw no confrontation with the Werners. Werner also described being assaulted by Lyons in the club bar after he had followed him there in order to "seek an explanation," something disputed by those present, who stated that the Werners were in fact the aggressors. Werner also described cuts and bruises to himself and his wife for which there was no evidence.[12]

But as the most senior British figure in Foochow, Werner's perfidy went unchallenged, at least initially. In the days following the incident, efforts were made by local figures to find an amicable solution. Letters of apology were proposed, conciliatory meetings were arranged. But after a week of such efforts, and to everyone's surprise and then utter consternation, Werner, acting

11 ibid.
12 ibid.

in his judicial capacity, served a letter of summons on Lyons, requiring him to attend the Consular Court that same afternoon on a charge of malicious damage to the consular lamp. The charge made no mention of any assaults on the Werners, a notable omission considering that this had originally been Werner's most serious allegation.[13]

Werner's office at the Consulate served as the courtroom. Werner's latest young vice-consul, Arthur Blackburn, appears to have been excluded from the hearing, with Werner accompanied only by his Chinese clerk. There then followed what was later described as a "Gilbertian" scene with Werner acting as "prosecutor, jury, and judge."[14]

At the outset of the hearing, Lyons agreed to plead guilty to damaging the consular lamp, but refused to plead guilty to the more serious offence of doing so maliciously. Werner would not accept this and a plea of not guilty was entered. The sole witness then produced by the court was the Chinese gateman, who spoke no English. Sometimes the Chinese clerk translated for the gateman, at other times Werner simply spoke with the man directly in Chinese, of which Lyons understood little, save that Werner was evidently pressing the gateman to say that Lyons was drunk, something the gateman failed to describe.

Lyons did eventually get to cross-examine the witness. According to a Foreign Office report on the hearing, "the man's replies (before he was stopped by the court) brought out the fact that after Mr Lyons had finished breaking the lamp and had finally gone back into the club, he, the gateman, looked up and saw Mr Werner on the verandah of his house."[15]

This was obviously not a version that accorded with Werner's

13 ibid.
14 Paul King, T. Fisher Unwin, *In the Chinese Customs Service*, (1924), p260.
15 UK National Archives, FO 228/1861 To and From Miscellaneous.

earlier reports of assaults.

It then transpired that neither the gateman nor the interpreting clerk had been sworn and were not therefore under oath – a major omission. Nonetheless, Werner pressed on, stating that he had in any case received a letter from Lyons only that morning in which he admitted to breaking the lamp. The punishment, Werner declared, "should" be imprisonment, but that he was being lenient and would only fine Lyons £5 (£2 for the lamp, the remainder going toward the cost of the summons).[16]

The fine was described in a diplomatic despatch as excessive.[17]

Werner had had his day in court, his own court, and had thus done himself irreparable harm. His use of judicial proceedings was seen as vindictive. He was also accused of grave impropriety in himself trying a case in which he himself had an interest. But worst was the evidence of his lying, a word not used in the lengthy Foreign Office report to his superiors in Peking. But its inference was plain throughout.

The Foochow Club incident proved to be the last straw for the British Minister in Peking, Sir John Jordan (1852-1925), an Ulsterman who had spent his entire career in China and Korea. Jordan had been on home leave at the time of the incident and heard of it from his deputy on his return. As a result, Werner's six-month home-leave was quickly brought forward in order to remove him from Foochow and China. Jordan then appraised the Foreign Office's Controller of Consular Affairs in Whitehall:

> Dear Mr Law,
> … after studying the whole dossier, I reluctantly came to the conclusion that Mr Werner could no longer, in the interests of public service, be retained as Consul of Foochow

16 ibid.
17 ibid.

and I wrote to him a letter in which I informed him that, in the event of his return to China, I should consider it my duty to recommend his transfer to another consulate where no assistant was required ... As the enclosed summary will show, Mr Werner's official career has been practically one continuous record of friction and trouble at almost every post he has held and he is, I am convinced, of such a morbidly suspicious temperament as to be constitutionally unfitted to carry on the duties of a Consul of a port of any size or importance. He has had four assistants, all men carefully selected by myself, during the past few years and has quarreled with three of them. The fourth was only at Foochow for three months. The situation has become an impossible one and men will not, if they can possibly avoid it, serve with Mr Werner whose quarrelsome idiosyncrasies have made his name a byword throughout China.

Mr Werner's last official act was one of simple insubordination. In spite of Mr Alston's warning that he should not write direct to other authorities in Peking, he sent me, before starting on home-leave, an official despatch date 15th December, containing a long indictment against his American colleague at Foochow whom he described amongst other things as a "ferocious enemy" and having written him "insulting and libellous despatches". Without consulting me he took upon himself to send a copy of this despatch and its 62 enclosures to the American Minister in Peking. I have censured this improper, and in my experience unprecedented proceeding in a despatch copy of which is enclosed.

I have thought it best, in the first instance, to deal with the matter in this semi-official way, but I am quite prepared to report the whole case to His Majesty's Secretary of State should that course be considered advisable.[18]

In the polite manner of official despatches of the time, this condemnation of Werner was as strong as it could get. The phrase
"in the event of his return to China" gave a good indication of
Jordan's desire that Werner did not do so. In his letter to Whitehall, Jordan also included a further report, where he listed out
"Werner's troubles at Foochow:"

With his assistants:

Moss, whom he charged with tampering with his correspondence, with uselessness as a consular officer, dishonesty and being dishonourable.

Harding, whom he charged at different times with studied rudeness, a low trick, lying, prejudice, native conceit,
contemptuous demeanour.

Blackburn, whom he warned away from his house and
charged with working antagonistically to him.

With the community in general:

During the last two years Werner has not been on ordinary
speaking terms with four married couples and six unmarried people. The causes of the rupture were various, e.g.
a charge by Werner against one man of running after his,
Werner's, wife; an imagined slight to Mrs. Werner: an omission to call on Mrs. Werner. Werner made charges against
the consular doctor, Moorhead, of professional misconduct.
Consequently out of a club membership of thirty-five
Werner was not on speaking terms with eight. He was on
far from good terms with the remaining members of the

18 ibid.

community, including two of his colleagues, the consuls for
Germany and the United States.[19]

Jordan cited another example:
Werner's attitude during the Kiukiang boycott, 1909
    The boycott arose from the death of a Chinese porter
alleged to have died as a result of a blow from a stick given
by an Englishman called Mears, employed as Superintendent of Police by the municipal council in Kiukiang.

A perusal of the voluminous correspondence shows that
throughout this period Werner was obsessed by the idea
of personal animosity directed towards him by various
members of the community, including the Commissioner
of Customs, the American Methodist Mission, the Agent of
the Asiatic Petroleum Company and others. He refers in his
despatches to underhand and illegal methods, untrue statements, bribery; biassed and hostile attitudes and so forth.[20]

Throughout these accounts, a recurring pattern emerges in Werner's behaviour: constant disputes and confrontations; unfound-
ed accusations of dishonesty and immorality; perceived slights
and mistrust; imaginary enemies and adversaries; and his voluminous letters of complaint.

    There were other barbed exchanges between fellow foreign-
ers and Werner. It was an age when communication was often
written, and much could be said between the lines by skilful correspondents. High standards of politeness and address would
be maintained throughout, usually signing off, with no sense of

19 ibid.
20 a) ibid., b) *The Correspondence of G. E. Morrison* vol 1 1895-1912, editor Lo Hui-min, (1976)
    pp523-524, (letter to I.V. Chirol, September 13, 1909, "Unfortunately we have a very infe-
    rior Consul in Kiukiang ...").

irony, as "I have the honour to be your obedient servant." The following are extracts from letters addressed to or concerning Werner dating from the same period.

From Mrs Skerrett-Rogers to Werner on the subject of their stolen property:

It is difficult to divine any useful purpose in the nature of the communication you addressed to me on the 25th ultimo by way of reply to two very simple queries. All I wanted to know could have been expressed by your stating that the Chinese authorities had been unsuccessful in their search for my property... Instead you seized the opportunity to lecture me on my irregular conduct, dilatoriness, breach of treaties, utilising my husband's compradore instead of yourself, failure to communicate with you or your assistant, and so on... You say your assistant was in the port during your absence, yet it is matter of common knowledge that you resent any assistant of yours (once you have quarreled with him) being consulted on consular business. I did not therefore apply to Mr Blackburn in my predicament, fearing, thereby, that I might antagonise you and jeopardize my interests.

From Mr Skerrett-Rogers to Werner:

As you say you are a barrister, it should be unnecessary for me to point out that the reporting of a subordinate to his superiors does not constitute "publication" ... your warning to me has about equal value. My wife did not quote me in any way, and one does not need to be a barrister to know that a husband is not liable for what his wife may do, say, or write on her own responsibility in such a connection as the present. However, I am perfectly agreeable to be held jointly liable for all my wife wrote to you, every word of which I second and support... You constantly write of the biassed views of others; does it never occur to you to look close to home? All things are possible, and it may be that you are invariably right, and the rest of the world utterly wrong, but, and I say it with all possible respect, I know little of what you have done to support you in such an optimistic view of yourself ... Believe me, Sir, I write to you more in sorrow than in anger and with the sincere hope that from the past you may acquire some wisdom for the future, covering, incidentally, a care for how you wantonly insult Irish people.[21]

From Vice-Consul Harding to the Embassy in Peking concerning Werner's state of mental health:

By the same mail as this letter Sir John Jordan will doubtless receive an official despatch from Werner containing a letter from me in which I request my removal from Foochow. This letter gives only the very latest action on his part which leads me finally to conclude that work under Werner, for me at any rate, is impossible. Since my arrival here I have made a note of a few occurrences which show Werner's extreme suspiciousness with all those he has to do, amounting to a form of mental disease; there is a Greek word for it which I have forgotten, but Gray no doubt will be able to supply it. I propose to communicate to you a few evidences of this disease, asking you to submit the letter to Sir John Jordan. It is naturally impossible for me to write such a letter as this through my chief (Werner)... Referring to Werner's charge against the Reverend Packenham Walsh, I have communicated the paragraph thereanent to the Bishop, who is shortly going home;

----

21 UK National Archives, FO 228/1861 To and From Miscellaneous; letters July 1913.

and I have a letter from him saying that my version of the occurrence is correct, but admitting that perhaps he should not have mentioned the matter to me at all. The poor Bishop was so upset that he came into the assistant's office immediately after leaving Werner and said to me, "Is the man sane? Is the man sane?"[22]

And by Doctor Moorhead to the Embassy on Werner slandering him, which also takes up the issue of his mental stability:

A gentleman recently informed me that Mr Werner in the reading room of the Club said to him that "Moorhead had seduced Miss (blank) and then had sent her away, under the excuse that she was suffering from (blank)". This gentleman knows the lady referred to, also her family, and he at once informed me of H. M. Consul's remark. He has subsequently given me a written and signed statement as to what passed, which I am ready to produce for your Excellency's inspection... this is one incident in a particular campaign to destroy my honour... The impressions conveyed by Mr Werner's letters and his last extraordinary statement in the Club, so malicious and so dangerous to himself, would seem to be a want of control perhaps more apparent to a medical man than the public, and pointing to a mental neurosis.[23]

Many of Werner's problems during his Foochow years appear to relate to his evident insecurities over his new wife. A British consular officer, a student interpreter in Peking at the time, later recalled that Werner, after his marriage to his young wife, "became madly jealous of all his Vice-Consuls, who he accused of

22 UK National Archives, FO 228/1861 To and From Miscellaneous; letter March 1912.
23 UK National Archives, FO 228/1861 To and From Miscellaneous; letter August 1913.

watching her in the bathroom, etc. The Legation used to bet on the arrival of complaints about the latest Vice-Consul. The final straw was a complaint about Blackburn, not only the mildest of men but one who had arrived in Foochow with a brand-new wife of his own."[24]

But Werner's problematic relationships with others long predated his marriage; the stresses of the latter probably merely exacerbated them. As early as 1896, the British Minister in Peking, Sir Claude MacDonald, later one of the heroes of the Boxer siege, wrote to Werner in Macau castigating him for his extensive correspondence with a Mr. Milisch and the language he had used. Sir Claude had felt obliged to apologise to the German *charge d'affaires*. And he required Werner to write a formal letter of apology. This Werner did, but only in a qualified way and with a very bad grace.[25]

Then in 1900, only a few months before the Boxer rebellion began, Sir Claude wrote to Werner again over a similar affair that coincided with his promotion to consul:

> Had not the recommendation for your promotion been made prior to your recent conduct towards Dr Underwood, I should seriously have considered the advisability of passing you over for promotion. The explanation for your conduct for which I asked you and which has now reached me is in my opinion altogether unsatisfactory and does not in any way rectify the phenomenal foolishness of your behaviour... I have now to instruct you to write without delay an apology to Dr. Underwood for the annoyance you have caused him, and to direct you to first submit to H.M. Con-

....
24 School of Oriental & African Studies library archive, PP MS 52 P.D. Coates collection; notes on interview with Sir Alwyne Ogden, October 3, 1973.
25 UK National Archives, FO 228/1224 From Canton, 41 to end.

sul at Foochow the terms of your apology for approval.

I must warn you that should any further cases of similar conduct be at any time brought and proved against you grave consequences will be exacted on yourself, for I shall be obliged to report to H.M. Secretary of State that I considered you quite unfit to hold the position of consular officer in H.M. service.[26]

P.D. Coates, author of *The China Consuls*, began his consular career as a student probationer in Peking in late 1937. When writing his history of the British consular service in China decades later, Coates observed that in its many years of existence (1843-1943), only two of the several hundred consular staff had been forced to retire under the provisions of a special 1887 Act of Parliament. Werner was one of them. Coates, who would have known Werner, or of Werner, described him as a byword for

maniacal quarrelsomeness, who should have been removed much earlier than he was.[27]

But in 1913, perhaps predictably, Werner did not go quietly from the consular service. He and Gladys travelled back to England for his hurriedly-granted six-month leave, going by train via Siberia, with Werner stopping at Peking on the way in order to put his case personally to the Minister, Sir John Jordan.

The meeting, yet another stormy confrontation, did not go well for Wer-

Sir John Jordan. (School of Oriental & African Studies)

26 UK National Archives, FO 228/1357 To and from Amoy and Foochow.
27 P.D. Coates, *The China Consuls*, (1988) pp440-441.

ner, and as a result, on his arrival in London in February 1914, he applied to the Foreign Office for permission to retire at the end of his current leave in June. The Foreign Office accepted his resignation and generously offered him the best financial option available, that being a full pension on medical grounds. All Werner had to provide was a doctor's report certifying him unfit. Werner then promptly upset this sensible process by obtaining a report declaring the exact opposite, that he was medically perfectly fit.

A Foreign Office internal report read: "The medical report shows him to be in the most robust of health. If we want to get rid of him, our only course would seem to be to remove him under the Act of 1887," (legislation enabling those unable to discharge their duties to be dispensed with). And then later: "The fact about Werner is that his condition borders on insanity ... though it is doubtful whether he could be considered insane in the legal sense."[28]

A close inspection of the archive file reveals that Coates appears to have got things slightly wrong, Werner was not in fact "forcibly" removed from office under the Act of 1887. Probably in order to spare everyone further embarrassment, the Foreign Office managed to persuade the Treasury that Werner's many years of service in "unhealthy ports" counted sufficiently to qualify him for a forty-year pension of £622, four shillings and five pence per year (his annual salary had been £800 plus housing).[29] In 1914, this pension amounted to a very healthy income in the UK, and in China, to which the Werners planned to return, it afforded a far higher standard of living.

Once his pension was safely confirmed, Werner then wrote another lengthy letter to the Foreign Office, this time attacking

28 UK National Archives, FO 369/683 China. Code 210 Files 2566 - 4199.
29 ibid.

Jordan and the many perceived injustices toward him, and requesting that this be officially recorded in the Foreign Office List,
an annual who's who publication, as the real reason for his retirement. This did not happen and the entire affair was brought to
an end.[30]

Notwithstanding the delay caused by Europe's slide into war
that July, the Werners made the journey back to China. It would
be over thirty years before Werner returned to the UK. Gladys
would never set foot in England again.

Werner's character can be summed up by the descriptions of
those who knew him: morbidly suspicious, possessed of a need
of control that amounted to mental neurosis, maniacally quarrelsome. As the exasperated Bishop remarked: "Is the man sane, is
the man sane?"[31]

Consequently, there can be little wonder why, years later, Arthur Ringwalt of the American Embassy did not take Werner's
murder claims seriously. Werner's behaviour consistently suggested a form of paranoia, or at least some form of crippling
personality disorder, which may have been made exacerbated
by social isolation in China. But Werner also had problems with
plain honesty and acknowledging the truth; he not only denied
any error of judgement at the time of his enforced retirement,
but also published in book form an entirely contrary account of
the affair, one in which he was advised against retiring and was
offered another consular post.[31]

Despite the absence of consular responsibility, Werner's conflicts continued in a retirement spent largely in pursuing his literary interests. He admitted enjoying numerous "paper-fights"
and "a fondness for controversy" through letters to journals and

....

30 ibid.
31 E.T.C. Werner, *Autumn Leaves*, (1928) pp678-679.

newspapers.[32] Werner was nothing if not consistent.

During his investigation of Pamela's murder in 1937 and beyond, Werner's mindset appears to have been fixed. "Once my husband gets an idea into his head there is no use trying to convince him to the contrary,"[33] was his wife's description in 1913. Her words appear equally pertinent after Pamela's death. Throughout Werner's quest, the American dentist Wentworth Prentice appears to have either sensibly and politely ignored his accusations, or at least kept his distance from him. But perhaps not always. For indeed Prentice's great mistake, if it can be so described, may have been expressing his condolences to the bereaved Werner soon after the crime, possibly in a very sincere American manner, but in a way that Werner found grating. Werner described his contact with Prentice thus:

> His attitude toward me after the murder, though I had not seen him for several years, created in my mind a very strong suspicion, as reported at the time. He was so servilely polite that it impressed me very forcibly that his attitude was prompted by something else than mere social courtesy. The idea it formed in my mind was that it was intended to put me in a friendly frame of mind toward him and disarm suspicion.[34]

So Werner, despite his considerable legal training, formed a strong suspicion of guilt merely on the basis of a man's friendly attitude. "Servilely polite" - by this innocuous means, Prentice unwittingly made himself a murder suspect for Werner. In all

---

32 "Men in the East", *Caravan* magazine, January 1937.
33 UK National Archives, FO 228/1861 To and From Miscellaneous; letter by Doctor Moorhead 27 August 1913.
34 UK National Archives, FO 371/25315/1510 Murder of Pamela Werner Code 10 file 1510, letter from E.T.C. Werner to the British Ambassador to China, October 1938.

probability, this was a chance encounter between the two men soon after Pamela's death. In a letter to the Foreign Secretary Anthony Eden in July 1937, Werner marked out Prentice and two others, easily identifiable, as the culprits:

> The gravest suspicion rests on a destitute British ex-soldier, an American ex-marine, and another American, all close friends and known to indulge in the grossest sexual excesses.[35]

Werner can only be referring to Pinfold, Knauf, and Prentice. Of vital significance is that the above letter predates Werner launching his own investigation, something he described as only commencing in September 1937 on his return from a two-month annual stay at Peitaiho, and after the police investigation had ceased.[36] It appears, therefore, that Werner had already decided upon at least three of his suspects before he began the process of gathering what he considered evidence. This was to prove a great misfortune for the three men, especially given Werner's intransigence.

Having already decided upon his suspects, Werner then went about finding evidence to support his conclusion. Rather than seeing where the evidence led, Werner worked the other way around, setting out to find material that supported his suspicions and directed him to where he wished to go.

Over the next few years, Werner outlined his progress with report after report despatched to the British Ambassador and the Foreign Office in Whitehall. To assist him, he made use of men

....

35 UK National Archives, FO 371/21004 China. Code 10 Files 2047 - 2396.
36 UK National Archives, FO 371/25315/1510 Murder of Pamela Werner Code 10 file 1510, letter from E.T.C. Werner to the British Ambassador to China, June 1939.

he described as "my secret agents."[37] He also offered a reward of $5,000 in the local newspaper for witnesses solving the murder.[38] Though presumably Chinese dollars, this was nonetheless an enormous sum of money in Peking at that time. Between the use of paid agents and the offer of a prodigious reward, Werner was possibly unwittingly laying himself open to unscrupulous individuals willing to provide whatever kind of spurious evidence the old man required. The Chinese police had similarly offered a $1,000 reward within three days of the murder, but they were unlikely to be quite so open to suggestion as Werner.[39]

In the circumstances, then, it is not surprising that Werner found ready and willing witnesses. Werner congratulated himself on locating his star witness, the young rickshaw coolie Sun Te-hsing in September 1937 from amongst the 50,000 or so of his kind he estimated as working in Peking (a contemporary city guide provided the figure of 44,169).[40]

Werner laid great stress on the importance of this man's evidence – despite some major variations in Sun Te-hsing's recollection of events outside the door of Number 28. As recorded by Werner himself, initially the young coolie had the suspects loading the woman's "dead body" onto his rickshaw at midnight,[41] but then in a later account Sun Te-hsing described the woman as being alive and groaning and subsequently pleading for his help before being bludgeoned to death near the Wall.[42] Nonetheless, Werner was so convinced by his rickshaw witness that in Sep-

37 UK National Archives, FO 371/25315/1510 Murder of Pamela Werner Code 10 file 1510, letter from E.T.C. Werner to the British Ambassador to China, October 1939.
38 "$5,000 Offered for Arrest of Werner's Murderer," *Peiping Chronicle*, January 26, 1937.
39 "$1,000 reward offered", *Peiping Chronicle*, January 10, 1937.
40 a) UK National Archives, FO 371/25315/1510 Murder of Pamela Werner Code 10 file 1510, letter from E.T.C. Werner to the British Ambassador to China, October 1938. b) *Guide to "Peking"*, published by *the Peiping Chronicle*, revised edition 1935.
41 UK National Archives, FO 371/25315/1510 Murder of Pamela Werner Code 10 file 1510, letter from E.T.C. Werner to the British Ambassador to China, October 1938.
42 E.T.C Werner, *More Memorigrams*, (1948) p192.

tember 1937 he took him to the British Embassy in order to meet Allan Archer, who had recently replaced Fitzmaurice as Peking Consul. As a result, Archer, who had not been in Peking at the time of the police investigation, in turn consulted Dennis and Botham who were both by this time back in Tientsin. Through them, Archer discovered that the the rickshaw coolie was already known to Chinese police, as very soon after the murder he implicated a number of Italian marines, as opposed to Prentice and the others on Werner's list.[43] Predictably, Werner did not like the response he got from Archer, complaining bitterly of the Consul's "myopic description" of the evidence as being "fantastic – valueless – and cannot be true.[44]

In the years that followed, aided by his "secret agents," Werner located several other dubious witnesses willing to tell him how they saw Prentice and Cappuzzo carry Pamela down the narrow staircase from the dentist's flat to the car, with Pamela plaintively uttering 'save life' in Chinese.[45] One other, fully two years after the event, managed to recall Pinfold spying on Werner's house the day before the murder.[46] And still another who allegedly worked inside Number 28 and could describe hearing a commotion, screams, a great thump, then silence. The same witness then related how the body was taken to the nearby private hospital run by a Korean named Doctor Kim for dismemberment before being returned to Number 28.[47] According to Werner, the British and Chinese police had apparently been too slow, too rude, or too incompetent to secure any of these witnesses.

....

43 UK National Archives, FO 800/299 Miscellaneous correspondence Volume (Clark-Kerr papers).
44 UK National Archives, FO 371/25315/1510 Murder of Pamela Werner Code 10 file 1510, letter from E.T.C. Werner to the British Ambassador to China, October 1938.
45 E.T.C Werner, *More Memorigrams*, (1948) p191.
46 UK National Archives, FO 371/25315/1510 Murder of Pamela Werner Code 10 file 1510, letter from E.T.C. Werner to the British Ambassador to China, June 1938.
47 ibid.

The theories and claims that Werner raised in his reports ranged from the purely improbable to the outright bizarre. In one scenario, he proposed that at least ten persons were involved in the murder, three of them doctors,[48] that the Korean Doctor Kim may have performed the mutilations in Prentice's flat, possibly with the help of Pinfold,[49] and that an ambulance - from the PUMC Hospital, no less - may have been used by them to transport the body.[50] Werner claimed Prentice had also committed a murder in the United States, thus either ignoring or being unaware that the dentist had not been home for fifteen years.[51] Werner also reported that Pamela wrote a note to him while she was being held prisoner at Number 28, but had been refused permission to send it. This despite Werner describing his daughter as having been previously stabbed in the face and having sustained a fractured skull.[52] Han, the Chinese Head of Police, was, Werner reported, "a Judas" who had deliberately misled the British police and consular officials,[53] used torture in his investigations,[54] was in league with the murderers[55] and, worse still, had been for many years "a close friend and co-sexualist" with Prentice.[56] Indeed, throughout his reports, Werner had all manner of people down as "sexualists" or "sado-sexualists": Prentice, Knauf, Cappuzzo, Kim, Han and Gorman.[57] Werner's lurid understanding

....

48 ibid.
49 ibid.
50 ibid.
51 ibid.
52 E.T.C Werner, *More Memorigrams*, (1948) p192.
53 UK National Archives, FO 371/25315/1510 Murder of Pamela Werner Code 10 file 1510, letter from E.T.C. Werner to the British Ambassador to China, October 1938.
54 UK National Archives, FO 371/25315/1510 Murder of Pamela Werner Code 10 file 1510, letter from E.T.C. Werner to the British Ambassador to China, February 1939.
55 UK National Archives, FO 371/25315/1510 Murder of Pamela Werner Code 10 file 1510, letter from E.T.C. Werner to the British Ambassador to China, June 1939.
56 UK National Archives, FO 371/25315/1510 Murder of Pamela Werner Code 10 file 1510, letter from E.T.C. Werner to the British Ambassador to China, October 1939.
57 UK National Archives, FO 371/35815 Murder of Pamela Werner. Code 10 file 714. Letter from E.T.C. Werner to the British Ambassador to China, October 1941.

of the word "sexualist" was evidently very different from that found in dictionaries (a sexualist is usually defined as a type of botanist). Nonetheless, whatever he meant by the word, Werner referred to all these men as "sexualists" purely on the basis that they were "well known to be so", at least according to Werner. He never produced any evidence to support such allegations.

Werner frequently alleged types of behaviour in his suspects that he personally disapproved of or had difficulty with. For instance, he appears to have been sexually repressed throughout his life, ergo his suspects were sado-sexualists who frequented a brothel. Werner was shocked by nudity and believed it to be a return to savagery,[58] ergo Prentice ran a nudist club outside Peking for the benefit of his fellow degenerates.[59] Werner abhorred drunkenness,[60] ergo the murderers were drink-filled at their murderous task.

Werner laid great stress on sexual propriety and was at pains to prove it in Pamela, so much so that he later published the following passage in one of his books, taken from the coroner's hearing:

Extracts from the evidence of Dr. John Preston Maxwell.

Coroner (Fitzmaurice): Could you tell me if at any time this girl had given birth to a child?

Maxwell: No, she had never given birth to a child.

Coroner: Is there any evidence to show at the time this murder occurred she was pregnant?

Maxwell: No.

Coroner: Is there anything more that you could state other than you have stated in your report?

58 a) E.T.C. Werner, *Autumn Leaves*, (1928) p520, & b) E.T.C. Werner, *Memorigrams*, (1940), p9.
59 UK National Archives, FO 371/25315/1510 Murder of Pamela Werner Code 10 file 1510, letter from E.T.C. Werner to the British Ambassador to China, October 1938.
60 E.T.C. Werner, *Autumn Leaves*, (1928) p519.

Maxwell: I do not think so, the parts were perfectly normal.

Coroner: Would you say definitely that it was the work of a sadist?

Maxwell: I should say certainly from the appearance of the body in general.

Coroner: And coupled with that is it consistent with one who might have some medical knowledge?

Maxwell: I think one could say definitely that it was not the work of an ordinary sexual sadist in this, that the uterus was left alone. The organs were left. A sexual sadist interferes with the uterus if he can get at it as a rule, that is the common thing I should say.

Coroner: Could it have been done by a man of not only knowledge of human anatomy but by a person who had knowledge of animals such as hunter or butcher?

Maxwell: Yes.[61]

Doctor John Preston Maxwell (1871-1961) was a notable British obstetrician and Christian missionary working at the PUMC who at the time of giving evidence was within a few months of retirement and his final return to England. Maxwell had spent most of his working life in China and had written extensively on the subject of foetal osteomalacia (a bone disease). He was a respected medical figure. The extract from the coroner's hearing is, however, a clas-

Doctor John Preston Maxwell, coroner hearing witness

....

61 E.T.C. Werner, *Memorigrams*, (1940), p151.

sic example of a specialist in one area (obstetrics) allowing himself to be led into giving his opinion on specialist areas outside his field of knowledge (criminal psychology and forensic pathology). Maxwell had no expertise in sadism or sexual behavior, hence his bizarre comment about the removal of uteruses and "ordinary sexual sadists." Nor was he qualified to comment on the skills required in the butchery meted out to Pamela's body. Consul Fitzmaurice ought not to have allowed this mistake to occur. In the event, Maxwell's opinions on these matters carried little in the way of evidential consequence at the hearing. But they registered with Werner, who certainly saw them as significant, and resulted in him later searching resolutely for "sexual sadists" who had either "medical knowledge" and/or were "hunters."

Almost anyone, it seems, could be considered to be a closet sexual sadist if sufficiently disliked by Werner. But Doctor Ugo Cappuzzo was perhaps particularly unfortunate in fitting the requirements of the profile in that he lived close to the ice rink, was an experienced surgeon, and liked to shoot geese in his spare time. There can be little surprise, then, that before long he too was included in Werner's list of suspects.

"Fantastic" was the word politely yet repeatedly used by Consul Archer to describe Werner's crime theories, or so Werner bitterly complained.[62] Werner's many reports to the Foreign Office also contained no actual evidence. He provided no statements or exhibits. It may be that his long, rambling reports to the Foreign Office, full of rumor and hearsay, were Werner's only actual notes on the case. In 1945, having lost his own copies of the reports as a result of the War, he enlisted the help of yet another long-serving British Consul, Alwyne Ogden, in arranging

....

62 UK National Archives, FO 371/25315/1510 Murder of Pamela Werner Code 10 file 1510, letter from E.T.C. Werner to the British Ambassador to China, October 1938.

Murder of Pamela Werner. Encloses copy of letter to Consul.
Investigation is being continued.

I Enclosure.

Peking

March 18   1939

///////// Copy.

His Excellency

Sir Archibald Kerr Clark Kerr, K.C.M.G.,

His Britannic Majesty's Envoy Extraordinary and

Ambassador Plenipotentiary,

etc.,   etc.,   etc.,
Shanghai.

Your Excellency,

In continuation of my report of October 5th
1938 and following dates I have the honour to enclose copy
of a letter addressed by me to Consul Archer on February 26th
1939, with some additional notes.

This letter points out the deceit practised on the
Consul by Captain Han, the Chinese Chief of Police, in misleading him as to the suspicion attaching to the No.28
establishment, where I have established beyond any possibility
of doubt that the murder of my adopted daughter was committed.

But for the failure of the three Consuls and two Scotland Yard detectives to see through this deceit, the criminals
would, in all probability, long since have been arrested and
brought to trial.

As pointed out in previous reports, Consul Archer's
attitude was not helpful but obviously hostile, though he
was supposed to be acting as Coroner in the case of the
brutal murder of a defenceless girl, under British and who was
Chinese protection. His arguments were always those of
counsel for the defendants (in this case the murderers)
instead of those of prosecutor. It surely must be a pretty
rotten sort of judicial administration where so unspeakably
atrocious a crime can be treated in so insincere and unconst-
itutional a manner. Instead of attempts to cover them up, the
mistakes of himself and his predecessors should have been
frankly admitted, and he should have started with a clean
slate. As it is, the mismanagement of the case has become
the laughing-stock of the foreign communities both here and
in Tientsin, as well as of the Club bar drinking coteries.
The jubilation of the murderers may be easily imagined.

The enclosed letter also impeaches the action of the
Consul in the Oparina, ricksha coolie, and Italian sailors
sections of the investigation. In the latter a most important

An example of a letter from Werner to the British authorities (UK National Archives)

for copies of his "evidence" to be returned to him in Peking from London.[63] Ogden worked in China for over three decades, commencing a year or so before Werner's retirement, and later in old age provided P.D. Coates with insightful memories of many of the consular staff he encountered, including his experience of Werner, whom he described as "completely mad."[64]

Through late 1937 and into 1938, with an excited Werner visiting him at the Embassy every few days, the beleaguered Consul, Allan Archer, Fitzmaurice's replacement, had his work cut out trying to calm the old man down. It could not have been an easy task, especially as Archer had very recently come into possession of new intelligence on Pamela's murder that he was compelled to keep secret from Werner. This new intelligence pointed the investigation in an entirely new direction and, unlike Werner and his agents, it came from a source Archer and staff at the Embassy considered entirely reliable—a man who also happened to be one of the most colorful and extraordinary men in all China.

63 E.T.C Werner, *More Memorigrams*, (1948) p205.
64 School of Oriental & African Studies library archive, PP MS 52 P.D. Coates collection, notes on interview with Sir Alwyne Ogden, October 3, 1973.

10

THE ENIGMA

BACKHOUSE

On February 11, 1938, about one year after the murder, Allan Archer, Consul in Peking, wrote to Robert Howe, the *charge d'affaires* stationed in Shanghai and temporarily the senior British official in China. The letter was marked "personal and secret."

My dear Howe,
Since my secret letter of the 18th December last and your
reply (in handwriting) of the 31st December on the subject
of the Werner murder, E.C. Werner has been pursuing his
investigations, with the result that he now considers both
the Pinfold-Prentice circle and a Russian circle known as the
Oparina family to be eliminated from suspicion in favour of
a story told by a certain rickshaw coolie named Sun Te Hs-
ing implicating Italian marines. This story was already in the
possession of the police in January 1937, but as it is not clear
to what extent it was adequately investigated before being
discarded I have called for a report from Dennis and Botham
in Tientsin before taking any new action on it.
    Meanwhile, however, there has been a surprising devel-

opment. Sir E. Backhouse, who is doing translation work
with the Japanese, has sent a verbal message to me by Dr.
Aspland [Dr Aspland was embassy doctor and present at the
autopsy] to the following effect:

His Japanese friends (including a Japanese General) talk
quite openly and boastfully to him about the Werner murder
case, say that everyone is on the wrong track, and that the
murder was committed by two Japanese, who were members of a Japanese Secret Vengeance Society which exists in
Peking, as vengeance for the Sasaki case. Details are given,
viz: that the girl was enticed into a Japanese restaurant in the
Japanese Hatamen Quarter by a certain Chinese named Tan
Shou Ching, who had at one time been one of the girl's Chinese friends but had a grudge against Werner; that she was
there deliberately murdered, and the body cut up by one of
the Japanese who had been a medical student; that a Chinese
rickshaw coolie named Te Fu Hai was given $25 to take the
body and throw it in the ditch; that the original plan had
been to murder Mrs Fitzmaurice but as they could not get to
her they chose Pamela Werner as the daughter of a retired
British Consul; that Dr. Ito, the Japanese dentist whom Mr
and Miss Werner had been attending, is also a member of
this Secret Society and intended to warn Pamela that she had
better not stay in Peking, but delayed doing so until too late;
that one of the Japanese has since been killed in the war and
the other is now serving somewhere at the front, but that Tan
Shou Ching and Te Fu hai are still in Peking.

Backhouse passes this history on to me through Aspland
as he feels if he did not let us know he might be guilty of
being an accessory after the fact, but he only does so on the
definite condition that it is not used in any way that would
involve him, as the Japanese have made it quite clear that if

he gives them away they will "get" him somehow, even if he were to return to England.

It seems incredible that the Japanese could invent all this in such detail merely in order to claim that Sasaki is avenged, and accordingly it looks as though we have the true story at last, and cannot use it to do anything. It explains so much that has hitherto been incomprehensible, and as Captain Han has probably known all along and been warned off any effective action by the Japanese I feel that it is quite impossible to go to him with such a story and try to get Tan Shou Ching.

If it were not for Werner, still frantically pursuing the murderers of his adopted daughter, over whom he took little interest or care while she was alive, I think we could now accept this story and drop, on political or diplomatic grounds, any further attempts to pursue it. As it is, I do not know what to do with Werner, as clearly I cannot tell him this story, or he would move Heaven and Earth for vengeance on the Japanese, get questions asked in Parliament etc etc and generally land us in an impossible diplomatic situation, as the Japanese would simply deny the story as fantastic.

I will let you know in due course the result of re-investigations into the story regarding Italian marines, over which I will go very carefully. Meanwhile, I have not shown this letter to anyone here, and I think that no one else should see it except Blackburn [the same Blackburn who was once vice consul to Werner in Foochow, but now embassy counsellor]. But I enclose a spare copy in case you wish to send it to someone in the F.O.

Would you let me know, if you have any views as to what I could do now?

Yours sincerely, Allan Archer.[1]

The source of this new intelligence was Sir Edmund Trelawny Backhouse, 2nd Baronet (1873-1944), a most remarkable man who for forty years lived an enigmatic and increasingly reclusive life in Peking. Born in England into a wealthy Quaker family, and Oxford-educated, Backhouse was an eminent sinologist with a one-time reputation for possess-

Sir Edmund Backhouse ing high-level contacts in Peking government circles. He was a gifted linguist, and certainly capable of conversing in Japanese with Japanese army officers.

Although addressed to Howe, Archer's letter was also read by the new British Ambassador, Sir Archibald Clark Kerr (1882-1951), who had only arrived in China a few days earlier, his predecessor having been badly injured during the Japanese invasion of the previous summer. Clark Kerr either already knew of the Werner case, or more likely was hastily provided with a briefing, for he added at the end of the letter:

> This looks to me like the truth at last and we are in the stark situation of knowing and being unable to do anything about it. I will tell Archer there is nothing to be done at the moment, but will take a copy to the F.O.[2]

Archer and Clark Kerr's unwillingness to take action over important new information on the brutal murder of a British subject

....

1 UK National Archives, FO 800/299 Miscellaneous correspondence Volume 2 (Clark Kerr papers), letter from Allan Archer, February 11, 1938.
2 ibid.

Consul Archer's letter reporting Backhouse's murder theory (UK National Archives)

is made understandable by the war and politics of the time. By February 1938, the Japanese firmly held the upper-hand in the Sino-Japanese War and already controlled most of the major cities in northern China. The conflict had already involved major loss of life, mostly Chinese. The Japanese military controlled the entire city of Peking, including the Chinese police. In this position of power, the Japanese had become increasingly arrogant and provocative in their dealings with other foreign nationals. Foreign governments were increasingly ineffective in restraining Japanese aggression in China whilst simultaneously slowly reducing their own military presence in the country. Britain's once-considerable influence in the region was fast on the wane.

The British officials also had the problem of the lack of supporting evidence for the new theory, plausible though it seemed to them. For safety's sake, Backhouse, living alone with his servants in a corner of the Tartar City, had insisted that his name not be mentioned, so raising the subject with the Japanese would probably point to Backhouse as its source. Finding evidence to confirm Backhouse's information would require the work of detectives. Dennis and Botham could no longer freely investigate in Peking, at least not without the cooperation of the Japanese, something that would surely not be forthcoming once they realized the suspects were also Japanese. To accuse the Japanese with or without substantiating evidence would have undoubtedly created a serious diplomatic incident, and might also have played into Japanese hands in their search for conflicts with the Western nations. In any event, any such action would require the consent of the Foreign Office, which in the political circumstances was unlikely.

The motive mentioned in Archer's letter was given as vengeance for the Sasaki case. Six months before Pamela's murder, two British soldiers, both military police, had been arrested over the murder of a young Japanese army officer named Kisaku Sasaki. Sasaki had been assaulted in the small hours of the morning by a pair of drunk uniformed servicemen who had left a bar off Hataman Street. At the time, though not yet actually in control, the Japanese military was present in Peking in large numbers. To Japanese fury, Consul Fitzmaurice, acting in his extraterritorial capacity as judge over accused British subjects, found in favour of the defendants, and there was no conviction. It was an incident the Japanese would not have forgotten. At the time of Pamela's murder, a heavily pregnant Mrs. Fitzmaurice was within days of giving birth to her second child and therefore not nearly as accessible as Pamela Werner cycling Peking's streets on her own.

Killing a consul's wife would have been an extreme act, even by the murderous standards of the Japanese militarists, one without precedent. But Archer, with first-hand experience of the anti-British climate in Peking, clearly thought the idea credible, as did Clark Kerr, the British Ambassador. Japanese antipathy toward the British was high during this period, and backed by

a concerted propaganda campaign. The Japanese sought to justify their hegemony and aggression in China by projecting themselves as the Far East's liberators. The valiant Japanese troops were nobly ridding the region of the cruel imperialist white men.

Gordon Creighton (1908-2003) was a young secretary at the British Embassy during 1935-1937. Although they never met face-to-face, he was also a secret embassy contact of Sir Edmund Backhouse.[3] Like the elusive baronet,

Gordon Creighton, Backhouse's Embassy contact

3 School of Oriental & African Studies library archive, P.D. Coates collection PP MS 52, letter from Gordon Creighton, April 29, 1989.

Creighton was also a linguist of considerable ability. Many years later in his retirement, Creighton wrote to P.D. Coates, recalling both the Sasaki trial and the murder of Pamela Werner:

> ... the murder of Werner's daughter, you will know, I am sure, that the affair was preceded by another grisly business involving the Japanese ... in a brawl in the Ch'ien-Men-Wai red-light area, one hot night in the summer of 1935 or 1936.[4]

At this point Creighton's memory appears to have let him down as he recalled *two* Japanese nationals being killed rather than just the one. He then continued describing how Japanese officials claimed this act was done:

> ... two soldiers allegedly of our embassy guard ... they produced bits of uniform, belt-webbing etc, allegedly torn from the British assailants. Everybody of course knew that that particular webbing was not worn by British personnel, but something very similar, or identical, was normal wear for U.S. Marines. The U.S. Embassy of course sat quiet and said nuffin, and the Japs clearly wanted to use the thing as a battering ram against Great Britain, not the Americans, since <u>we</u> were still the key power in the Far East and in China - not the Yanks. Fitzmaurice as H.M. Consul in Peking conducted the Consular Court Enquiry into the charges, and I as Assistant Chinese Secretary had to interpret and question lots of witnesses, pimps, whores (Chinese and Koreans), rickshawmen, bystanders, etc. So I took a great interest in all those goings on ... The killing of Werner's daughter took place also while I was still in Peking, and it

4   School of Oriental & African Studies library archive, P.D. Coates collection PP MS 52, letter from Gordon Creighton, April 29, 1989.

interested me vastly, as I feel sure it was a Japanese revenge
act.[5]

"A battering ram against Great Britain," and a highly political
case. From court case notes held in the UK National Archives, it
is possible to discern what may have have happened on the night
of 26-27 May 1936 and thereafter.

What appears certain is that towards midnight on that Tuesday night, two foreign soldiers in uniform, both white men, visited two bars in the Tartar City consecutively. This was in no way
unusual as the bars were frequented by soldiers of many nationalities, and indeed the bars relied on such custom. The soldiers
appear to have been what was described as "fighting drunk." At
least one of the pair began gratuitously assaulting various Chinese and Koreans quietly minding their own business, resulting
in five or more people sustaining minor or moderate injuries.
The soldiers then quickly left the second bar and entered the
street. The assaults might not have excited much attention had
the pair not then happened to cross the paths of two Japanese
soldiers, both of them off-duty but in military uniform. The two
Japanese were attacked without warning. One of them managed
to break away while the other, a young officer named Kisaku
Sasaki, was not so fortunate. Most likely struck with some form
of blunt instrument rather than being merely punched, Sasaki
sustained a fractured skull and died of a cerebral hemorrhage.
Either the blow or the resulting fall killed him, it was difficult to
tell which. All these facts went largely undisputed. The identity
of the perpetrators, however, was entirely another matter.[6]

Japanese officials, understandably furious and keen to make
political capital from the incident, quickly implicated British sol-

....

5   ibid.
6   UK National Archives, FO 676 247 Criminal case, Sasaki and Ohnishi.

diers. Seeing a diplomatic incident developing, the British Embassy immediately confined all British soldiers in Peking to the compound and seized the log detailing personnel movements in and out of the barracks.[7] Two weeks later, with several British soldiers accused of the crime, Chief Inspector Dennis, summoned from Tientsin, conducted a formal identification parade of suspects at the Embassy. This event was attended by staff and victims from one of the bars concerned, passers-by, and also by the second Japanese soldier present when the fatal attack took place. None of the witnesses could identify any of the men in the lineup as being involved in the street attack on the two Japanese. But a barmaid identified two British soldiers, Cook and Hunt, as being involved in an assault inside a bar.[8]

There then followed an abuse of judicial process which ought not to have been permitted. Japanese Embassy staff suddenly produced a further four witnesses, all reputedly bar staff, none of whom had previously provided statements or spoken to the police. On being admitted to the lineup, three of these *new* witnesses identified Cook as being involved, and Hunt as an accomplice, though with some inconsistency.[9]

While the offence took place on Chinese territory, all British citizens in China were subject to British law under the extraterritoriality agreements dating from the 1840s, in the same way that all Japanese were subject to Japanese law. After the identification parade, Consul Nicholas Fitzmaurice, in his capacity as judge, rejected the charge of murder as there was no direct evidence to link either soldier with the crime. Not only did this outrage the Japanese but it placed enormous importance on the outcome of the sole remaining charge of causing bodily harm to another

....

7 ibid.
8 ibid.
9 ibid.

Japanese man inside one of the bars, for which Cook alone stood trial a few weeks later.[10]

The trial, in the Embassy compound presided over by the British Consul, began at the end of June 1936 and lasted eight days, during which witness after witness gave conflicting, doubtful or inconsistent evidence, all of which was revealed as such by an able British defence lawyer. The Japanese doctor could not even confirm on what day he had completed his rather inadequate autopsy as he had neglected to record the date. On the final day, Fitzmaurice found Cook not guilty, but not before the Japanese officials, seeing the way things were going, had already made a point of walking out of the court in disgust.[11]

Cook and Hunt were both military police tasked with patrolling Peking's bars and clubs in the search for drunk British soldiers or for those out without leave of absence. Furthermore, they had at some time prior to the fatal incident designated some of the more notorious bars as being out-of-bounds, a policy that cost several Chinese and Korean-run bars a good deal of trade. As a result, Cook and Hunt were both known to, and unpopular with, the bar owners. The soldiers' regular patrols (designed to address the sort of violent behavior they were accused of) ensured that they were easily recognizable by many bar staff. Cook and Hunt had often worked together, but the barrack log exhibit showed that they had not done so on the night in question. Neither had either of them possessed the necessary time or opportunity to cover the distances involved and behave in the manner of which they were accused. In the circumstances, it is difficult to see what other verdict Fitzmaurice could have brought.[12] The identity of the soldiers responsible for the death of Kisaku Sasaki

....

10 ibid.
11 ibid.
12 ibid.

remained unknown, and as a result of the not guilty verdict, as both Backhouse and Creighton observed, the frustrated Japanese may well have felt a desire for revenge. Or perhaps they simply regarded it as expedient to feel so.

Archer's letter to Clark Kerr concerning Backhouse's Japanese intelligence, marked as it was "personal and secret", was known to only a handful of British diplomats, and did not become public for many years. Clark Kerr's collection of private letters was opened to view by the UK National Archives in 1972. Certainly, Werner appears not to have been aware of it and its allegation. The letter was not entered into the outgoing register of embassy correspondence, as was normal procedure. Similarly, although Clark Kerr may have taken a copy with him to the Foreign Office as he indicated, there is no official record of it arriving there.

Unlike Archer and Clark Kerr, however, a few men in Whitehall possessed information about the information's source, the extraordinary Sir Edmund Backhouse, a character so peculiar that Werner appears quite straightforward by comparison.

Backhouse was born in 1873 into an old and wealthy Quaker family with roots in Cornwall and Lancashire. His father was made a baronet, a title Edmund, the eldest of five children, inherited along with the prefix of *Sir*. After schooling at Winchester College, Edmund attended Merton College, Oxford, where he soon showed his credentials for being the black sheep of the family. Living extravagantly among a clique of fashionable homosexuals and socialites, he soon racked up large debts. Declared bankrupt and without finishing his degree, Backhouse left England and arrived in China in 1898, just in time to be caught up in the Boxer siege, during which he failed to distinguish himself owing to the sudden development of a bad back which incapacitated him.

Backhouse lived the rest of his life in Peking supported, it is surmised, partly by a family allowance, partly from his extraordinary talent for languages and the translation of documents, partly from book royalties, and partly from various business interests. For some years he worked as a translator for the famous *Times* correspondent George Morrison ("Morrison of Peking"). Backhouse, always a peculiar figure and increasingly reclusive in his later years, died in Peking in 1944 while the city was occupied by the Japanese.

Charming and unfailingly polite, Backhouse's reputation was that of a sinologist and sage, a book collector living the life of a Chinese scholar. In his final decades, he even dressing like one; robed and sporting a long beard. His remoteness only added to his mystique.

Backhouse, came to wider attention in 1976 with the publication of Hugh Trevor-Roper's book *Hermit of Peking; the Hidden Life of Sir Edmund Backhouse*.[13] The book revealed another, secret, side to Backhouse, that he was a serial fraudster.

In addition to George Morrison, Backhouse also worked with J.O.P. Bland, another China correspondent for *The Times* and in 1910, Bland and Backhouse collaborated in writing the book *China Under the Empress Dowager*. Backhouse both provided and translated the Chinese sources, whilst Bland composed and polished the final text. The book was an international best-seller. Coming so soon after the Empress Dowager's death (in 1908) and on the eve of the revolution that wiped away her dynasty, it captured the moment. The book was largely based on the diary of an elderly courtier named Ching-shan, who met his death with the defeat of the Boxers in 1900. Backhouse said he had himself discovered the diary during the general free-for-all of looting and destruction that followed the lifting of the siege of the

13 Sir Hugh Trevor-Roper, *Hermit of Peking; the Hidden Life of Sir Edmund Backhouse.*

legations, of which Backhouse was a part. Backhouse had either been allocated or had simply seized Ching-shan's Peking home as a spoil of war, with what remained of its contents, scattered documents included. The diary, Backhouse said, had been only moments from being burnt by a group of Sikh soldiers before his timely intervention.

China Under the Empress Dowager provided what purported to be the first in-depth account of events leading to the tumultuous Boxer rebellion from the perspective of the Chinese court, and it cemented Backhouse's reputation as a Chinese scholar of rare ability. But the whole project was based on what was almost certainly a lie. Ching-shan's diary, donated by Bland to the British Museum in London, was finally judged an elaborate fake, but it was not until 1936 that a public claim of forgery was made, by a British journalist in Shanghai, William Lewisohn. A painstaking study by him revealed that the diary was a clever pastiche of passages and quotes borrowed from elsewhere. Backhouse dismissed Lewisohn's findings and thankfully for him, the start of the Sino-Japanese War in 1937 brought a convenient end to this ruinous discussion of Ching-shan's diary.

The affair of the courtier's diary was not the only time Backhouse was accused of deception. Another incident in 1915 involved the sale of a large consignment of rifles and ammunition from China to Britain. China was officially neutral in the European conflict, so a private business deal was arranged, funded behind the scenes by the British government. Backhouse was chosen to be the facilitator. He was already in Peking, spoke excellent Chinese, and was said to possess contacts with highly-placed Chinese officials. The British Embassy in Peking, it was emphasized, could not be seen to have a part in the deal. Backhouse was to work alone and he alone was to negotiate and make all the arrangements. Two million pounds sterling of British Government money was transferred to a bank in China, and initially things seemed to go well. Backhouse reported having made contact with the appropriate Chinese officials and ascertained the existence of quantities of suitable rifles stockpiled in various parts of China. London was delighted. But then the operation ran into problems. Backhouse reported delays in securing the right people and in arranging shipping of the weaponry from locations across China to Hong Kong. Finally on September 22, the Embassy sent word to London that the ships carrying the arms cargo had been assembled off the port of Foochow and would sail down the Chinese coast to Hong Kong. But the ships never turned up. In early October, they were reputed to have been diverted from Hong Kong to Canton, at which point the British Minister in Peking, Sir John Jordan, decided to break cover and went personally to see the Chinese President, Yuan Shikai, who, to Jordan's surprise, said he knew nothing of the arrangement. Jordan went to see Backhouse at his home, and took him to a meeting with the President's principal aide, Liang Shih-i. Jordan made Backhouse brief Liang on events to date, to which a sceptical Liang suggested that Backhouse must have been duped, as China had nowhere near such amounts of munitions to sell.

A downcast Jordan reported the situation to London, and there was immense disappointment all round. The consensus was that blame was to be placed on the perfidious Chinese and splits among its generals and ministers. Backhouse had done all he could and was not to blame. The Government in London had a war to fight and no time for an investigation or recriminations. But not so for Jordan. The stress and failure of the operation had affected him deeply. He felt humiliated, and his conclusion from subsequent investigations led him to believe that it was not Backhouse who had been duped, but he himself. The secret negotiations Backhouse had supposedly been involved in, the nameless Chinese officials who had failed to deliver, the ships that had never been seen containing rifles by the tens of thousands that had in fact never existed. The whole thing, Jordan concluded, had been a Backhouse fantasy. Two million pounds sterling of government funds had been moved to a bank in Peking, but thankfully not lost.

For Backhouse, the end of one fraud seems to have opened the door to another. The day Jordan visited Backhouse, he had been in a meeting with an American businessman named George Sylvester Hall of the American Banknote Company, who was in China hoping to win a contract from the Chinese Government. Like many others, Hall found Backhouse to be charming, well-informed and above all, well-connected. Left standing alone outside Backhouse's home as Backhouse disappeared in the car of the British Minister, Hall was impressed. He knew nothing of the circumstances, but knew he had just witnessed none other than the British Minister call on Backhouse in order to take him to an urgent meeting with China's leaders.

Backhouse became the American Banknote Company's agent in Peking. He was seen as the man with both the expertise and the contacts to win the company the Chinese contract it was seeking. President Yuan Shikai, who had been busy trying to make himself into another emperor, died suddenly in 1916 but most fortunately, or so it seemed, Backhouse was on close terms with Tuan Ch'i-jui, the new Prime Minister and Minister of War. Working completely independently – not for the first time – Backhouse negotiated a contract for the American company. Hall was unhappy that he was excluded from this process, but the contract when it came was enormous, involving the supply of 650 million banknotes over thirteen years. In late 1916, Backhouse travelled in triumph to New York to report it. He was greeted by the company directors, all pleased to meet this "treasure of an agent." Hall was promoted. Back in Peking in December, Backhouse handed Hall the contracts for the order, written in Chinese and signed by the President and Tuan Ch'i-jui. In exchange he received £5,600 in commission, plus various expenses, including $320 he had used to bribe his way into seeing the new President. All was good and everyone was happy.

Except the orders for the banknotes failed to arrive. As the months slipped by, Hall grew increasingly concerned and by March 1917 the situation had become "a very grave and serious matter." Backhouse bought a little time, referring to problems with bribes and securing an interview with the Prime Minister, and Hall continued to trust his baronet-agent. Indeed, so totally taken in was Hall that before leaving China he also personally invested in various Backhouse schemes, going fifty-fifty with him in purchasing a collection of Chinese curios. Hall had never seen the curios, and acted entirely on Backhouse's recommendation. He was also persuaded by Backhouse to enter into the unlawful purchase of a pearl jacket of the late Empress Dowager, a once-famous item still kept in the Imperial Palace. Hall even lent Backhouse his revolver pistol as back-up should the planned trespass-come-burglary of the Palace and dealings with the eunuchs therein go awry. Hall provided 50,000 Chinese dollars as his half of the arrangement. Backhouse reported a partial success in this caper; he had not secured the entire jacket, but managed to cut off 344 pearls (of which he later showed Hall only one) before making a dramatic escape from the palace by firing the revolver (presumably without killing anyone). The pearls, Backhouse insisted, were so valuable that Hall was certain of an excellent return.

Hall waited in America. But he saw no more of the other pearls than his company did of orders for banknotes. Time, letters and telegrams proved of no use. By the late summer of 1917, Hall, professionally compromised and considerably out of pocket financially, finally came to see Backhouse as "a crook" and decided to track him down. He caught up with Backhouse in Peking just as the latter was leaving China - or so he claimed - to take up a new role in France, helping to manage the Chinese Labour Corps as part of the war effort. Hall once again fell for the Backhouse charm, and after a brief meeting, he sent a telegram to New York explaining that Japanese pressure had apparently caused the Chinese Government to repudiate the banknote contract and that Backhouse had returned his commission to him. Backhouse, meanwhile, was reportedly in Japan, where he claimed to be on a mission to bribe the Foreign Minister. This, according to baronet, would help smooth the way with the Japanese in order that the banknote contract could in fact go ahead after all.

Hall finally realized he had been played for a fool and went to the US Embassy with the banknote contract, and then with the American Minister to see the Chinese Prime Minister, Tuan Ch'i-jui, allegedly Backhouse's close friend. Tuan declared his signature on the document to be a fake. He also said he had never heard of Sir Edmund Backhouse. An appalled Hall sent a telegram to New York: "We have ended all relations with Mr Backhouse, who has obviously been crooked. Deceived both Embassy and ourselves."

Hall subsequently pursued Backhouse across the world through his lawyers, and his tenacity paid off. A year later, in November 1918, the two men met for an out-of-court settlement in Japan. Backhouse got his curios returned to him, whilst Hall in turn received £10,650, a huge sum that included payment for his legal expenses.

For six years, Backhouse had also been the Chinese representative of the British shipbuilders John Brown & Company. His role had been to arrange the purchase of battleships by successive Chinese governments. His services with John Brown were terminated at about the same time as his problems came to light with the Banknote Company. The shipbuilder, needless to report, did not sell a single ship to China.

Considerably less tenacious than Hall were the curators of the Bodleian Library at Oxford, the university where many years before Backhouse had failed to complete his degree and left creditors in his wake. As ever, Backhouse's relations began well. In 1912 and then a few years later, Backhouse made enormously generous gifts of old Chinese books and other documents to the Library. The first required twenty-nine crates for shipment, weighed four and a half tons, and consisting of 17,000 manuscripts. The second was even larger. Everyone at the Bodleian was thrilled with these acquisitions, the scale of which was almost overwhelming. With the first gift alone, the Library quadrupled its Chinese collection. This, at least, was not a fraud.

In 1920, Backhouse wrote to say that he had further precious gifts for the Library. All he required was £1,000 in advance to help with their freight. The Curators readily agreed. Backhouse wrote again reporting yet more wonderful acquisitions – 30,000 volumes from the Palace Library in 150 cases. Very soon, Backhouse's advance from the Bodleian totalled £2,495. There followed delays and excuses, with Backhouse appealing for the Curators' patience and understanding. And then Backhouse disappeared. It turned out he had been staying with his family in Scotland, but had tried the patience of his family once too often, having borrowed money from them on the strength of the sale of yet more spurious pearls. Dear old Uncle Edmund was no longer welcome. For a long time thereafter, the family supplied Backhouse with a personal allowance, on the understanding that he *remain* in China. For a time the Bodleian Curators continued to give Backhouse the benefit of the doubt, but eventually the advances were written off.

After the early 1920s, Backhouse's visits to Britain ceased. "Going native," wearing the robes of a Chinese mandarin and growing a long beard, he appears to have remained in China for the rest of his life, increasingly living the life of a recluse. This was possibly owing to inclination, but it may also have been prudent to keep his distance from various foreign lawyers and courts.[14]

But there were further Backhouse tales, some unavailable to Trevor-Roper due to time disclosure rules at the UK National Archives. On its publication, Trevor-Roper's *Hermit of Peking* caused quite a stir. Gordon Creighton, who as a young man had worked at the British Embassy in Peking and translated in court in the case of the British soldiers accused of murdering the Japanese officer, was most definitely not impressed. Defending Backhouse in no uncertain terms, he wrote to a former *China Service* colleague:

> I think it is totally monstrous that a silly shit like Trevor-Roper (just because he was Trevor-Roper) should have been allowed to get away with writing that stupid book. Trevor-Roper had never been in China or anywhere in Asia ever in his life. He had probably never been into a Soho Chinese take-away. For silly sods like him to pose as experts on China is ridiculous.[15]

Trevor-Roper, however, did not pose as a Chinese expert, and never purported to be one. He merely wrote about one particular

....

14 Sir Hugh Trevor-Roper, *Hermit of Peking; the Hidden Life of Sir Edmund Backhouse.*
15 School of Oriental & African Studies library archive, P.D. Coates collection PP MS 52, letter from Gordon Creighton, April 29, 1989.

individual, a foreigner in China, the records of whose activities were largely kept in foreign archives. The evidence he found was overwhelming. (Though Trevor-Roper's reputation was to suffer a blow some years later over his commentary on what turned out to be bogus "Hitler diaries," his work on Backhouse remains unaffected).

As a Backhouse contact at the British Embassy in the 1930s, Gordon Creighton had good reason to feel disappointed in the charge that his former informant was a lifelong fraudster. It cast doubt upon the information Creighton had received from him, information which had then been passed on to London as important intelligence. For in 1936, a few months before Pamela Werner's murder, Backhouse had returned to playing the part of British secret agent.

With his knowledge of languages, the now ageing Backhouse was apparently earning a living translating documents for a wide variety of people. The political situation in the China of 1936 was becoming ever more complicated. The Chinese government of the Kuomintang, with its tenuous control over much of the country, had established an ascendancy over the Chinese Communists and the northern warlords, but were losing out to Japanese pressure. It was in this political and military maelstrom that Sir Edmund Backhouse decided to make his mark once more. His first subject of intelligence was the Communist subversion of a Chinese newspaper.

The *Shih Chieh Jih Pao* (World Daily News) was a Chinese-language newspaper based in Peking. It had a circulation chiefly among students and educated Chinese. On September 11, 1936, from his private address in the Tartar City, Backhouse wrote to Gordon Creighton at the Peking Embassy:

Dear Mr Creighton,

... you might like to know that I was given a letter in Russian to translate for the *Shih Chieh Jih Pao* from the supreme office of the Secretariat, Union of Soviet Socialist Republics, in the Kremlin, on official paper. It continues the subsidy of gold roubles 250 a month to the *Shi Chieh Jih Pao* but instructs it to concentrate on attacking Hitler and his regime, Mussolini and Japan, the latter in so far as the censor allows, but to go-slow in attacking Great Britain. It is dated August 12th 1936. I am not allowed to copy it but carry it in my head. I am also told on high authority that Japan is instigating the attacks on the Empire in the *Ch'en Pao*: decadence of Britain, ignominious surrender to Mussolini, possible withdrawal of extra fleet from Mediterranean at his dictation, Greece and France cancelling their undertakings with Britain regarding cooperation, imminent separation of Canada from the Empire and the like. Excuse my temerity in mentioning these extraneous matters.

Yours sincerely,

E. Backhouse.[16]

Creighton soon replied stating that "such material is very much appreciated, and we are most grateful to you for passing it on to us."[17]

Backhouse responded with a second translation of instructions from the Soviets to their tame Chinese newspaper. He apologized for not being able to provide a copy of the original Russian before going on to give a summary of Soviet thinking in

....
16 UK National Archives, FO 371/20273 China. Code 10 Files 1895 (papers 6428 - end) – 2153.
17 ibid.

that part of Asia:

> ... the Union of Soviet Socialist Republics does not envisage
> any activity by the party in Tibet for the present. It would
> irritate the Tibetan hierarchy and cause grave reactions in
> India and London. There is no need to attack Great Britain
> for designs on Tibet, because her imperialistic policy is long
> ago dead and the Soviets' concern is not in that direction ...
> The journal should stress the importance of extending So-
> viet influence from Turkestan into Kansu and South Mon-
> golia to counteract the Japanese menace.[18]

Backhouse added that he wondered what the Soviets would
think if they knew the newspaper was so slack as to let a foreigner like himself near their correspondence. And then observed
that "the Chinese are strangely naive for all their cunning and
disingenuousness."[19] In a third letter, Backhouse let Creighton
know of the newspaper's reply to Moscow, which he had translated into Arabic for them for added security:

> We learn that Japan is sending agents into Tibet. One or two
> comrades on the staff of the Panchen Lama could do useful
> spade work with the young Tibetans, just as the Soviet did
> formerly in Outer Mongolia with the student class there ...
> If "Grasshead" (Chiang Kai-Shek) were eliminated, China
> would go Soviet within a month and make face to our ag-
> gressors ... the local authorities (in Peking) are friendly but
> forbid large meetings. Small assemblies are "winked" at
> and we have many comrades in the 29th Army, especially

18 ibid.
19 ibid.

among the younger officers and sergeants.[20]

Creighton wrote again, wanting to know from Backhouse the names of those really running the newspaper, if not the official owner. Meanwhile the letters were marked "secret" and despatched to London. In a covering report entitled "Russian Propaganda in the *Shih Chieh Jih Pao*," Creighton's superior at the Peking Embassy, D. J. Cowan, wrote with perhaps a degree of scepticism: "It is all very mysterious because this newspaper is perhaps the most independent and incorruptible, and we have hitherto failed to detect any signs of "Sovietization" in its presentation of news or its editorials. Nevertheless, we should be glad if the information supplied by Sir Edmund might be treated as strictly secret."[21]

In London, Backhouse's *Shih Chieh Jih Pao* reports were met with a cautious response. A Foreign Office official with responsibility for China dryly observed: "This is all in a day's work for the Soviets. The remarks about Tibet and Britain's harmlessness are interesting. To say of an Empire that her imperialistic policy is long ago dead sounds like a veiled hint that the old lion is getting toothless, and the Russians and Japanese appear to be in agreement about that. Then he added as an aside: "the source is useful."[22]

His superior agreed. Though it was not fed back to the Peking Embassy, the opinion in Whitehall appeared to be that the intelligence was most likely a deliberate ploy by the Soviets to spread misinformation.

A month later, in November, Backhouse wrote to Creighton with yet more intelligence. This time he set his sights higher. In-

20 ibid.
21 ibid.
22 ibid.

stead of general information about relatively local issues, he went for one of the most worrisome international issues of the day – the prospect of a military alliance between Germany and Japan; the Anti Comintern Pact. News of the pact reaching fruition was overdue, as Backhouse would have well known. He claimed that he had again translated a secret Soviet intelligence document concerning the pact for Chinese Communists. The original document had been written in Armenian by the Soviets for security purposes. Armenian was another of Backhouse's many languages. Marked "top secret", the Embassy sent the Foreign Office a copy of Backhouse's treaty by a telegram dated November 2, 1936.

> "Treaty. The two contracting States hereby agree to form a defensive alliance against the Soviet and to come to each other's assistance in case of aggression against either party by the Soviet International or such provocative action by the Soviet as may compel either party for the sake of national prestige to take up arms against the Soviet.
>
> The treaty is to be for a period of ten years and to be automatically renewable for an equal period unless notice of withdrawal be given by either party at extirpation of nine years. But contracting States agree not to make a separate peace in case of war being forced upon them by the Soviets.
>
> Declaration A. Germany undertakes to extend recognition to Manchukuo, latter State being vitally affected by Soviet aggression in order that Manchukuo may be invited to become party to alliance between Germany and Japan.
>
> Declaration B. Germany renounces all claim to mandated territories under Japan's administration and will approve their incorporation in Empire of Japan.
>
> Declaration C. Japan will support Germany's claim to re-

turn Kamerun (boundary of 1912) and German east Africa."[23]

This time, London took the report far more seriously. The file went as far as Anthony Eden, the Foreign Secretary, reaching his desk on November 30. Unfortunately for Backhouse, his secret intelligence was overtaken by events while en route to London. Only a few days earlier, on November 25, Germany and Japan signed the real pact, of which the Foreign Office had just received details.

Before reaching Eden, the file was minuted by officials in the Far East department. The first of whom, Nigel Ronald, had to look up Backhouse in a copy of *Who's Who* before commenting that although the document might of course be a Russian forgery, few Russians would be able to read Armenian script and that writing the alleged treaty in this language would indeed have ensured greater secrecy.

His superior, Mr. C.W. Dade, then made the following informed analysis:

The document is an odd mixture of text and paraphrase. The first paragraph is at variance with the apparently authentic text we have now received. Declaration A seems rather improbable as we know that Japan does not want recognition of Manchukuo; she may possibly think Germany is a safe exception as a non-member of the League, but the risk of her example being copied would, I should have thought, outweigh the advantage of having Manchukuo as a formal accessory to the part. We have had no indication that Germany particularly wants to recognise Manchukuo.

23 UK National Archives, FO 371/20286 Japan. Code 23 Files 303 (papers 7279 - end) – 539.

I am inclined to think there is a good deal of guesswork in this document.[24]

"I agree," wrote Anthony Eden in conclusion on the very same day, underlining Dade's comments. "It may be, as Mr. Ronald suggests, an early draft. Or it may be a deliberate forgery planted on us by the Russians". And then Eden added: "Backhouse is under a cloud; though I don't wish to insinuate that he would be party to a fraud of such a kind."[25]

"Under a cloud." These were strong words coming from Eden, who was well known for his gentlemanly politeness. Perhaps Eden possessed information on Backhouse that others under him did not.

Nonetheless, some months later, after prompting by a Peking Embassy unaware of London's actual assessment of the Backhouse material, a letter was despatched to Sir Edmund from London, signed by Eden himself, "thanking him for what he has done."[26]

A little over a year later, Backhouse was again supplying the Peking Embassy with political intelligence, this time with his account of the revenging Japanese and their involvement in the Pamela Werner murder, and this time using Graham Aspland, the embassy doctor, rather than Creighton as the channel. Again, Backhouse's role as a jobbing translator had led him to sensitive intelligence, only this time it was the Japanese themselves who had sought him for the task rather than the Communists. Or so he would have people believe.

Backhouse's report in February 1938 giving the Japanese as suspects in Pamela's murder carries many of the hallmarks of

....

24 ibid.
25 ibid.
26 UK National Archives, FO 800/297 Knatchbull-Hugessen, Sir Hughe: Miscellaneous correspondence.

his previous frauds: carefully constructed, hard to disprove, the information provided had to remain a secret, somehow the recipients felt privileged or indebted; Backhouse's image as a man in-the-know with high-ranking contacts was enhanced. Had Backhouse ever met a covert communist newspaper editor or Japanese general? Were the Communists and Japanese so short of their own translators that they turned to an eccentric British baronet and trusted him with confidential documents? Possibly. There would have been few native English speakers in Peking in those days with Backhouse's language capabilities. The reference to a male friend of Pamela is of interest, for it hits upon the important subject of boyfriends, a factor to be explored later. But, beyond that, Backhouse's intelligence reports to the Embassy of 1936-1938 have to be considered in light of the numerous fantasies advanced by him over the years.

However, the embassy staff members Archer, Aspland and Clark Kerr appear to have believed Backhouse. Archer: "It seems incredible that the Japanese could have invented all this in such detail." Much of Backhouse's information was probably available to any educated person in Peking who kept abreast of the political climate, news and gossip. The details of the Sasaki case featured in local newspapers. Of the suspects Backhouse referred to, two were anonymous Japanese, one allegedly already dead, the other vaguely serving somewhere on "the front." He named two Chinese, a Tan Shou Ching and Te Fu Hai, both of whom were allegedly "still in the city." Described as a student and a rickshaw coolie, in ordinary peacetime circumstances the pair might be traceable, but less so in a time of war. The Japanese Doctor Ito, however, could certainly be easily found. A Doctor Ito was mentioned as playing in golfing pairs on the sports page of *the Peiping Chronicle*[27] and he was possibly the same dentist Pamela visited on the morning before her death. Doctor Ito's presence in Peking would have been common knowledge. Backhouse, however, could have confidently expected the Embassy staff not to approach Ito to ask if he was a member of a secret Japanese society and knew of the murder plan in advance. But even if they had unexpectedly done so and Ito had flatly denied knowledge or involvement, Backhouse could simply have remarked that of course he would, what else did they expect? But Backhouse surely knew that would *not* happen, as he had in effect required the Embassy staff to keep all the intelligence he supplied a secret. He had tied their hands.

Having passed on his Japanese theory, Backhouse had not quite finished with the Werner murder. At some point during 1941, prior to the attack at Pearl Harbour, with life outside the Legation Quarter becoming ever more difficult for foreigners, Backhouse was forced to leave his home in the Tartar City and moved to one of the small green-roofed houses inside the British Embassy compound, where space was available following the withdrawal of the military guards redeployed to Europe. Backhouse moved into a house he shared for a short time with, of all people, E.T.C. Werner.[28] The pairing must have made for a peculiar domicile.

Notwithstanding the Japanese information that he had passed on to Consul Archer three years before, of which he now made no mention, Backhouse provided encouragement to Werner's own peculiar theories. He told him that as a result of his investigations, he too was convinced that Prentice and Cappuzzo were responsible. This action by Backhouse could perhaps be seen as his humouring the old man by telling him what he wanted to

27 *Peiping Chronicle*, society & sports column (golfing pairs), May 12, 1937.
28 E.T.C. Werner, *More Memorigrams*, (1948), pages 202,217,223.

hear. But he didn't merely nod and agree with Werner. He went further, volunteering that his information came from a friend who was a secretary in the Italian Embassy and that Cappuzzo had been ordered by the Ambassador to leave his large home in the Embassy compound. The suggestion was that this was punishment for a sexual impropriety of some kind.[29]

Werner was encouraged by this intelligence, coming as it did, from a man of such standing and respect. So much so that he later recorded their conversation in a passage in his final book, describing it as: "Information communicated to me by Sir Edmund Backhouse, who, unknown to me, had been carrying on an independent investigation and, later on, was sharing with me House No. 7 in the British Embassy Compound."[30] But like so many people in China and beyond, Werner lacked insight into the true nature of the genial old gentleman with whom he shared a residence. Backhouse's story appears in any event to be untrue; the Italian diplomatic archive records how Cappuzzo remained living in the same embassy-owned house outside the compound throughout his many years stay in Peking.[31]

Backhouse was nearly ten years younger than Werner, but he was to predecease him by a similar timespan. In fact, Backhouse had only a few more years to live and would not survive the War. But he had at least one more substantial fraud left in him.

---

29 ibid.
30 ibid.
31 Archivio Storico Diplomatico, Rome, archive "Le Rappresentanze Diplomatiche e Consolari Italiane a Pechino 1870-1952, folder 186, file 9043 "Cappuzzo".

11

THE DIPLOMAT

DAVID JOHN COWAN

ON DECEMBER 16, 1937, only a month or so before receiving Backhouse's Japanese information, Consul for Peking, Allan Archer, wrote in secret to Robert Howe, British *charge d'affaires*. The subject was again the Werner murder. At the time, Howe was traveling from one Chinese-controlled city to another in an effort to stay near Chiang Kai-Shek and his government as they retreated from Nanjing ahead of the Japanese war machine.

My Dear Howe,

Referring to your secret telegram for me of the 21st November on the subject of the Werner murder case... Herbert [Consul General in Tientsin] had heard, or thought he had heard, the same name mentioned in Tientsin.

I had a conversation with Herbert here some two weeks ago, and we agreed that Dennis, the Chief of Police in Tientsin, should have Herbert's informant up and see what he had to say. I now show some correspondence in original showing the result, which you may like to see and possibly show to McNeill or Priestwood [crown prosecutors at the

British court in Shanghai]. It is very strange, but I do not
know what can be done on this line.

Poor old Werner is actively pursuing researches in the
Peking underworld, Russian, Chinese, and American, writes
me long letters, and comes and sees me every two or three
days... his clues, such as they are at present, point in the direction of certain Russians and American ex-marines, and not
at all in the direction of "some member of the Embassy"...

Yours sincerely, Allan Archer.[1]

Robert Howe had evidently recently asked Archer to investigate
the disturbing suggestion that "some member of the Embassy"
had been involved in the Werner murder. Unfortunately, the
police report that Archer refers to in his letter has not survived;
Dennis's conclusions are therefore unknown.

Word of involvement of "some member of the Embassy"
would have been particularly distressing for Robert Howe, for

the name carefully left out of the letter was that of an old colleague of his,
a senior diplomat and former soldier.
He had been a friend of Howe's, and
war and fate had made them as close
as brothers. Howe felt bound to him,
so long and traumatic was their shared
experience. The man's name, "the
name mentioned in Tientsin," was that
of David John Cowan, holder of the
Military Cross. At the time of the murder, Cowan held the top diplomatic
rank of First Secretary at the Peking

*David John Cowan.
(courtesy of William Cowan)*

....

1   UK National Archives, FO 800/297 Knatchbull-Hugessen, Sir Hughe: Miscellaneous correspondence.

Embassy.

Throughout 1937, rumours concerning the Werner murder had swirled through Peking's foreign community. One particular claim was that the murder "had been hushed up because clues led too close to the British Embassy," as reported by Ida Pruitt (1888-1985), an American social worker attached to the PUMC Hospital and a woman who heard much of the foreign society's news, and its gossip.[2] If unsubstantiated by evidence, such talk of clues that led "close to the British Embassy" could have been dismissed as idle speculation, but it transpired that there may be more to it than mere baseless whispers. In the aftermath of the crime, Cowan had vividly described to a colleague in the Tientsin consulate "how the murder and mutilations would be done".[3] The First Secretary's dramatic demonstration with a sword sounds like it may not have been intended as a serious one, but the concern it generated among the consulate staff would suggest that they felt otherwise. Howe realised that the matter needed investigating.

Robert George Howe was something of a rarity in the British diplomatic service. His humble background did not fit with the conventional image of a British diplomat and his career demonstrated the possibility of advancement without the need to be "someone's son." Howe had been born in the East Midlands town of Derby in 1893, one of five children whose father was a near illiterate steam locomotive cleaner, and also a Congregationalist Christian, a faith his son also quietly held throughout his life. Howe won scholarships to the fee-paying Derby School and then, in 1912, to Cambridge University, where he studied

---

2 Hoover Institution Library & Archives, Nym Wales Papers 1931-1998 (Helen Foster Snow), Sian Incident, box 17.
3 School of Oriental & African Studies, PP MS 52 P.D. Coates collection; notes on conversation with Sir Alwyne Ogden, October 3, 1973.

mathematics at St Catherine's College.[4] Howe did not finish his degree. In August 1914, imbued with a spirit of patriotism and adventure, he volunteered to join his local regiment, the Sherwood Foresters, and was commissioned as a second lieutenant. After training in Plymouth, Devon he was billeted at the country home of local Cornish gentry, where he fell in love with the family's daughter. Howe's unit sailed from Devonport to support the ill-fated Gallipoli campaign in Turkey where he commanded a wiring unit laying and repairing barbed wire overnight in no-man's-land between the Allied and Turkish trenches. In October 1915, with the Gallipoli campaign an obvious failure, Howe and his unit were evacuated to take part in the Salonika campaign in Macedonia, on the border between Bulgaria and Greece. Here, Howe was to experience another Allied defeat.

It was in this forgotten corner of World War One that Howe's path crossed with that of David John Cowan of the Connaught Rangers (known from the War onwards as *John* to everyone other than his parents). Twenty-one years of age, like Howe, at the outbreak of war, Cowan had been a medical student before volunteering in August 1914. He was the only child of devoted parents who lived in Gordon Square in London, where his father was a civil engineer.

Some twenty years after the end of the War, after many separate diplomatic postings, both men found themselves serving in China, where Cowan was posted to the Embassy in Peking. On February 4, 1937, less than a month after the murder, in a rare opportunity for the two friends to meet up, they were both guests of the Peking Rotary Club, where the outgoing and sociable Cowan was the Club's invited speaker. The story he chose for his audience, injected with a good measure of humour, was of the

----

4 Sir Robert George Howe, *Inherit the Kingdom*, unpublished autobiography.

thirty-four months and eleven days' captivity he and Howe experienced in Bulgaria.[5] Howe's role that day at the Rotary Club was to simply sit, listen and smile at Cowan's account of the dramas and privations of that time. Decades later, in retirement in the 1970s, he wrote of the same period in his unpublished autobiography. Bulgaria was a seminal event in the lives of both men.

Armed conflict between the emerging, newly-independent states in the Balkans in 1912 and 1913 had been instrumental in the origins of World War One, but the region thereafter became a sideshow. In July 1914, Austria invaded the small state of Serbia, but was surprisingly beaten and forced to retreat. Bulgaria, meanwhile, was not keen to engage, and as a consequence, it was courted by both sides. Eventually, in September 1915, the Bulgarians agreed to mobilize and join the Central Powers, and Serbia, attacked by Austria to the north and Bulgaria to the east, was overwhelmed. France and Britain helped the Serbs by sending troops to the port of Salonika in neutral Greece with the intention of marching north and linking up with their beleaguered allies. This became known as the Salonika or Macedonian campaign. The Allied forces, some hastily transferred from Gallipoli, arrived too late and were too few in number. They advanced to the mountainous border of Macedonia but were outnumbered, outgunned and then thrown into retreat. Howe and Cowan were both part of this and were wounded, captured and imprisoned in Bulgaria for the next three years. The pair made several unsuccessful escape attempts together. At the end of the war, they were released in dire physical condition, Cowan with malaria and Howe with the influenza virus that in 1918 and 1919 killed millions.

Howe left for England before Christmas 1918, but Cowan

---

5 "D.J. Cowan addresses Peking Rotary Club", *Peiping Chronicle*, February 5, 1937.

stayed on in the Balkans for a further six months working with Military Intelligence. After the War and their return home, the lives of Cowan and Howe continued to have much in common. Both men soon married, to sweethearts who had waited for their return from captivity. Rather than resuming their studies at university, they both passed a competitive entrance examination and joined the Diplomatic Service; Howe entered in late 1919, Cowan in 1922.[6] Both men commenced their new careers at the junior rank of third secretary. Howe's first posting was to Copenhagen, whilst Cowan's was to Budapest.[7]

Cowan and Howe had joined a changed diplomatic service. Prior to their amalgamation in 1918, Britain's Diplomatic Service (largely dealing with political matters) and its Foreign Office (largely dealing with everything else) were separate bodies. Previously, entrants into the Diplomatic Service received no pay during their early years of service and had to guarantee £400 per year from their own resources.[8] In effect this meant that the Service and its subsequent career structure was only open to the sons of gentlemen with wealth and connections. The likes of Howe, a locomotive cleaner's son from Derby, would have been excluded. As would also Cowan and the great number of young men from minor public schools. Women, of course, did not feature at all.

Cowan and Howe spent the next fifteen years or so serving in one diplomatic posting after another, with occasional stints at the Foreign Office in London. Both were promoted slowly yet steadily to the rank of First Secretary. After Budapest, Cowan's next overseas posting was to Helsingfors in Finland, then a return to Sofia in 1929. He was in Belgrade in 1932, before being posted to

6 UK National Archives, Foreign Office list.
7 ibid.
8 Diplomat in Peace & War, Sir Hughe Knatchbull-Hugessen, John Murray publisher (1949), page 13

Peking in February 1935.[9]

Howe preceded Cowan's arrival in China by several months, arriving there the previous year to become Counsellor at the Embassy, a senior position just beneath that of Ambassador. Prior postings, in addition to Copenhagen, had been to Belgrade, Rio de Janeiro, and Bucharest.[10] Although both now in the same country, the two friends had little opportunity to meet. Cowan was

Robert Howe, Shanghai, 1937

based in Peking—for much of the time being in charge of British interests in the old capital— while Howe was usually traveling in regions elsewhere. Nonetheless, on his visits to Peking, Howe was struck by the scale of not only the Legation Quarter, but also of the British compound itself. Other postings had involved relatively modest housing and facilities, whereas in Peking:

> The British Legation compound was a town in itself. It housed, beside our diplomatic staff a British regiment with their barracks, a dairy farm, vast stables and school for students, and all the necessary modern conveniences like central heating, electric light and sewage.[11]

Living conditions at the Embassy had evidently improved since Werner's early days when the daily collection of night-soil

9   UK National Archives, Foreign Office list
10 ibid.
11 Sir Robert George Howe, *Inherit the Kingdom,* unpublished autobiography.

There was also another important change: the
?eking was in fact officially no longer the Em-
st Government under Chiang Kai-shek had
 .. ιegions further to the south and had chosen Nanking, a city far to the south, as the capital. In addition to this,
not for the first or last time, Peking was renamed. It was now
officially called Peiping, meaning "northern peace."

This shifting of China's capital placed many of the foreign
ambassadors and ministers in an awkward position, Britain's
included. For many, Peking's climate and facilities were more
agreeable than those of Nanking, a hot and humid city with considerably less charm. Most foreign diplomats had no desire to
move from the Legation Quarter. As a result, a compromise was
made, with many nations splitting their staff between the two
cities, with ambassadors and senior diplomats often roaming between the two and making use of upgraded consulate buildings.

Like many other nations, Britain now provided the superior
rank of ambassador, instead of minister, to represent them in
China. Britain's Ambassador to China from late 1936 was the improbably named Sir Hughe Knatchbull-Hugessen, or "Snatch" to
his friends. His short stay in the country was to prove eventful,
ending in him being shot and invalided home. Not long after
arriving in Peking, Sir Hughe visited a number of Chinese cities and met with Chiang Kai-shek to discuss the brewing crisis
with Japan. As a result, with Knatchbull-Hugessen traveling and
Howe based in Nanking, for much of the time, Britain's most
senior diplomat in Peking was the First Secretary, D. J. Cowan,
who had added a working knowledge of Chinese to his set of
language skills.[12]

Despite the mounting political tension between China and Ja-

....

12 UK National Archives, Foreign Office list.

pan, life in Peking for many foreigners carried on much as usual. Legation parties and the social scene continued to be legendary, including high jinks such as junior diplomats recklessly walking round the high parapet of the Peking Hotel, and the provision of "lethally" concocted cocktails that rendered unsuspecting recipients senseless.[13] Ordinary life too could be dangerous. While out riding in the country, Knatchbull-Huggesen's twenty-one-year-old daughter, Elisabeth, was struck in the head by a spent bullet fired by an unseen assailant. She survived, thanks to her future husband who immediately dug the bullet out with the improvised use of a large key.[14]

Then in his early forties, Cowan now had a wife and two sons, and a responsible role. But he was nonetheless socially active, featuring regularly and more often than any other member of the Embassy in the society column of *the Peiping Chronicle*. During early 1937, in the weeks and months following Pamela Werner's murder, the newspaper reported Cowan, amongst other things, playing hockey with the Peking team (alongside his sporting fifteen-year-old son); sharing his home with visiting dignitaries; attending dog shows; running children's skating events; and holding open-house evenings at the Embassy.[15] Cowan was a well-known and popular figure.

At no time was Cowan's high profile role in Peking society more evident than at the Embassy celebrations to mark the coronation of George VI in May 1937. The Ambassador was away in Nanking, and it was left to Cowan to organise the all-day programme of events in the Legation Quarter: the firing of a royal salute, a religious service, a reception and buffet lunch, children's sports, village sideshows, an evening supper, fireworks and final-

13 Sir Berkeley Gage, *It's Been a Marvellous Party*, limited edition publication (1989), p56.
14 Diary entry of Elizabeth Young (née Knatchbull-Hugessen). Young family documents.
15 *Peiping Chronicle*, articles and notices February-April 1937.

George VI coronation celebrations, British Embassy, May 1937;
Cowan in the foreground. (Courtesy of William Cowan)

ly, a celebratory ball. The day was a great success, and met with much praise and congratulations, with Cowan described as having quite "a genius for the decorative."[16] Tall, jovial, resplendent in his dark blue diplomatic uniform complete with his campaign medals and Military Cross, albeit with his tunic looking rather on the tight side, newspaper photographs of the celebrations showed a beaming Cowan in his element.

Sadly, the good times for him were nearly at an end. No one present for the coronation celebrations could have imagined just how catastrophic the next few months would turn out to be for the genial British First Secretary. The escalating armed conflict provided the catalyst.

During the night of July 7, Chinese and Japanese troops clashed at the Marco Polo Bridge outside Peking. More than one hundred Chinese soldiers were killed, but many foreigners in the city initially assumed that it was just another spat that would soon blow over.

....

16 British Community of Peiping to Celebrate Coronation Today", *Peiping Chronicle*, May 12, 1937.

"Local trouble beyond the triple walls of Peking - just another incident," was how British resident Hope Danby initially assessed matters. But she then described how, over the following days, "a distant shadow grew hourly in the darkness – it approached nearer and nearer until the whole city was affected by it. Anxiety and perplexity were felt by everyone, Chinese and foreigners alike. Then came the week when all Europeans and Americans living outside the walls and in the city were ordered into the Legation Quarter by their consuls."[17]

Having sought refuge at the home of a friend in Legation Street, Hope Danby found herself with a view into the compound of the Japanese Embassy and saw that it was crowded with Japanese civilians who feared being massacred. But within a few weeks, the fighting in the Peking area was over. The Chinese forces were defeated and retreated. The Japanese army, which for years had already exercised a presence in the city, now marched through its streets as conquerors.

Hope Danby's account continues:

> "And one day, hearing a loud and continuous rumbling of heavy vehicles, I went and stood in the Long Peaceful Way, the wide thoroughfare near my house, and watched a seemingly endless line of Japanese soldiers go by. With them was every imaginable type of war equipment, guns, tanks, mortars and cars. The parade had been staged to impress the populace with the sight of Japanese strength, but few Chinese witnessed it. Wisely enough, they had stayed at home behind barred doors - this they always did in times of trouble."[18]

17 Hope Danby, *My Boy Chang*, (1955), p136.
18 ibid., p137.

Peking was to remain in Japanese hands for the next eight years, until August 1945. The fighting just outside it had been brief and thankfully the city and its unique architecture emerged virtually undamaged. By early August, the British Embassy published a notice in *The Peiping Chronicle* cautiously suggesting that it was safe for British residents to return to their homes outside the Legation Quarter.[19] Many foreigners wondered if the charmed life they had enjoyed for so long might yet continue as before. As was custom, many of them, Werner included, set off for the beach resort of Peitaiho to escape the summer heat.

But the conflict that had begun on the Marco Polo Bridge spread to encompass much of northern and coastal China, with the destruction and killing raging with far greater intensity. The Japanese were determined to subjugate all of China.

The British Ambassador, Sir Hughe Knatchbull-Hugessen found himself caught in the fighting. On August 26, he set off from Nanking to Shanghai with a couple of aides in two embassy motor vehicles. The weather was fine and both vehicles prominently flew Union Flags. It didn't help them. On an open road, they were strafed by a Japanese aircraft and the Ambassador was shot. "The bullet came through the open window, straight through me and lodged in the woodwork of the car behind me," he later recorded.[20] The car immediately stopped in order to assess the Ambassador's wounds, only to be bombed by a second aircraft. While the others scattered into paddy fields for cover, Sir Hughe could only spread himself helplessly across the seat of his bloodied car. The bombs dropped wide, and there followed a frantic two-hour drive to find a hospital in Shanghai with an aide standing on the car's running board to keep watch for more airborne attacks. The Ambassador was lucky to survive. A bullet

....

19 *Peiping Chronicle*, notice in social column, August 1, 1937.
20 Sir Hughe Knatchbull-Hugessen, *Diplomat in Peace and War*, (1949), p121.

Richard Dennis (in uniform, centre left) and Sir Hughe Knatchbull-Hugessen (centre right), Tientsin, 1936. (courtesy of Diana Dennis)

had passed through his abdomen and exited close to the spine, fracturing the vertebrae but without damaging the cord.

By any standards, the shooting of an ambassador was a major diplomatic incident. Within a day, the Japanese Ambassador arrived at Sir Hughe's hospital bed. Though lying bandaged in great pain, Sir Hughe nonetheless thought it best to admit him so he could see the injuries for himself. Sir Hughe later remembered: "He came and muttered a sentence to his interpreter. When it was translated I was listening for the word "regret". But I only heard "sympathy". I could not refrain from saying in somewhat outspoken terms exactly what I thought of the whole business. There was an awkward silence." But there was still no apology.[21]

Back in the UK, the British press were vehement in their condemnation, but the Japanese government was bullish. It was

---

21 ibid.

winning the war in China and showed no intention of asking for the forgiveness of a fading colonial power it intended to replace. The British Prime Minister, Neville Chamberlain, was in favour of sending the Japanese "a sharp note." The Foreign Secretary, Anthony Eden, advocated the withdrawal of the British Ambassador to Tokyo, but this option was ultimately overruled at Cabinet level.[22]

Robert Howe was on furlough in Cornwall at the start of these hostilities. Returning with his wife to her family home after a long walk, he was greeted by his agitated mother-in-law with the news that the Foreign Office had been urgently telephoning all day. The message was that the Ambassador had been shot and Howe was to leave immediately for China to deputise for him.[23]

Howe arrived in Hong Kong via a state-of-the-art modern flying-boat to Egypt, followed by an ancient Vickers aircraft with numerous stops for refuelling. From Hong Kong he sailed to Shanghai on a Royal Navy destroyer, one with the suitable name of *HMS Daring*. During the journey they passed, quite literally, under the guns of the Japanese fleet that was busy shelling the Chinese coastline. As Sir Hughe's stand-in, Howe spent the remainder of 1937 traveling from one Chinese city to another to keep in touch with the Chinese Government whilst simultaneously overseeing the interests of thousands of British subjects who found themselves in a war zone. Shanghai with its huge International Settlement was by far the greatest concern and had the most to lose. But Nanking was Howe's first destination. He and a few colleagues managed to arrive there by stealth. Avoiding the dangerous roads, they sailed by river in a humble Chinese junk, thereby going completely unnoticed by the Japanese.[24]

....

22 UK National Archives, FO/954/6 Private Office Papers of Sir Anthony Eden, Earl of Avon, Secretary of State for Foreign Affairs.
23 Sir Robert George Howe, *Inherit the Kingdom*, unpublished autobiography.
24 ibid.

By this point Peking was in comparison a military backwa-
ter with the Japanese steadily tightening their control. Numbers
of Chinese journalists were arrested and their newspapers "voluntarily" closed down.[25] Shops were searched for "books assailing Japan."[26]As an exception, the English language newspaper
Peiping Chronicle was permitted to continue, but it was soon under new – Japanese – ownership.

From the very start of the conflict in July, British interests
in Peking were largely in the hands of Cowan, the most senior
British official on the ground. Communication with senior colleagues outside the city was unreliable, and travel dangerous.
Cowan was therefore left to deal with matters himself.[27] It was
a stressful situation, and one that soon led to his undoing. That
August, the following wire report appeared in newspapers
around the world:

> Big Battle Averted by Briton's Grit - Peking Clash of Japa-
> nese and Chinese Stopped.

> How Major [sic] Cowan, M.C., British Charge d'Affaires,
> saved the lives of hundreds when he courageously intervened
> to prevent street fighting in Peking was told in a despatch sent
> to the Foreign Office yesterday by "The Daily Mail" and other
> newspaper correspondents in the city. By his commanding
> personality, supported by the pressure of the British Embassy,
> he called on both sides to desist. Each was unwilling to agree
> without assurances from the other. Undaunted by the difficul-
> ties he negotiated now with one side, now with the other. At
> last, impressed by his strict impartiality, the Chinese and Japa-

25 Newspapers in City Suspended, *Peiping Chronicle*, August 2, 1937.
26 "Police Search Shops for Books Assailing Japan", *Peiping Chronicle*, August 11, 1937.
27 Sir Robert George Howe, *Inherit the Kingdom*, unpublished autobiography.

nese were pacified and agreed on peace. Appalling slaughter
was averted. The situation here is returning to normal. Britons
and other foreigners are preparing to leave for their homes
outside the city.[28]

Lionel Lamb (1900-1992) was a newly-arrived vice-consul in Peking, and though he had only known Cowan a few months, his
recollection of the newspaper report was damning:

> I never could make out how this story originated, but we
> suspect that whatever the facts, Cowan gave such a story to
> the Press, probably at the Club over a few gins. The Japs nev-
> er seriously intended to bombard Peking, as they knew that
> Chinese resistance in North China would soon crumble.[29]

Lamb appears to have been correct – the story is not supported
by known events. In fact, though initially it probably went unnoticed, Cowan was struggling badly with the pressures brought
about by the War and the sheer volume of work it created for
him and the Embassy. Almost overnight, arrangements had to
be made for hundreds of often eccentric and demanding British
subjects to be given refuge in the Legation Quarter, many inside
the Embassy compound itself. And then their subsequent safe
return to their homes. There was the loss of British property to
catalogue – stolen, requisitioned or damaged by the Japanese.
There were compensation claims to negotiate, the demands of
hundreds of telegrams to and from the Foreign Office which
required regular updates about the latest hostilities,[30] together

28 Articles in: the *Daily Mercury*, Mackay, Queensland, August 4, 1937; the *Advertiser*,
Adelaide, August 2, 1937; *Cootamundra Herald*, August 4, 1937.
29 School of Oriental & African Studies, MS 380730 Sir Lionel Lamb collection, notes commenting on newspaper cutting.
30 UK National Archives, FO 371/20953 China. Code 10 File 9 (papers 5107-5448).

Victorious Japanese soldiers parade through Peking, 1937. (Alamy)

with scores of reports to write and cipher on political events and Japanese propaganda. And, entirely extraneously, the submission of accounts of the current levels of *Mu Tsai,* a common form of slavery in China whereby the poor sold their daughters as indentured household maids to the wealthy.[31]

The pressures on Cowan were mounting. His apparently reasonable request for the British Government to provide travel expenses home for the wives and children of Foreign Office staff in China was rejected by the Prime Minister, Neville Chamberlain, on the basis that Hong Kong still appeared to be a safe enough refuge.[32] On top of this, Cowan was short-staffed (his second-in-command was ill and incapacitated), the summer heat was at its height, preventing him from sleeping, he feared for the health of his elderly father back in London, and he was without the support of his wife who had already left for the Peitaiho resort with their sons.

Increasingly exhausted, Cowan kept up with his wide-rang-

31 ibid., FO 676/273 Slavery.
32 ibid., FO 366/992 Correspondence, diplomatic records.

ing duties through into September, even ensuring that routine events such as a horse-race meeting outside the city went ahead as planned. Belatedly, his efforts did not go entirely unnoticed, with the Foreign Secretary Anthony Eden writing to him expressing his appreciation for his good work during the conflict.[33] But it is not clear whether Eden's letter arrived in time for Cowan to read it. By September, Cowan's telegrams and reports to London began to portray a lack of acumen, with him complaining in forthright terms about minor disputes over security arrangements with the American Embassy that he ought to have been able to resolve locally. He then almost contradicted himself by praising the abilities of Colonel Marston of the US Marine Corps (the same commanding officer who recommended that Knauf be recalled to the USA).[34] These oddities attracted some bemused comments by those processing the reports in London. Strangely, given events over the next few days, Cowan's last report of September 27 was one of his more lucid, a detailed appreciation of how the Japanese were attempting to establish a puppet government in the region.[35] But on the same day, the embassy doctor, Graham Aspland, recorded:

> Owing to the strain of work during the last two months
> and sleeplessness to which the climate of North China is
> very conducive, Cowan has had a complete nervous break-
> down and it is imperative that he be granted leave out of
> this country away from all conditions that have contributed
> to his present condition.[36]

Cowan's junior colleague at the Embassy, George Young, took

33 ibid., Foreign Office general index for 1937.
34 ibid., FO 371/20954 China. Code 10 File 9 (papers 5452-5963).
35 ibid., FO 371/20956 China. Code 10 File 9 (papers 6540-7546).
36 ibid., T 164/169/9 Cowan, D J, First Secretary, Peking: nervous breakdown and death gratuity paid to legal personal representative but death compensation refused.

over his duties. Cowan was confined to his bed and arrangements made to evacuate him home as soon as possible via Tientsin. A colleague present related how Cowan:

> ... puts the illness down to a reversion to War Shock fol-
> lowing his hard treatment as a prisoner of war in Bulgaria.
> Cowan told him that he had a similar attack in 1918 (which
> was before he entered the diplomatic service) which lasted
> three or four months. The doctor says "As soon as the fight-
> ing commenced round Peking, the excitement began and
> increased daily until it reached the stage of absolute de-
> mentia". When Cowan left China no-one anticipated a fatal
> ending.[37]

D. J. Cowan died of a heart attack en route to the UK on the *S.S.
Dunera* on October 26, 1937 while crossing the Indian Ocean. He
was buried at sea. He was only forty-one years old. A Foreign
Office report described how the transport ship's medical officer
consulted a psychiatrist at Singapore who advised that Cowan
should not be landed there but continue, apparently thinking
that he might recover. On the contrary, it was conceded, his mental condition worsened and he died before reaching the next port.
The report concluded:"I think there can be no doubt that Cowan's breakdown at Peking was due to the strain under which he
had been working ever since the hostilities began in July last. He
was in charge the whole time and his anxieties must have been
considerable increased by the wounding of the Ambassador. He
certainly did not spare himself."[38]

Cowan's youngest son was only a small boy at the time of
his father's death. The pair had been close. As well as possess-

37 ibid.
38 ibid.

ing early memories of visiting the Royal Palace in Belgrade with his father and playing with the Yugoslav King's sons, then later kite-flying in dusty and windy parks of Peking, Cowan's son later recalled rather candidly: "My father smoked and drank too much."[39] Perhaps he did, but he would hardly have been alone in such habits. Werner's objection to the drinking culture of the colonial club was one of his most perpetual complaints, and probably his most apposite.

Throughout the previous century, the rate of attrition among the Foreign Office personnel in China had always been high. Death or retirement due to ill-health were common. P.D. Coates discovered that of the ninety British entrants that joined the "China Service" between 1897 and 1920, five committed suicide. In 1926, six breakdowns due to overwork or nerves were recorded in the previous two years alone.[40] Gordon Creighton, on arriving in China as a new recruit, was warned that on top of regular illnesses (he later caught typhus), one in four would die young, one would take to drink, one would go mad, and that only the fourth would survive to become a consul-general.[41] These words of warning were not without some truth.

In late 1937, following the sudden death of Cowan, Howe had a great deal on his plate, not least of which were the politics of being British *charge d'affaires* in a country at war. For a brief period he met weekly with the monk-like Chiang Kai-shek and his much-admired English-speaking wife Soong May-Ling in Nanking. Each time, he conveyed the good wishes of His Majesty's Government in their struggle against the Japanese. It was all he was able to offer. Britain would commit itself no further. Chiang and his wife were at least polite in expressing their thanks for

39 Unpublished autobiography of Richard Cowan (1931-2015), son of D.J. Cowan.
40 UK National Archives, FO 369/1940 China. Code 210 Files 4563-6117.
41 School of Oriental & African Studies, PP MS 52 P.D. Coates collection, letter from Gordon Creighton, April 29, 1989.

this mere verbal support.

Nanking would soon fall to the advancing Japanese with the Chinese government and forces retreating westward to Hankow. As a result Howe coordinated his staff's evacuation of Nanking jointly with the American Ambassador Nelson T. Johnson. Two naval ships were used for this purpose, the USS *Panay* and HMS *Bee*, both sailing upstream on the Yangtze River. Japanese planes attacked the ships, and the *Panay* was hit. A week later, the Japanese army entered Nanking and massacred many of the inhabitants. Estimates range from 40,000 to 300,000, but the actual number will never be known as the Japanese destroyed the records.

On top of all this, Howe also had to confront the rumour that his dead friend, Cowan, had been involved in Pamela Werner's murder. Whatever the substance of the allegation, Howe felt compelled to discreetly make enquiries. Chief Inspector Dennis's services were called upon once again.

There were a few strange aspects. Cowan had not attended Pamela Werner's funeral on January 15, 1937, which would have surprised many given that he was the most senior British representative in Peking and the murder of the young British woman had shocked the entire foreign community. The Ambassador, Knatchbull-Hugessen, was in Nanking[42] and Consul Fitzmaurice represented the Embassy at the well-attended ceremony in the small British cemetery outside one of city's western gates.[43] Botham and Han were among those present, as were Hugh and Agnes Mackenzie from Tientsin. The elderly Doctor Aspland, who had assisted with the post mortem, acted as a pallbearer, as did Constable Pearson, police officer for the British Embassy, who had attended the original crime scene beside the wall. The short fu-

....

42 *Peiping Chronicle*, society column, January 15, 1937.
43 "Lewis C. Arlington and William Lewisohn", In Search of Old Peking, (1935), p249.

neral service was conducted by the Embassy Chaplain.[44] Absent throughout was First Secretary, D. J. Cowan. Nor thereafter, during the months of police investigation, was Cowan quoted as making any public comment on the murder. Not a word from the man who otherwise featured regularly in the news and social columns of *the Peiping Chronicle*.

Perhaps Cowan's absence from any official event connected with the murder was noted by some at the time, or perhaps comments began months later after his sudden illness and death. Maybe the rumor originated from his disturbing antics showing how such injuries as Pamela's could have been inflicted. Mental illness at the time carried a great stigma, and the full circumstances of Cowan's sudden departure and subsequent death may have only been known by a relatively small number of people. The rest of the foreign community, left substantially in the dark, were free to speculate and spread rumors.

And spread they most certainly did. In her notes from the period, the American journalist and Peking resident Helen Foster Snow recalled the shocking murder of her neighbor Pamela Werner (whom she had never met), and her discussing the subject with Ida Pruitt, the social worker at the PUMC. Snow heard the following from Ida Pruitt who "knew everyone in Peking": "Ida said that the murder was hushed up quickly because clues led 'too close to the British Embassy'".[45]

Such a damaging rumor was one that Howe would have felt obliged to investigate, painful though it must have been for him, concerning as it did his close friend: a friendship he likened to that of "Jonathan and David".[46] Helen Foster Snow, however, did place Pruitt's assertion about clues leading to the British Em-

....

44 "Last Rites Held for Miss Werner", *Peiping Chronicle*, January 16, 1937.
45 Hoover Institution Library & Archives, Nym Wales papers 1931-1998 (Helen Foster Snow), Notes on the Sian Incident Box 17.
46 Sir Robert George Howe, *Inherit the Kingdom*, unpublished autobiography.

bassy into perspective: "This was the classic Chinese reaction to every such thing – they always blamed the British Embassy for everything that went wrong, and called every foreigner they disliked a 'British agent'".[47] Nor would Cowan's reputation have been helped by the Japanese policy of anti-British propaganda, which by December 1937 was well underway.

Pruitt's rumor relating to "clues that led too close to the British Embassy" probably represented the tip of the iceberg of stories circulating concerning the Embassy, and probably Cowan. But such rumors were never accompanied by any evidence. Dennis's report to Archer on the "someone at the Embassy" has not survived, but whatever it contained, Howe appears not to have felt the need to pursue the matter any further – and it would have been out of character for the "strong" and "straightforward" Howe to ignore real evidence.[48] The strong likelihood is that the Cowan connection to Pamela Werner was nothing more than a widely-circulated rumor, with nothing concrete to link the man with the crime. All the factors are circumstantial: Cowan was in Peking on the night Pamela was murdered. But so were many others. Cowan made no public comment on the case, and had no discernible involvement in the murder investigation. To have done so would have undermined Fitzmaurice, who as Consul had judicial responsibility in the case, so Cowan's not going to the funeral amounts to evidence of nothing. In short, it appears that there was no case against Cowan.

It is notable that Werner, who was quite content to assert the guilt of other men on the flimsiest of evidence, and who could not have failed to hear the rumor involving "someone at the Embassy," never once made reference to it. On the other hand, Werner

....

47 Hoover Institution Library & Archives, Nym Wales papers 1931-1998 (Helen Foster Snow), Notes on the Sian Incident Box 17.
48 Sir Berkeley Gage, *It's Been a Marvellous Party*, (1989), p55.

was peculiarly biased in his selection of suspects. His letters and books were littered with excoriating criticism of the performance of many members of the Foreign Office, but he never questioned their moral integrity. Werner accused Embassy officials of being woefully idle or incompetent, but never of being corrupt. Somehow Werner appears to have retained respect for the institution to which he once belonged; a respect that prevented him from repeating a rumor that one of its members was involved in his daughter's murder.

"Sad Loss to British Community; Sudden Death of Mr. Cowan" was the headline in *The Peiping Chronicle* of October 28, two days after the diplomat's death. The newspaper then continued, warmly:

> "The news of Mr. Cowan's death will come as a great shock to a wide circle of friends in Peiping, for he appeared to be in the most robust health. Mr. Cowan will always be remembered here as a genial and generous personality who sacrificed his time, his energies and finally his health to the interests of the British community in Peiping and never failed to use his influence for the general welfare during a critical period.[49]

In contrast to this, his Embassy colleague Lamb much later recalled, rather less generously: "Cowan was not a commanding personality, except perhaps in build."[50]

The reality probably lay somewhere between these two contrasting descriptions, or even encompassed them both.

....

49 "Sad Loss to British Community", *Peiping Chronicle*, October 28, 1937.
50 School of Oriental & African Studies, MS 380730 Sir Lionel Lamb collection.

12

THE JOURNALIST

GEORGE GORMAN

FOLLOWING COWAN'S sudden death, the Foreign Office soon assigned another senior and experienced man to assist at the British Embassy in Peking. John Greenway (1896-1967), a diplomat of the same age and rank as Cowan, was transferred from Stockholm.[1]

Greenway, however, was slow to arrive in Peking in early 1938 and subsequently stayed only a few months. He was at the Embassy just long enough to encounter Werner in a difficult interview concerning his latest theories relating to the now-closed murder investigation.[2] Perhaps unsurprisingly, Greenway recalled Peking as: "A very odd place, full of curious characters, and eccentricity of some kind is normal among foreign residents who have been there for a long time."[3]

But if Greenway's staffing of Peking was a temporary measure, it was the Embassy's youthful Second Secretary, George "Gerry" Young (1908-1960), aged twenty-nine, who appears to

1 UK National Archives, annual Foreign Office list.
2 UK National Archives, FO 371/23513/1510 Murder of Pamela Werner. Code 10 file 1510, letter from E.T.C. Werner to the British Ambassador to China, October 1938.
3 J.D. Greenway, *Fish, Fowl and Foreign Lands*, (1950) p14.

George Gorman with his daughter, early 1930s. (Courtesy of Deborah Mcfarlane)

have taken on the challenge of overseeing Britain's diplomatic affairs in Peking. He was an able public servant and his intelligence reports were well received by Whitehall. Very soon, writing "in the absence of the Ambassador," Young was confident enough to inject his reports with a dose of humour, at the expense of another British subject, George Gorman.

Gorman, editor of the magazine *Caravan*, had recently joined *The Peiping Chronicle* as editor, following its change of ownership into Japanese hands (simultaneously dropping the nationalist "Peiping" and reverting to its former title, *The Peking Chronicle*).[4]

Despite being employed by the Japanese, Gorman nevertheless a few months later found himself enmeshed in trouble with their security services when he produced his camera at the wrong time and place, much to the delight and amusement of Young at the Embassy, who reported to London:

> I have the honour to enclose a further cutting from the 'Peking Chronicle', in which the editor, Mr. George Gorman, describes his experiences at the hands of the Japanese police during a visit to Jehol by means of the newly-opened Peking-Jehol railway.
>
> The news that the Japanese had picked on Mr. Gorman, who is North China's leading pro-Japanese propagandist,

---

4 *Peking Chronicle*, Notice, November 1, 1937.

GRAEME SHEPPARD

as their first victim, proved a source of considerable gratifi-
cation to the breakfast tables of Peking, where the journalistic pablum provided consists for the most part of his daily
hymns in praise of the Rising Sun.

Surprisingly, and much to the delight of many in Peking's foreign community, George Gorman had actually published an account of his experience of Japanese custody in an article entitled
"All the Fun of the Jehol Jail."[5] By this time, Gorman had been
working in China as an apologist for the Japanese Government
for many years. It had not made him popular.

"The traitor," wrote one of his wife's relations. "He knew
what was going on all along and of course the Japanese would
use him just as long as he was useful to them."[6]

With the Japanese military now a triumphant occupying force
in Peking, Gorman had become a figure of scorn for many European residents. For different reasons entirely, he had also become
a subject of intense dislike to Werner.

Werner's animosity towards Gorman had been a recent development. Prior to Pamela's murder, the two men appear to
have got on well. Both had found the other useful owing to their
mutual interest in publishing. Werner needed an outlet for his
writings, while Gorman needed articles to fill *Caravan*. But their
working relationship broke down some time after January 1937.
And for once on Werner's part, it was done with valid reason:
the police had found compromising evidence that suggested that
Gorman's relationship with Pamela had not been one that Werner would have tolerated.

While D.J. Cowan's connection with the Werner murder ap-

5 "All the Fun of Jehol Jail", *Peking Chronicle*, April 10, 1938.
6 Deborah McFarlane, *Britain & Japan; Biographical Portraits*, volume VIII, compiled & edited by Hugh Cortazzi, (2013), pp507-524.

pears to have existed only in the minds of some of Peking's foreign community – it was without supporting evidence and only conceived months after the event – George Gorman's relationship to Pamela was another matter.

In the days following the discovery of Pamela's body, the British police made a thorough search of her small bedroom at the Werner home. This was a routine police action in the search for evidence of the offence or offender, and intelligence relating to the victim's activities, lifestyle and associates. Among Pamela's few belongings in her spartan bedroom, police found her "minutely detailed diary."[7] In one entry, which would have been no earlier than the previous summer, Pamela described being at a picnic where "Mr. Gorman made love to me."[8] As with all the case exhibits, the diary is now lost to us, its fate unknown, but at the time it would have been seized as police evidence. At what point in the investigation Werner got to hear of its content is unclear.

The day before she was murdered, Pamela had visited the Gorman home, close to the French ice rink, for afternoon tea.[9] On the evening after the murder, Gorman called at Werner's home with the police, ostensibly to check on the welfare of Pamela's father, and entered the compound, the main building and even Pamela's bedroom. This intrusive visit, made under the shrewd guise of being a concerned "family friend," soon featured in the next edition of *Caravan*.[10] Whatever Gorman's initial motive might have been, he was quick to take advantage of the situation.

In the circumstances, the strong likelihood is that the police would have closely examined Gorman's involvement with Pamela and he may even have been treated as a genuine police sus-

7 E.T.C. Werner, *Memorigrams*, (1940) p147.
8 UK National Archives, FO 371/23513/1510 Murder of Pamela Werner. Code 10 file 1510, letters from E.T.C. Werner to the British Ambassador to China, February 1939 & June 1939.
9 "The Pamela Werner Case", *Caravan* magazine, February 1937.
10 ibid.

pect.

George William Aloysius Gorman was a well-known figure in Peking. Born in 1888 in Liverpool in northwest England, Gorman's parents were second generation Irish immigrants in a city with a large Irish community. His father was a bookkeeper. After leaving the local Catholic school in his mid-teens, Gorman worked briefly as a cotton merchant's clerk before quitting Liverpool for good in 1905 and working his passage to Canada. It was the start of a much-travelled career in journalism which had him working for newspapers on three continents.[11]

In Quebec, Gorman secured a cadetship on the *Montreal Star* newspaper. Intelligent and industrious, he appears to have taken well to the newspaper industry and remained in it all his life. Further positions, and promotions, followed at other newspapers in Boston and New York before he returned to Canada and Fort William (now Thunder Bay) in Ontario in or before 1911. There he married and had a daughter.[12]

Whatever his later loyalties, at the outbreak of war in Europe in 1914, Gorman, age twenty-six, volunteered for the Allied cause and joined the Canadian Expeditionary Force. He saw active service in France, achieving the rank of company sergeant-major, before a heart condition led to him being medically discharged in 1917.[13] Gorman's first marriage ended on his return to Canada. His second wife, Aileen Brown, thirteen years younger than him, was a fellow journalist he met while working for the *Vancouver Star* in British Columbia. It was in Vancouver that Gorman made friends within the city's expanding Japanese community, a friendship that developed into a strong admiration of the Japanese nation and the positive aspects of the national character. It

11 Deborah McFarlane, *Britain & Japan; Biographical Portraits*, volume VIII, compiled & edited by Hugh Cortazzi, (2013), pp507-524.
12 ibid.
13 ibid.

was a sentiment at odds with his employer and the *Vancouver Star's* influential owner, Victor Odlum. Odlum had earlier stood for the federal election on a "White Canada" platform and was opposed to the province's increasing "Yellow" population.[14]

In 1926, having reputedly resigned from the *Vancouver Star* over Odlum's anti-Japanese views, Gorman, with his wife and infant daughter, made the bold decision of relocating to Japan, where his basic command of the language and pro-Japanese sympathies were noted by the Foreign Ministry. In Tokyo, Gorman made good use of his Japanese contacts to secure a position as editor to an English-language newspaper, not in Japan itself, but in Peking, with the Japanese-owned *North China Standard*. It was the start of a largely successful relationship between Gorman and the Japanese authorities, lasting fifteen years.[15]

Most of Gorman's personal correspondence has been lost, and without supporting evidence beyond his many pro-Japanese newspaper reports, it is difficult to glean what his true motives may have been in connecting himself so thoroughly with Japan's imperial regime. Certainly there appears to be no evidence of any great financial reward. But Gorman, an opportunist and of an independent mind, presumably saw an opportunity to advance his career away from the crowded newspaper industry of North America. Working with the Japanese in the Far East may well have appealed to his sense of adventure. It is also probable that Gorman felt a genuine admiration for what was a rising nation.

In all, Gorman had two lengthy spells working in Peking – 1926 to 1930 and 1936 to 1939 – punctuated by several years in Manchuria. In 1930, with the closure of Peking's *North China Standard*, Gorman, with his wife and now two children, took up the position of adviser to Japanese regional interests and later

---

14 ibid.
15 ibid.

became the editor of a Manchurian newspaper, again Japanese-owned.[16]

In 1931, following the so-called Mukden incident, Japan transformed mineral-rich Manchuria into the Japanese-run state of Manchukuo which was subsequently provided with its own puppet government and currency, and the former Chinese Emperor Puyi as its nominal head. There could be little doubt in Gorman's mind that he was serving a nation bent on the military subjugation of its neighbours. Nonetheless, Gorman played along.

During the early 1930s, despite his close relationship with the Japanese, Gorman was also a foreign correspondent in the Far East for the respected British newspaper the *Daily Telegraph*. The British Ambassador in Tokyo took great exception to this, and in 1934 warned the Foreign Office that one of Gorman's Manchukuo telegraphs to the *Daily Telegraph* was "deliberately misleading" and commented on how ... "it is considered undesirable that a serious English newspaper should have such a representative at this time. Gorman was also described as ... an Irish Canadian ... who is a paid Japanese propagandist and his whole attitude is very anti-English."[17]

Whitehall was less strident, but agreed. After discussion, one senior figure observed:

> ... I feel pretty sure that if we can make a good case against Gorman the "Telegraph", which is a friendly and helpful newspaper, will probably dispense with his services at the earliest opportunity.[18]

16 ibid.
17 UK National Archives, FO 395/514 General. Code 150 Files 92-105; report by Sir Robert Clive, Ambassador to Japan, November 26, 1934.
18 Ibid., report by Sir Arthur Willert, December 17, 1934.

George Gorman, third from left, among a group of journalists, 1938

Gorman ceased working as correspondent for the *Daily Telegraph* the following year. What role the Foreign Office played in his departure is unknown.

By 1936 Gorman was back in Peking and living in the Legation Quarter, this time running the cultural magazine, *Caravan*.[19] Subtitled the "Magazine for the Far East," *Caravan* appeared monthly, price one yuan. With a modern, fresh image and high quality photographs – color on the front page – the magazine featured lengthy articles of regional interest, to which Werner was an occasional contributor. With unfortunate timing, the January 1937 edition of *Caravan* contained a rather flattering four-page Gorman biography of Werner, the article forming part of the magazine's *Men in the East* series. Pamela, alive at the time of the magazine going to print, did not get a mention, but the article was available to anyone in Peking who wanted to learn more about the murder victim's father.

At this time, Gorman's children, a girl and a boy, were in their

19 UK National Archives, FO 371/23513/1510 Murder of Pamela Werner. Code 10 file 1510, letter from E.T.C. Werner to the British Ambassador to China, June 1939.

early to mid-teens, some five years younger than Pamela. And although the girl in particular was both intelligent and mature for her age, Pamela's friendship with them was perhaps another example of her degree of social immaturity. Though the Gormans had only returned to Peking from Manchuria the year before, and Pamela had spent much of that time at school in Tientsin, she knew the family well enough to call on them for tea the afternoon before her death. What is unclear is whether Pamela knew the Gormans through her father, or whether it was the other way round.

Other than a mutual interest in publishing, Gorman and Werner had very little in common. There was a twenty-four-year age gap between them, not to mention different backgrounds, careers and personalities. Despite his unpopularity, Gorman was socially outgoing and attended the golfing events and various parties and gatherings mentioned in *The Peiping Chronicle*, as one would expect of a diligent journalist. He was also Roman Catholic and attended Mass daily throughout his life. The reclusive Werner was, by contrast, a declared atheist and thoroughly disapproved of Gorman's club-bar drinking habits;[20] like so many of his contemporaries, Gorman was a heavy drinker.[21]

However useful their working relationship had been, the falling-out between Werner and Gorman after the murder was complete and irrevocable. The February 1937 edition of *Caravan* featured Gorman's long article covering the crime in great detail. Given the case's notoriety it was obviously a story that Gorman felt he could not ignore. Though the article's tone was serious and unsensational, Gorman nonetheless described, in the third person, his taking the liberty of entering the Werner home

---

20 ibid.
21 Deborah McFarlane, *Britain & Japan; Biographical Portraits*, volume VIII, compiled & edited by Hugh Cortazzi, (2013), pp507-524.

as a "family friend," with Han and other police, to discover an overwhelmed Werner hours after the discovery of his adopted daughter's body. Gorman went on to describe the house's interior and Werner's sorry condition. This would quite understandably have angered Werner.

Towards the end of his "scoop", Gorman went on to speculate in general terms as to motives for the crime and what kind of person may have been the perpetrator. He was probably doing no more than transcribing the chatter that passed amongst the foreigners in Peking. Nonetheless his doing so enraged Werner, who complained bitterly that Gorman's words were "criminally libellous and *sub judice*."[22] Despite his much vaunted legal training, in these particular complaints Werner was wide of the mark, as Gorman had neither named nor implicated anyone, and no criminal prosecution had taken place.

The bad feeling between Werner and Gorman would have been of little concern to the Chinese and British police, whose sole interest would have been in establishing whether or not Gorman had any meaningful connection with the murder.

As a working journalist, editor and a married man with children, Gorman may well have had a strong and conclusive alibi as to his whereabouts on the evening of the murder. Nonetheless, the police will no doubt have explored the circumstances of Pamela's visit to the Gorman home for tea on the day before her murder. How long had the Gormans known her? Who was there? Between what times? Who invited whom? What was said? What were Pamela's plans? What is not known is whether Gorman himself was even among those present for tea that afternoon.

As to Gorman's talking his way into the Werner home the day after the murder, this may have been viewed by the police as an

22 UK National Archives, FO 371/23513/1510 Murder of Pamela Werner. Code 10 file 1510, letter from E.T.C. Werner to the British Ambassador to China, June 1939.

act of journalistic opportunism - distasteful perhaps, but unlikely to amount to anything more. Whilst it is the case that murderers, for one reason or another, often have a habit of returning to the scene of the crime, the Werner home, however, was *not* the crime scene, and there is no suggestion Gorman knew of the existence of any diary entry. Even if Gorman *had* known of Pamela's diary it would surely have been difficult for him to search for, find and destroy that or any other possibly incriminating evidence under the noses of the investigating police.

Undoubtedly of great interest to the police would have been the comments in the diary, where Pamela wrote that at a picnic: "Mr. Gorman made love to me." While the assumption today is that of sex, the words probably held a different meaning for a young woman in the 1930s. It is likely that Pamela was merely alluding to Gorman flirting with, or flattering her rather than there being any sexual contact. Pamela was an attractive nineteen-year-old at the time of her death, while Gorman was a married man of forty-eight. It is impossible now to know what, if anything, went on between them, real or imagined, at what was most likely an outing attended by at least several other people. By modern standards, however, it probably amounted to very little.

Werner asserted that Gorman was "interrogated" by police.[23] Given the existence of the diary entry, it is highly probable that police did indeed speak with him, possibly even in a formal setting and under caution. Gorman may have denied any knowledge of the picnic matter, or dismissed it as a figment of the imaginative mind of a young woman, or perhaps even admitted to a harmless impropriety. But whatever the case, police enquiries into Gorman as a suspect appear very soon to have

23 ibid.

ended. Despite Gorman's general unpopularity, nowhere is Gorman mentioned in connection with the crime. Nowhere, that is, except by Werner:

> "I hereby deliberately accuse Gorman of lying, protecting a murderer, and trying to mislead the officials when he wrote that Prentice, his friend and co-sexualist, was at the cinema when Pamela was inveigled into his flat."[24]

Gorman therefore joined the Werner list of Prentice's nefarious friends. Though in the small world of the Legation Quarter it is quite possible the two men knew one another, Werner's basis for the allegation that Gorman wrote protecting Prentice by lying and providing a cinema-going alibi remains a mystery (it appears nowhere in Gorman's *Caravan* articles on the murder). But *The Peiping Chronicle* did run adverts for at least three Peking cinemas showing films that evening.[25]

Werner also charged that Gorman published his *Caravan* article outlining likely murder scenarios in an effort to deflect suspicion from himself,[26] which is stretching logic. Conversely, by the same reasoning, the magazine *not* covering the crime may equally have led to Gorman being accused of avoiding the issue.

Werner's sudden clash with Gorman left the former in a potentially awkward position when it came to his latest book, *Memorigrams*, a volume published in Shanghai which is best described as a mixed collection of Werner's views and anecdotes. Largely compiled before the murder, it was not published until 1940, which gave Werner the opportunity to add a lengthy chap-

24 UK National Archives, FO 371/35815 Murder of Pamela Werner. Code 10 file 71; letter from E.T.C. Werner to the British Ambassador to China, December 1941.
25 *Peiping Chronicle*, adverts for the Peking Pavilion, Capitol and Chen Kwang Theatre cinemas, January 7, 1937.
26 UK National Archives, FO 371/23513/1510 Murder of Pamela Werner. Code 10 file 1510, letter from E.T.C. Werner to the British Ambassador to China, March 1939.

ter about Pamela's murder. The latter included a long, rambling address to the murderer: "one of those course, vulgar cads who know nothing of the joys of refined homes and pretty children, living happy, pure lives, as contrasted with your degraded, bestial existence", also a fulsome diatribe against all the police and officials Werner considered to be incompetent (some of the chapter's text had appeared in *Caravan* magazine in June 1937 in the form of an open-letter to the unknown murderer, though on that occasion without its criticism of others). George Gorman wrote part of *Memorigram's* introduction, presumably before the two men's falling out. This did not deter Werner from forcefully condemning the journalist in the ensuing pages by reporting the "made love to me" diary entry and his own allegation that Gorman had tried to deflect suspicion from himself.[27]

Gorman's unpopular tenure at *The Peking Chronicle* lasted just two years. In September 1939, the same year that intelligence reports claimed Gorman had received payments from the Japanese for supplying them with anti-British propaganda, Gorman was dismissed from the newspaper, ironically, for his pro-British sympathies against Germany.[28] Whatever the reality of Gorman's attitude towards Britain, it appears to have been surpassed by his dislike of Germany born of his experiences during World War One.

Following his Peking dismissal, Gorman and family relocated to Yokohama, Japan where he worked as an editor on yet another Japanese-owned English language newspaper. Less than two years later, in the spring of 1941, with the War in Europe worsening and tensions mounting in the Pacific, his wife Aileen moved with their two children to Australia for safety. Gorman

....

27 E.T.C. Werner, *Memorigrams*, (1940) p3 & p148.
28 Deborah McFarlane, *Britain & Japan; Biographical Portraits*, volume VIII, compiled & edited by Hugh Cortazzi, (2013), pp507-524.

remained working in Japan. It would be many years before he next saw his daughter. Fate would have it that he never met his wife or son again.

In Australia, where Japan was already perceived as a real threat, Gorman's wife found herself under surveillance by the Government's security services. Her mail was intercepted and her movements monitored. By late 1941, her husband had begun giving bi-weekly broadcasts on a Japanese Government radio channel, telling Australian and American audiences how Japan wanted to stay out of the expanding war. The press in Australia dubbed Gorman "Lord Haw Haw of the East." None of which could have made his wife's life any easier.[29]

But Gorman's cordial relationship with his employers was about to come to a precipitous end. Like a great many Europeans and Americans in those parts of the Far East controlled by Japan, Gorman woke on the morning of Monday, December 8, 1941 to a changed world. On the other side of the international dateline, Japan had raided the American naval base at Pearl Harbour in Hawaii, resulting in the death of over two thousand American servicemen and causing severe damage to the US Pacific Fleet. Thousands of expatriate civilians in the Far East suddenly discovered that their home countries were at war with Japan. No longer were they neutral foreigners, entitled at least in principle to a degree of protection. They were now enemy aliens at the mercy of the Japanese military. The first that many knew of the war was a hammering on the door by Japanese soldiers.

Despite Gorman's many years of support for the Japanese cause, he received worse treatment than many other enemy civilians who found themselves in the wrong country at the wrong time. He was arrested at his home in Yokohama that afternoon,

29 ibid.

delivered to a local police station and on the following day to a nearby internment camp. There, Gorman was held for a few weeks before being interviewed by agents from the government's Foreign Affairs section. They wanted to know whether Gorman was in the service of a foreign government and had engaged in spying on Japan. Not content with Gorman's denials they transported him to a cell at Yokohama's Gumyoji prison.[30] Stripped of his belt, braces and neck-tie, Gorman spent four winter months in isolation in an unheated cell. Bedding was basic and prison food limited. A man of average stature, Gorman lost over twelve kilograms in weight.[31] He later estimated that he was interviewed between forty to fifty times, each lasting on average of between four to five hours. Ironically, it was suggested to Gorman that he "had imparted into my editorials a flavour which was anti-Japanese and particularly anti Japan's allies." The examiners' main bone of contention, however, was a compromising but un-posted letter they had found in Gorman's home written to R.H. Scott, Chief of the Far Eastern Bureau of the Ministry of Information in Singapore, advising him on the most effective methods of conducting anti-German and pro-British propaganda in Japan.[32] (Sir Robert Heatlie Scott (1905-1982) was a "China Service" consular officer. Captured after the fall of Singapore, he was tortured in Changi prison).

Gorman admitted to the letter's authorship sending his interrogators into a fury. He was beaten and the interpreter gravely informed him that this admission of espionage would mean confinement to prison and probably execution.[33]

But he survived. In April 1942, he was released from prison

---

30 ibid.
31 ibid.
32 UK National Archives, FO 371/31839 Committee of Enquiry into the treatment of British subjects in Japanese controlled territory. Code 23 file 867 (papers 7071-7634).
33 ibid.

and kept under house arrest at a hotel. Then in July, he was repatriated aboard the Japanese liner the *Tatatu Maru* along with
over a thousand other foreign nationals. Also on board was the
British Ambassador to Japan and staff of the Embassy along with
a crowd of assorted British nationals, all of whom had spent the
previous eight months confined to the Embassy compound in
Tokyo, and for whom Gorman appears to have been *persona non
grata*.[34]

The *Tatatu Maru* exchanged its cargo of foreign nationals for
Japanese at the neutral port of Laurenco Marques (now Maputo
in Mozambique). There, Gorman took the opportunity of giving
an interview to a correspondent from the British newspaper, *The
Times*. Japan, Gorman explained, was strong and determined,
and its people were enthusiastic for continuing the war. Gorman
reckoned that the only way Japan could be beaten was by sea.[35]

On his arrival in England some six weeks later, Gorman was
promptly arrested, this time by British intelligence officers under
Defence Regulation 18(b).[36] The wartime regulations gave extensive powers of detention and internment of alien nationals and,
as exemplified by Gorman's case, included persons suspected of
aiding or supporting the enemy. Detention could be for as long
as was deemed necessary. Gorman was given what he later described as "a thorough grilling."[37] Nevertheless, he was subsequently released after two weeks in custody. In the UK, records
of wartime interviews under 18(b) remain closed to public inspection; the accusations levelled at Gorman remain unknown.

Discarded callously by the regime he had long supported,

....

34 Deborah McFarlane, *Britain & Japan; Biographical Portraits*, volume VIII, compiled & edited by Hugh Cortazzi, (2013), pp507-524.
35 "Policies Behind the War", *The Times*, August 31, 1942.
36 UK National Archives, FO 371/35815 Murder of Pamela Werner. Code 10 file 71; covering
report remarks.
37 Deborah McFarlane, *Britain & Japan; Biographical Portraits*, volume VIII, compiled & edited by Hugh Cortazzi, (2013), pp507-524.

Gorman later commented: "I bore no ill-feeling toward the Japanese whom I admire sincerely." A lifelong outsider, when convenient and to suit the occasion, Gorman had described himself as either British, Irish, or Canadian. On his return to Britain, Gorman applied to join his wife and children but Australia refused him entry (his marriage was in any event over). Canada, his home for many years, also refused him entry.[38] Alone and initially unemployed, Gorman had little choice but to remain in Britain for the remainder of the war.

Of all the men linked in some way with the murder of Pamela Werner, Gorman met with the most opprobrium from his contemporaries, some of whom described him as a traitor. Unfair perhaps, as Gorman was never actually in league with his own country's enemy. And like nearly every foreigner in Japan, Gorman was arrested after Pearl Harbour. If he was a traitor, he was not a wartime one.

As an experienced journalist, Gorman must have realised at some point that he was working for a tyranny. And yet he continued doing so. As editor of *The Peking Chronicle,* he oversaw blatant Japanese propaganda – "Steps to Sino Japanese Cultural Union Revealed; Make Peace with Japan, Paper Says, There is yet time for Agreement"[39] – even as Japanese troops were slaughtering innocents in Nanking. By the standards of the time, which provide the only meaningful moral judgement, Gorman's work in China, though never actually traitorous, progressed steadily from what many foreigners as opportunistic and adventurous, to distasteful and eventually morally abhorrent.

As to the murder of Pamela Werner, scorned by many in Peking though he was, and close enough to events to generate a

....

38 ibid.
39 *Peking Chronicle*, a) "Steps to Ensure Sino-Japanese Cultural Union Revealed", & b) "Make Peace With Japan Paper Says", November 24, 1937.

measure of gossip, there was no primary evidence linking Gorman with any aspect of the crime. Unless they were extremely incompetent, the British and Chinese police would no doubt have looked closely at the three circumstances that linked Gorman with Pamela. But even placed together, they amounted to no more than evidence of friendship or acquaintance, appropriate or otherwise. The fact that Gorman was at liberty and writing lengthy articles on the subject a month after the murder strongly suggests that police enquiries proved negative.

13

WAR IN THE PACIFIC

ARRESTS AND INTERROGATION

FOR THE FOREIGNERS in Peking, Pearl Harbour changed the world. Many were in disbelief, unable to conceive that such an audacious attack on Pearl Harbour could really have happened.

At the *Hotel des Wagon-Lits*, guests of all nationalities gathered in the lobby, not knowing what to do. The British and Americans sat in little groups in a state of shock as if waiting to be arrested. Suddenly, the main doors of the hotel burst open and a group of Japanese soldiers marched in armed with rifles and bayonets, swords and pistols. Guests braced themselves as the soldiers dispersed in pairs throughout the hotel's ground floor, covering stairs, entrances and exits, only for nothing further to happen. The soldiers left the hotel in the same manner in which they had arrived. It appears to have been no more than a show of force.[1]

One problem the Japanese occupiers faced was the sheer number of foreigners resident in the city. Arresting them all on day one was logistically impossible, and in most cases unnecessary. The Japanese needed to prioritize their targets and immedi-

....

1   Hope Danby, *My Boy Chang*, (1955), p167.

ately set about doing so.

In a breach of diplomatic rules, Japanese soldiers entered the British compound via the main gates on horseback and tore down the Union Flag. The Embassy staff were confined to the grounds, and no foreign visitors were permitted.[2]

A few hours earlier, while the streets of the Legation Quarter were filling with Japanese soldiers and machine guns, the Embassy staff had set about burning sensitive documents and codes. The faces of those engaged with the same task in Tientsin Consulate were reportedly black with smoke.[3]

The British Embassy had been virtually unguarded. Due to the war in Europe, the small garrison of British soldiers had been withdrawn the previous year. The only other foreign troops of significant number left anywhere in China were American, including a recently reduced detachment of US Marines guarding the American Embassy in the western corner of the Legation Quarter.

Long before Pearl Harbour, it had been argued by many in Washington that American troops in China were in an untenable position and rather than protecting American interests in the region, they were becoming an increasingly vulnerable target in an escalating war zone. Calls for their withdrawal were resisted for reasons of national prestige and the desire not to be seen as giving in to Japanese pressure. Finally, a month before Pearl Harbour, the order had been given for the orderly withdrawal of the remaining US troops. Packed to go and with their compound stripped, the last of the "China Marines" were scheduled to leave China on the SS Harrison only two days after the Japanese attack. The men had been so close to avoiding capture.

....

2 ibid., p169.
3 School of Oriental & African Studies library archive, MS 380697 Woodall, John Emmett, pamphlet, The Tientsin Grammar School after Pearl Harbour.

While the American compound was surrounded by the new enemy, a flurry of radio messages was sent between US Marine Corps commanders in bases across north China. A decision was made: troops were ordered to comply with the demands of the overwhelming Japanese forces.

In Peking at one o'clock that afternoon an affecting ceremony, as strange as it must have been tense, occurred inside the American compound. In freezing winter air, the entire Marine Corps guard fell out, smart in their forest green uniforms and winter fur hats. The sentries on the gates joined them. A company of Japanese soldiers marched in and stood opposite their foes. A long pause was followed by the American commanding officer, Colonel Ashurst, giving the order to "sound retreat." To the sound of a bugle, the Stars and Stripes was solemnly lowered, carefully folded, and handed to the Colonel. The Colonel gazed at the flag for a while, then handed it over to the Japanese officer taking the surrender. There followed another long pause while the Japanese officer reflected, then handed the colors back to the Colonel, who nodded in appreciation. The marines then stacked arms and returned to barracks as prisoners. In total, 204 US Marines in North China entered four uncertain years of captivity on the first day of the Pacific War.[4]

Elsewhere, foreign banks across Japanese-occupied China were closed and telephone lines disconnected. Foreign interests, including concession administrative buildings, ports and power stations, were all taken over,[5] as were even the social clubs and racecourses.

Tension had existed in Tientsin as early as 1939 when Japanese barricades had blockaded the British Concession following

4 United States Marine Corps in North China 1894-1942, Chester M Biggs, Jr., McFarland & Company (2003), p207.
5 School of Oriental & African Studies library archive, MS 380697 Woodall, John Emmett, pamphlet, The Tientsin Grammar School after Pearl Harbour.

its refusal to hand over a number of alleged Chinese assassins. The Japanese soldiers humiliated British subjects going in and out, by strip-searches which left them standing literally naked in the street. In December 1941, the Japanese marched in and occupied the entire concession, arresting its civil leaders and police,[6] including Chief Inspector Richard Dennis. The story was much the same in Shanghai, effectively bringing to an end the century-old Treaty Port era. Pamela's old school, the Tientsin Grammar School, was on the list for a visit by the Japanese military, as related by its young headmaster, John Woodall:

> By mid morning normal routine was interrupted. A Japanese major, several officers and a civilian interpreter, with ten or a dozen soldiers with fixed bayonets burst into the school. Having briefed the Chinese staff on no account to offer resistance or behave offensively if and when soldiers turned up, the head boy Yang saw that it was so. In my study civilities, though brief, were exchanged and I asked what they wanted.
>
> "Where is your safe and money?"
>
> "Here is my safe and here are my confidential files in it."
>
> "But where is your money?"
>
> "TGS accounts are dealt with by the B.M.C. Accountants and they take in and pay out the money."
>
> "But why is there no money here?"
>
> "Because in the terms of the Trust Deed all monies are dealt with by the B.M.C."
>
> [Woodall produced a Japanese dictionary and showed them the words trust and trustees, but it failed to help.] At this stage we were stymied. They just could not understand

---

6 Desmond Power, *Little Foreign Devil* (1996), p162.

why I had no money.[7]

A few weeks later, the TGS ceased to be a school for English-speaking Tientsinners and was converted into a Japanese girls' school. Woodall was ordered to leave. He and his colleagues attempted to carry on working, holding secret classes in nine different locations across Tientsin. But he was soon detained by the Japanese and warned to stop; the assemblies were unlawful, as was the unauthorised teaching of the English language to children.[8]

Personal experience of the first days and weeks of war varied amongst Peking's foreigners, depending partially on nationality. Those on Werner's list of suspects provide a good example. As an Italian citizen, Doctor Ugo Cappuzzo carried on life unmolested; Fascist Italy had entered the War in Europe six months earlier and was a fellow Axis ally of Japan. Reserve US Marine Fred Knauf was, predictably, immediately arrested. He and a handful of other retired marines in Peking found themselves incarcerated with their colleagues from the regulars who had surrendered at the American Embassy.[9]

The American dentist Wentworth Prentice, however, fared better, at least initially. His private dental business had probably suffered in recent years due to the slow, steady exodus of customers as Western governments recommended that their citizens leave troubled China. After Pearl Harbour, Prentice probably feared arrest and the closure of his practice, and with it financial ruin. But as luck would have it, he was assessed as harmless by the Japanese and allowed to continue practising dentistry.

A few weeks later, a no doubt relieved Prentice found him-

---

7 School of Oriental & African Studies library archive, MS 380697 Woodall, John Emmett, pamphlet, The Tientsin Grammar School after Pearl Harbour.
8 ibid.
9 "Knauf Tells of Far East", *Mosinee Times*, March 1, 1944.

self, as did ten other American and British citizens, duped by a fellow foreign resident into signing a joint letter addressed to *The Peking Chronicle*:

> We, the residents of the Anglo-American community here in Peking, take this opportunity to express our sincere gratitude and appreciation to the Japanese Army for the lenient treatment and kind consideration shown to us during this abnormal situation that we find ourselves in.
>
> There has always been rumours that the Japanese Army imposes hardships on some civilians and suppresses others, but this has been disproved right here in Peking, as we are not arrested or interned, but quite free and comfortable.
>
> To further show our sincere appreciation, we hereby assure the Japanese military authorities that we wish to cooperate with them as much as possible to preserve peace and order.
>
> The treatment which the Japanese Army has accorded us is an example of the good spirit which must have the admiration and approval of the whole world, and we hope that other countries may learn of this in due time.[10]

The letter would have been excellent propaganda for the Japanese, especially considering "the gratitude and appreciation shown by those who signed it during this abnormal situation" - meaning the war. The man behind the letter, with his name heading the signatures, was American citizen David Laughlin (1899-1982).[11] Laughlin, like Fred Knauf, who he knew well, was a former corporal in the China Marines and long-term resident

10 "Americans and Britons Thank Japanese Army", *Peking Chronicle*, December 27, 1941.
11 US National Archive, report by counselor of US Embassy China, 894.20211/575, 17 August 1942.

of Peking. According to intelligence compiled during this period by American Embassy staff, Laughlin had been a paid informer for the Japanese long before the outbreak of the war. While not connected to any school or college, he had earned an uncertain living teaching English to Japanese and Chinese. Tellingly, in the first months of 1942, while most Americans in Peking were forced to move to smaller quarters due to a lack of money, Laughlin moved to superior accommodation. In the understated opinion of Richard P. Butrick, American Counsellor in Peking, Laughlin made his "doubtful loyalty" doubly the worse by sending his own "expression of regret" to the Japanese authorities, referring to what he described as American atrocities in the Philippines.[12]

Prentice, perhaps horrified by his ill-judged early association with Laughlin, reported to the Embassy how the man had been trying to ingratiate himself with leading figures in the American community in Peking in an effort to establish himself as the liaison figure between them and the Japanese authorities. In order to stymie such a move, Counselor Butrick issued a memorandum requesting the Japanese only to deal with American citizens through the representatives of a proposed American resident committee. This committee was formed in late January 1942 by Doctor Reinhard Hoeppli, a doctor formerly at the PUMC who had been recently appointed the new Swiss Consul, with the task of looking after the interests of many of Peking's foreigners.[13] Laughlin's influence in that perfidious direction was therefore curtailed.

It would not have been difficult for the Japanese to identify targets, having been in control of Peking since 1937. But Laughlin was thought to have provided information leading to the

....

12 ibid.
13 ibid.

arrest of eleven US citizens, including Knauf.[14] Knauf later reported that the reasons for his detention were never explained to him, but he reckoned he was found "not guilty," though it was not clear of what. True to character, he boldly told his captors through an interpreter: "You're through, you haven't a chance, my country will defeat you."[15]

Knauf shared a prison with some 160 regular Marines, but unlike them he was released a month later on the condition that he lived within the walls of the city. His savings were frozen and he was kept under surveillance by Chinese and White Russian agents.[16] Meeting up with the Swiss Doctor Hoeppli, he expressed the opinion that Laughlin had considerable influence with the Japanese authorities. Knauf's comments on Laughlin were subsequently included in Counselor Butrick's report to Washington, to which someone annotated next to Knauf's name: "reputation not good."[17] Knauf's name remained tainted by his allegedly nefarious Peking business dealings of previous years.

Throughout all these early wartime events, E.T.C. Werner remained in Peking, having moved from his courtyard home to the house in the British Embassy compound he shared with Backhouse. Werner had continued writing letters to London concerning his investigations of Pamela's murder until almost the last minute – the last of his missives to reach the Foreign Office was posted just six days before the attack on Pearl Harbour, after which no further reports appear to have left China.[18] – and rather questionably, Werner then took to also sending his reports to the Japanese, his country's enemy, hoping for their help in the

14 ibid.
15 "Knauf Tells of Far East", *Mosinee Times*, March 1, 1944.
16 ibid.
17 US National Archive, report by counselor of US Embassy China, 894.20211/575, August 17, 1942.
18 E.T.C. Werner, *More Memorigrams*, (1948), p205.

investigation.[19]

Werner's appeal to the Japanese for assistance brought him no positive results. It was not the first time he had appealed to them. Prior to 1941, Werner met with several Japanese police and embassy officials, men who were probably keen to exploit a retired British consul if only to spread misinformation. Still rankling over the Sasaki case, the Japanese told Werner that it was common knowledge throughout Peking that Pamela's murder had involved officials from the British Embassy engaged in a shocking cover-up. Without any mention of evidence to support these allegations, Werner reported that the Japanese were adamant that, like Sasaki, Pamela had been a victim of drunk and murderous British soldiers. The British consuls, they alleged, had not only been incompetent, but also corrupt in making sure the truth did not emerge. But the Japanese failed to convince Werner. Not only did this theory clash with his own involving Prentice, Knauf, and Cappuzzo, but his faith in the British establishment was such that he could not credit its officials with such corruption. Werner did not believe in conspiracies in which the Sasaki case or that of his daughter had been deliberately hushed up.[20]

Over the next year, like every Allied national in China, Werner and his list of suspects were subject to the same slowly tightening grip of the Japanese occupation: queues for everything, foreigner registration, identity cards and passes, the wearing of armbands, the registration of property, the confiscation of vehicles, radios, binoculars and cameras. On top of these impositions many foreigners were evicted from their homes to make way for Japanese nationals. After the relatively easy opening months of war, life became increasingly difficult.

....

19 ibid., p187.
20 UK National Archives, FO 371/23513/1510 Murder of Pamela Werner. Code 10 file 1510, letter from E.T.C. Werner to the British Ambassador to China, June 1939.

The British resident Hope Danby described how some restrictions were overcome:

> The diplomats and their families only left their compounds
> when they obtained passes to visit their dentists. It trans-
> pired that the Japanese were particularly sympathetic to
> anyone who had tooth-ache. Of course everyone soon be-
> came aware of this and often one or other of the interned
> officials was to be seen in Legation Street, stepping jauntily
> along. Never had a dentist parlour been so popular.

Wentworth Prentice was suddenly a busy man. Hope Danby,
who unlike Werner evidently thought well of the American, remembered her conversation with him:

> "Say, ma'am," said the American dentist who was still
> allowed to carry on his practice, "you'd think that my
> waiting-room was the Palm Court at Miami Beach, it's that
> popular. Somehow word goes round when certain people
> have appointments with me and their friends drop in to see
> them. A kind of reception is held."
>
> "Yesterday I met some other internees – not diplomatic
> ones – being marched here under escort," I said. "The Japa-
> nese must consider them more dangerous than the diplo-
> mats - there were four soldiers with fixed bayonets guard-
> ing them, and a couple of plain-clothes detectives as well."
>
> "That's a different matter," he said, a smile wrinkling
> his kindly face. "When those professors and doctors come
> into the room it clears like magic. Unsheathed bayonets
> have their special effect, I find. I get down to my work
> without saying a word more than necessary, for the soldiers
> are as suspicious as good watch-dogs. But each time I do

as little as possible. Those prisoners haven't large gardens like the diplomats in which to exercise, and I reckon it does them the power of good to get out in the fresh air as often as possible."[21]

Prentice may have been referring here to several senior foreign doctors of the PUMC, who for some unfathomable reason were selected for strict house-arrest, their enormous and well-equipped hospital having been taken over by the Japanese.[22]

Soon after her visit to Prentice, Hope Danby left China on an early repatriation ship. A few months later, in October 1942, Chief Inspector Richard Dennis similarly left China, traveling as chance would have it on the same repatriation ship, the *SS Narkunda*, as George Gorman. Dennis had endured months of Japanese captivity in a small cage, and described this in a typed statement while sailing back to the UK. His evidence was later used at the United Nations war-crime trials, supporting charges of unlawful arrest, false imprisonment, ill-treatment and starvation by the Japanese.

Dennis described how, on the May 4, 1942, he was summoned to the office of the Japanese officer in control of the seized British Concession in Tientsin. Once there, "he told me that I was required at the Japanese Gendarmerie Headquarters in the Japanese Concession for questioning. I had no illusions as to what this foreboded."[23]

Dennis spoke little or no Japanese and the interpreter had a poor grasp of English, but it was made evident to Dennis that his offence had been reporting Japanese military activity to the British authorities. Guessing which incident this referred to years

21 Hope Danby, *My Boy Chang*, (1955), p184.
22 ibid., p169.
23 UK National Archives, TS 26/806 Tientsin and Peking: false imprisonment: R H Dennis.

before, Dennis asked his captor when it was that Japanese military law had come into force in Tientsin. In July 1937, came the answer, the date of the Marco Polo Bridge incident and the start of the Sino-Japanese War. Dennis pointed out that British subjects were not subject to any such law until December 8, 1941. His protest was met with silence.

At the time, the Foreign Office in Whitehall found it difficult to judge the seriousness of the situation in the wake of the Marco Polo Bridge incident. Was it a skirmish, or would it develop into something larger? The answer proved to be the latter, but in the meantime intelligence was requested from Tientsin, a city through which Japanese troops would travel if the fighting escalated. The Foreign Office approached Tientsin's British Municipal Council for help. Dennis was assigned the job. The Japanese interrogators produced official reports written by Dennis bearing dates from July 4, 1937 to the middle of August 1937, addressed to the British Garrison in Tientsin. On his release from custody, where he spent ninety-four days in a wooden cage, Dennis was unsurprisingly in poor health and had lost thirty-four pounds in weight.[24] Dennis' career in the Far East was effectively over.

Though repatriation ships had begun sailing, they were too few and far between. In 1942 approximately 14,000 Allied nationals remained in Japanese-occupied China,[25] the majority in Shanghai or Hong Kong. Some were merchants or workers caught out by world events; others were embassy and consular staff required to remain at their posts. There were missionaries and hospital staff and others, like Werner, Knauf, Prentice and Backhouse, for whom China was home. Some families had been there for several generations. Hope Danby recalled that one old-school British national refused to leave Peking even after being

24 ibid.
25 Greg Leck, *Captives of Empire* (2006).

offered a place on the same ship as her. He was near sixty, he pointed out to her, and had nothing in England and no chance of finding work there. If he left China he would lose everything he had strived for during the previous forty years.[26] The man's feelings were quite understandable, but it was a forlorn position to hold.

26 Hope Danby, *My Boy Chang* (1955), p214.

14

CAPTIVITY

SAINTS AND SINNERS

IN EARLY 1943 the Japanese began to round-up and intern all foreign enemy civilians in occupied China. British, American, Dutch and Belgian nationals were to be concentrated into over a dozen of what the Japanese euphemistically called "civilian assembly centres" scattered across China. The stated aim was "not only to forestall espionage activities but also to stabilize the living of enemy aliens."[1] It may in part have been a response to the wholesale internment of Japanese persons in the United States.

Foreigners in Peking and Tientsin were transported 600 kilometres south in crowded trains to a large former American Presbyterian missionary compound three miles outside the town of Weihsien in the province of Shandong.[2] A few exceptions were made for poor health with some elderly British and American subjects permitted to remain at the Embassy. Backhouse was one such lucky soul. For the rest, there was no chance of escaping the round-up in a country where Caucasians were instantly recognizable.

....

1 *Peking Chronicle*, article dated to March 1943.
2 E.T.C. Werner, *More Memorigrams*, (1948), page i.

Over several days in late March 1943, by order of local Japanese commanders, the men, women and children arrived as ordered at Peking railway station, bringing only what they wore or could carry. Among their number were Werner, Prentice and Knauf who were soon to be confined together in a camp 200 yards by 150 yards surrounded by barbed wire, an electrified fence and machine guns.

For most of the 1,800 internees, Weihsien camp, or to use the mission's Chinese name, "Courtyard of the Happy Way", was their cramped home for the next two and half years, up to and beyond Japan's defeat in August 1945.

Compared with some other internment camps in China, the inmates at Weihsien inherited a relatively sound camp structure. The mission huts and other buildings, built fifty years before, though largely basic in construction, were at least serviceable. The Japanese had cordoned off the best accommodation, the mission staff housing, for their own use. The remainder consisted of blocks of classrooms over several storeys, a church, a hospital, a bakery, a few kitchens and rows of huts containing what used to be living quarters for students. It had all suffered considerable neglect since the mission's enforced closure, particularly the hospital which had been stripped of valuable equipment by the Japanese. The overflowing toilets were at once identified as a health hazard, as was the inadequate water supply. The mission's trees and gardens improved the general atmosphere but there was a great deal of work to be done to make the camp habitable.[3]

That there were so few deaths and relatively little disease at Weihsien camp during its existence was testament to the spirit, industry and organizational skills of the people interned there. Thrown together by circumstance, they comprised a disparate

---

3 Langdon Gilkey, *Shantung Compound* (1966), p146.

group of individuals from nearly every walk of life, including missionaries, teachers, police officers, artists, writers, doctors, clergy, engineers, merchants, and businessmen.

It was often said in China, however, that there were only two distinct groups of foreigners: the Christian missionaries, and everyone else. Thus there were two contrasting mindsets often separated by a gulf of misunderstanding that sometimes led to downright hostility. One young Christian internee at Weihsien, disappointed by the poor behavior of a good many of his fellow Protestant missionaries, later wrote of his time there, quoting from the *Threepenny Opera:* "For even saintly folk will act like sinners; unless they have their customary dinners".[4] Despite such tensions and petty arguments, overall the Weihsien camp internees achieved a remarkable feat in holding their community together.

Although subject to rules and whims of a Japanese commander and a handful of police staff, the camp was in effect run by the internees themselves. The Japanese required the formation of committees with chairmen elected by the internees to preside over each of the nine chief concerns: food supplies, education, engineering, quarters, finance, employment, medical, discipline and general affairs. To their great credit the inmates made the camp administration work both efficiently and for the benefit of all. Each person had their own task according to their skills. Privations were in the main part shared and everyone, with few exceptions, pulled their weight.

Within a few months of the camp's opening, the Swiss Consul from Tientsin paid a visit of inspection. He reported on the overcrowding which had families squeezed into small rooms intended only for single students, with the other internees sleeping

....

4   ibid., p111.

Blocks 24 (left) and 23 (right), where Werner and Prentice possessed beds respectively; a photograph of Weihsien camp taken before the war

in one of the nine dormitory buildings, each having space enough for a bed, but little else. Electric lighting was inadequate, ventilation was poor, and stove heaters carried a risk of asphyxiation. There were queues to use the primitive toilets, the waste from which fed into cesspools with no overflow mechanism. The limited water supply, manually pumped from wells, was sited in close proximity to the cesspools. All drinking water had to boiled and the supply was so limited that internees were rationed to one cold shower every five days. Above all, there was a shortage of such basic provisions as food and medical supplies.[5]

One role was easily filled by the medical committee: Wentworth Prentice, the only dentist in the camp, was allocated that position having had the foresight to bring with him all the equipment he could carry from his practice in Peking. Luckily, a dentist chair was found discarded amongst the camp's debris,[6] and so equipped, Prentice and a young male Greek dental technician[7]

5   UK National Archives, FO 916/1036 British subjects in China - internment; June 1943.
6   Langdon Gilkey, *Shantung Compound* (1966), p13.
7   a) Greg Leck, *Captives of Empire* (2006), & b) Weihsien camp list, compiled Ron Bridge.

Eric Liddell (Eric Liddell Centre)

were able to ensure that at least the basic treatment of fillings and extractions was possible. Thus, even in captivity, dentistry remained central to Prentice's life. His other important role in camp life was to play second violin in the camp's symphony orchestra,[8] just one of the many forms of entertainment organized by the captives.

In his later years at the camp, Prentice was allocated a bed in block twenty-three, the largest, most architecturally impressive of the camp's buildings, complete with central bell-tower and balconies.[9] Here, he shared a cramped dormitory room with a dozen or so other single men. Chalk lines marked out individual's personal space around beds. Privacy at Weihsien was almost non-existent.

Another occupant of Block 23 dormitory was the Olympic medal-winner and Christian missionary, Eric Liddell, a hugely popular and inspiring man. Liddell, or "Uncle Eric" as he was known to the young children, somehow found time and a kind word for everyone, both Christian and non-believer alike. One fellow internee later described Liddell as the finest Christian gentleman he had ever met.[10] Another wrote that it was a rare thing indeed to meet a saint, but that Liddell was as close to one as anyone he had known. When Liddell, aged 43, died suddenly of a brain tumour in February 1945, five months before liberation, the latter witness recalled how the whole camp was stunned and

....

8 Interview and camp pamphlet provided by Peter Bazire, July 2013.
9 Weihsien camp list, compiled by Ron Bridge.
10 Norman Cliff, *Courtyard of the Happy Way* (1977)

felt an emptiness resulting from his loss.[11]

Liddell had close links with Pamela Werner. By 1937, he had married Florence Mackenzie, the eldest daughter of Hugh and Agnes Mackenzie of Tientsin, with whom Pamela lodged the year prior to her death. Liddell and Pamela would have met at the many Mackenzie family gatherings.[12] Later, the unfortunate Liddell entered Weihsien camp alone: prior to Pearl Harbour, Liddell's pregnant wife and their two young daughters had prudently left China for Canada and as luck had it, Hugh and Agnes Mackenzie, along with the rest of their children, had been on furlough in Canada and thus also avoided internment.[13]

Werner, who was not a fan of religion, shared a small room in Weihsien's Block 24 with another elderly gentleman, and yet another missionary, an American about the same age as himself.[14] Accustomed to privacy, Werner predictably loathed his years at Weihsien, describing the experience as:

> ... a life of socialism, threatening to develop into communism, deprived of liberty, almost of individuality. Each internee was a working ant... It was not a voluntary association of kinsmen for their mutual benefit, such as are the village communities which precede and later form the constituent elements of the city-state. To a lifelong confirmed individualist this was repugnant and harmful, the poor quality of the food, association of people not at all congenial, the monotony, lack of communication with the outside world, etc., acting deleteriously.[15]

11 Langdon Gilkey, Shantung Compound (1966) p192.
12 Interviews with Louise McLean & Findlay Mackenzie, 2014.
13 Tribute to Hugh Mackenzie by Union Church Tientsin, January 15, 1944 (Mackenzie family document).
14 Weihsien camp list, compiled by Ron Bridge.
15 E.T.C. Werner, More Memorigrams (1948), p1.

Another resident in Block 24 was Desmond Power, a young man of twenty on arrival at the camp. Born and raised in Tientsin, Power had been a pupil at the Tientsin Grammar School and, although several years younger than Pamela Werner, he had been on a nodding acquaintance with her, recalling her as being quiet and shy. During his time at the school, Power had heard that Pamela's father was regarded as a gentleman and a sinologue. Newly arrived at the camp, however, Power's half-brother warned him not to worry about "old man Werner going around accusing this and that person of murdering his daughter." Power soon got to notice Werner: "Someone pointed him out to me in the block's roll-call line saying that he was a pitiful case, at times pointing an accusing finger at people in the camp saying: 'You did it!' Most internees felt as I did that the poor fellow was unable to escape from his personal grief."[16]

Power did not register at whom Werner pointed his accusing finger, but there can be little doubt that Prentice and Knauf were his targets.[17]

Fred Knauf, unlike the majority of the internees, spent only six months at Weihsien. He initially shared one of the small hut-like rooms with Prentice. As the first arrivals at the prison camp, before the housing committee decided such details, the internees simply chose their own rooms and roommates, thus confirming that the two men were at least reasonably acquainted with one another. Like all the student rooms, Prentice and Knauf's room was tiny, only nine feet by twelve feet, but such was the overcrowding in the camp that not two but three men were required to share this space. Going by the description, which according to a camp housing officer was that of a "wan and paper-thin dope addict", the room's third occupant appears to have been Knauf's

16 Correspondence with Desmond Power, 2013.
17 P.D. Coates, *The China Consuls* (1988) p441.

associate and fellow former US Marine, David Laughlin.[18] For all his cosiness with the Japanese, Laughlin had not won any better treatment than any other foreigner.

"Straight, strong and sour," was how the same observant housing officer remembered Knauf, who seemed never once to smile. He thought Knauf's attitude to life was negative, unhappy and self-destructive.[19] Perhaps this was the case, but some allowance has to be made for the trying situation in which Knauf found himself; one of incarceration, and in close proximity to Werner.

Knauf left in September 1943 in the first and only group of Weihsien Americans selected for repatriation,[20] but Prentice and Laughlin remained. Why the Japanese permitted a known US Marine reservist to escape their custody is a mystery. Although Knauf was by this time fifty years of age, he nonetheless possessed a good deal of military intelligence and familiarity with north China that the US armed services may have found useful. Perhaps his release was simply a Japanese oversight.

Constantly hungry at Weihsien, Knauf found the long journey to freedom even worse. He and the other selected internees were loaded onto rail cars with pigs for company for the three-day train ride to Shanghai. Sabotage to the rail line by Chinese guerrillas caused long delays. There was little food and even less water, to the extent that Knauf wondered if they might die of thirst. In Shanghai, Knauf and the others boarded the *Teia Maru*, a former French ocean liner appropriated by the Japanese. Approximately fifteen hundred Americans and Canadians were crammed onto a ship that Knauf judged only possessed capacity for six hundred. Knauf described it as "a mad house."[21]

....

18 Langdon Gilkey, *Shantung Compound* (1966) p23.
19 ibid., p2.
20 *Mosinee Times;* articles featuring letters from Knauf to his sister, October 28,1943, May 5, 1944, March 1, 1944.
21 ibid.

A full month later, after stops at Hong Kong and Singapore where more internees were packed onto the already overcrowded ship, the *Teia Maru* reached Goa in India, where it was met by the International Red Cross exchange ship, *Gripsholm*, chartered by the US Department of State. The two ships were moored side by side, and the Japanese and Allied nationals stepped across two gangways simultaneously at opposing bow and stern ends, a screen preventing them from viewing one another.[22] The exchange took about an hour, and Knauf and his compatriots found themselves free.[23]

Sailing via South Africa and Brazil, the *Gripsholm* reached New York in early December. Back in Knauf's hometown of Mosinee, Wisconsin, the town newspaper had been covering news of their local boy's release since October. Fred had not been "home" since 1924, and the only photograph available was decades-old, with a young Knauf in his blue full-dress uniform. Knauf's brothers and sisters in Mosinee had been provided with confusing accounts of his whereabouts for the previous two years, including the erroneous information that he was a prisoner in the Philippines.[24] Finally, they could expect him back by Christmas, but Knauf disappointed them. He wrote explaining that he was taking some rest in Washington D.C., but he was healthy and felt as good as he had aged twenty. As for a return to Mosinee or a long term future in the US, he had other plans: "It's too expensive in this country... I will never be satisfied here and I am going back to the Orient the first chance I get."[25]

Meanwhile back in Peking, unlike the majority of his compatriots, Backhouse was spared the rigors of Weihsien camp. Age

22 Kokansen website, Bob Hackett and Sander Kingsepp; Stories of Diplomatic Exchange and Repatriation Ships.
23 *Mosinee Times*; articles featuring letters from Knauf to his sister, October 20, 1943, May 5, 1944, March 1, 1944.
24 ibid.
25 ibid.

sixty-nine in March 1943, he was nearly ten years younger than Werner, but physically frail. Having abandoned his home and most of his belongings in the city, Backhouse had been residing for several years in the British Embassy compound, where he occupied one room in a small house shared for part of this period with Werner. The accommodation suited Backhouse well. The war also brought Backhouse a congenial new associate, the Swiss Consul, Doctor Reinhard Hoeppli, who latterly inspired Backhouse to compose his last literary project.[26]

Doctor Hoeppli, a bachelor in his late forties, had been Professor of Parasitology at the PUMC since 1930 and possessed no prior consular or diplomatic experience. Following the medical centre's appropriation by the Japanese in 1942, Hoeppli was made an honorary consul by Switzerland and given the interests of American, British, and Dutch nationals to protect as best he could.

Hoeppli fulfilled his new role enthusiastically. During his visits he met Backhouse, who by then had developed a venerable aspect with his long white beard. Dressed in ankle-length native gowns with a black Chinese hat, Backhouse shuffled along, slow on his feet, and wore a rosary as a necklace. He had recently become a Roman Catholic, adopting, in the style of the convert, the name of Paul Backhouse, in which fashion he signed documents. He had not lost his ability to charm, and Hoeppli was another to fall under the spell of his gentle manner and courtesy, beguiled by his knowledge of society, lively intelligence and wide breadth of conversation. He also took a delight in Backhouse's taste for good food, which, despite his apparent poverty, involved the partaking of out-of-season strawberries and asparagus, along

---

26 Postscript by Reinhard Hoeppli to *Decadence Mandchoue, the China memoirs of Sir Edmund Backhouse,* February 1946.

Backhouse in his last years,
the Catholic convert

with fine wines from Bordeaux and Burgundy.[27]

Hoeppli became very fond of his new friend, and encouraged Backhouse to talk of his life and experiences. But Hoeppli was never entirely taken in by him. He recognised that Backhouse's late conversion to religion in 1942 was in part motivated by a fear of approaching death, and partly to a cynical hope that the Church may provide him with money and a home should Britain not do so. Referring to the sacraments, Backhouse remarked that "if they don't help, they will at least do no harm."[28]

Hoeppli was aware of rumors concerning Backhouse's past, including the questionable veracity of the famous court diary which had given rise to Bland and Backhouse's literary sensation decades earlier. Backhouse, Hoeppli realised, was sensitive to criticism, and it was a measure of the two men's closeness that he was able to raise the subject of the diary with him. The result was that Backhouse declared that he had found the diary as he translated it and had acted in good faith. Asked whether in light of recent research he still regarded the diary as genuine, he answered that "I did not falsify it," and did not commit himself.[29]

Hoeppli appeared to be willing to accept Backhouse's word on the subject, or at least push no further, perhaps wishing that such tales were indeed true. Hoeppli expressed his reserved judgement a few years later:

....

27 ibid.
28 ibid.
29 ibid.

> There can be no doubt that nature had given Sir Edmund
> not only a prodigious memory but also an extraordinary
> power of imagination. This last made his stories particu-
> larly vivid and fascinating, but obviously represented to a
> certain extent a danger to their truthfulness.[30]

Hoeppli's sympathetic attitude toward Backhouse was perhaps related to the fact the he had no comparative versions of the events described to him by Backhouse.

One of Backhouse and Hoeppli's conversations was in relation to the murder of Pamela Werner. Although he recorded none of the names involved in the discussion, Hoeppli described Backhouse telling him of his inside knowledge of a famous recent Peking murder. There can be little doubt it was the case of Pamela Werner. Having written to the British Embassy in 1938 revealing that he knew the Japanese were the perpetrators, Backhouse then told Werner, a few years later, that he too had investigated the case and had found that Werner had correctly identified the suspects. Backhouse had a third version for Hoeppli:

> ... Sir Edmund not only explained it (the murder) in detail
> as a case of mistaken identity, but gave the name of the
> culprits, their subsequent fate and death, the source of his
> information and also the reason why at that time the pros-
> ecution had to be stopped.[31]

This "mistaken identity" version may have been a variation of the revenge theory Backhouse supplied to the Embassy, but if it was, Backhouse fails to explain his new assertion that case "had

30 ibid.
31 ibid.

to be stopped." It is also unlikely that Backhouse would, during this delicate period of house arrest, have risked implicating the Japanese again. Hoeppli noted how careful Backhouse was to avoid upsetting the occupying forces, so much so that he spent a good deal of time praising both the Japanese and their allies, the Germans, whilst at the same time bitterly criticizing the British, despite Backhouse receiving the largesse of British relief funds while housed in the British Embassy compound.[32]

Whoever Backhouse provided as suspects in his account of the murder to Hoeppli, he appears over time to have created three separate versions of the Werner murder for three separate recipients.

Hoeppli heard so many engaging stories and anecdotes from Backhouse, that he suggested the old man write them down to preserve them. He further agreed to pay Backhouse out of his own pocket for his time and labour. The latter readily acquiesced. Saying that he had lost his personal notes and diaries when fleeing his home in 1939, Backhouse relied purely on his prodigious memory as he sat on his verandah and wrote page after page in his thin spidery longhand.

Two manuscripts of memoirs were written between December 1942 and the following June: *Decadence Mandchoue* and *the Dead Past*. The first of these works described his early decades in China, and the second, his childhood and youth in Europe. In both works Backhouse talks of politics, history and culture, lacing the engaging narrative with elaborate details of sexual affairs between himself and myriad figures, of both sexes, including a former prime minister, Oscar Wilde, and even the elderly Empress Dowager Tzu-hsi, for whom, Backhouse claimed, he was an amusing foreign sexual plaything.

....

32 UK National Archives, FO 369/3429 Will of Sir Edmund T. Backhouse. Code 210 file 2818.

The manuscripts relate stories concerning many artists, scholars and literary figures, most of whom were safely dead. His memoirs gave ample opportunity to display his erudite prose with their frequent quotes and discourses in many different languages, with hundreds written in Chinese script. Backhouse also found opportunities to slight former colleagues. Though unnamed, he described the *Times* correspondent George Morrison, who died in 1920, as "inquisitious" and "perfidious".[33]

Bland, meanwhile, again unnamed but identified as his co-author of *China Under the Empress Dowager,* was a "detestable personality" and *la lie du peuple,*[34] which translates roughly as "the dregs of society."

Backhouse finished the memoirs just before his health deteriorated. In the summer of 1943 he entered the French Saint Michael's Hospital where he died, probably from a stroke, on the January 8, 1944. Within a few hours of his death, an unnamed young Chinese called at Hoeppli's office asking after the Will and whether he knew of a large diamond Backhouse had promised to bequeath to him. Hoeppli had to disappoint the young man; at the end, Backhouse possessed virtually nothing to leave to anyone.[35]

Two days later, after a funeral service at Peking's Saint Joseph's Church, Backhouse was buried in a Catholic cemetery among the graves of a number of notable missionary Jesuits. It is not known who attended, but it is most likely that Hoeppli was there, and perhaps Backhouse's alcoholic Chinese servant, a loyal man according to the Swiss doctor, who in a peculiar relationship played the dominant role over his employer.

Soon after Backhouse's death, Hoeppli had the original mem-

---

33 *Decadence Mandchoue, The China Memoirs of Sir Edmund Trelawny Backhouse,* chapter II.
34 ibid.
35 UK National Archives, FO 369/3429 Will of Sir Edmund T. Backhouse. Code 210 file 2818.

oirs typed into four copies by his Chinese secretary and all copies remained in Hoeppli's sole possession for almost three decades. A postscript was added to the manuscripts by Hoeppli in 1946, explaining how he met Backhouse and the events surrounding their creation. Backhouse's instructions, Hoeppli noted, had been that both works would be eventually published, but until that unspecified time, Hoeppli must not share them with anyone. To respect Backhouse's dying wishes, and the sensibilities of the reading public, Hoeppli did nothing with the memoirs except take them back to Switzerland and give directions that on his death the four copies were to be distributed to the British Museum, the Bodleian Library, the Bibliotheque Nationale, and Harvard College Library.[36]

Hoeppli died in February 1973. Only then were the memoirs made available for study as Hoeppli intended. The Bodleian Library asked the Oxford University historian Hugh Trevor-Roper to take delivery of its copies and make an assessment of them on its behalf. This Trevor-Roper did, resulting in his book, *Hermit of Peking*.

What is to be made of Backhouse's last great project? His revelations of relentless sexual activity with the rich, the famous and the notorious, including no less than the Empress Dowager; what veracity can be attached to any of it? Is it credible that Backhouse as an active homosexual secretly cavorted in all-night sessions with the Empress, who was by then in her late sixties? (Backhouse attributed his ability to meet her requirements to the court-supplied aphrodisiacs).

If one considers Backhouse's memoirs in isolation from his now-established frauds, it is perhaps possible to concede that the *essence* of his sociosexual lifestyle among the great and the good

....

36 Postscript by Reinhard Hoeppli to *Decadence Mandchoue, the China memoirs of Sir Edmund Backhouse*, February 1946.

may contain a degree of accuracy. But it is also possible, and more probable, that it rather reflects the life Backhouse *wished* he had led.

15

The End of An Era

Liberation

On August 15, 1945 Emperor Hirohito announced his country's acceptance of the Potsdam Declaration: the war in the Far East and the Pacific was over. The announcement took many Japanese by surprise. Despite the dropping of atomic bombs on Hiroshima and Nagasaki, they had expected the Empire to fight on. Regardless of the surrender, huge areas of the Far East, including much of China, continued to be occupied by Japanese troops, and would remain so for some time.

In the lead-up to Japan's surrender, the Weihsien internees weren't sure what to believe. The propaganda and talk had been only of Japanese victories, but the rumors and hints in the newspapers suggested otherwise. Food supplies worsened and the camp guards started to get drunk and fight with each other.

One sagacious American was heard to quip: "We are in a race against time. The longer it takes the the warring Japanese to come to terms with the warring Allies, the more certain our chances of running afoul of the warring guards. And there's not a damned

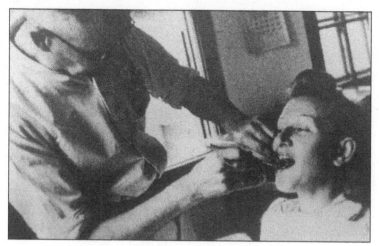

Wentworth Prentice in the Weihsien camp

thing we can do about it except sit tight and hope for the best."[1]

One day that August, it was the turn of the young inmate Desmond Power to sit in Wentworth Prentice's camp dentist chair. The air had been thick with rumors of a Japanese surrender. The check-up went smoothly and ended with an astonishing revelation. Out of the blue, Prentice shook the young man's hand and said the war was over and that they would be freed in a few hours. How Prentice discovered this is not known, but it was indeed the day Japan surrendered. At last, the rumors became reality.[2]

Freedom was not instantaneous. It arrived several days later, heralded by the deafening sound of low-flying aircraft which brought the internees rushing out of their huts, unsure if they were to be bombed or rescued. The aircraft was American and an advance party of seven Office of Strategic Service (OSS) team members parachuted into a nearby field. The excited captives charged past Japanese guards at the camp gate to greet their lib-

---

1 Desmond Power, *Little Foreign Devil* (1996), p212.
2 Correspondence with Desmond Power, 2013.

erators and carry them shoulder-high back into the compound.[3]

August became September, and with the Japanese no longer a threat, the Chinese nationalists and communists immediately resumed fighting one another. By day, the peasant farmers could be seen harvesting, but by night shelling and small arms fire were heard close by. Lines of communication simply weren't safe and the American forces commander had the unpopular task of delaying the internees' departure from the camp. To the grateful relief of the Weihsien inmates, supplies of food and clothing were parachuted into the adjacent fields which led to a race to beat the local Chinese to the crates. Conflict was inevitable, and had to be managed via interpreters, such as Desmond Power. On one such drop of stores an irate American serviceman ordered the farmers to get their thieving hands off the goods. The Chinese obeyed, but only after one replied with some eloquence:

> Tell the soldier of the foreign invasion country that this is our land, not his. Tell him that for the last three years the Eastern Ocean Devils confiscated our seed grain to feed you Western Ocean Devils. Tell him that in sustaining you, we were brought to ruin.[4]

Rail lines and bridges had been damaged by the Chinese fighting and so, finally, in October the Americans flew the Weihsien internees to Peking and Tientsin, much to the excitement of those who had never travelled by plane. Thus it was that after an absence of two and half years, Werner and Prentice returned to Peking.

A week or two earlier, a British Major-General had reported on conditions in north China:

....

3 Desmond Power, *Little Foreign Devil* (1996), p218.
4 Ibid., p225.

Peking like Tientsin is quite undamaged and on the surface
well run under Japanese control... The monuments and the
places of historic importance in the city are still intact and
in fact well looked after. I was able to pay hasty visits to
the Temple of Heaven and the Forbidden City with both of
which I was duly impressed. From a more practical point
of view the Peking Club has been rescued virtually intact
together with its funds from the Japanese and is now func-
tioning normally... The Embassy is in good order and has
been well looked after by the resident engineer who has not
been unduly interfered with by the Japanese. The Chancery
records were apparently all removed but a small proportion
have now been returned and it may be that the remainder
will follow... From the outside all seems normal. I had the
pleasure of hoisting the Union Jack again over the main
gate to the delight of the internees inside the compound
and to the surprise I thought of a considerable number of
Japanese soldiers looking on from outside.[5]

The chancery office was probably where the Embassy kept records relating to Pamela Werner's murder. It is not clear what
constituted the "small proportion" of records returned, nor if
any of "the remainder" did indeed follow. Also unknown are the
quantity and nature of materials destroyed by the Embassy staff
before being repatriated in 1942. In any event, no official records
concerning Pamela Werner appear to have made it to London.

The visiting British Major-General went on to write that he
thought the American armed services' large presence in North
China had a stabilizing effect which could afford Chiang Kai-

---

5   UK National Archives, FO 916/1333 British subjects in China - internment. Report of
    October 18, 1945.

shek's government the chance to get a grip on that part of the country, and even Werner found nice words to say about the US armed forces, expressing his gratitude to the Colonel in command of the camp for his "gallant comrades' kindness and friendship, as well as that of the overwhelming generosity of the great American nation"[6] in liberating and evacuating them from Weihsien. Praise indeed from a man who did not give it lightly.

Unlike the Allied soldiers who were soon to leave for home, many of the newly-liberated British internees had less to celebrate. For most, there would be little or no opportunity to pick up the threads of their previous lives in China. In 1943, during the height of the War, the British and American Governments relinquished the rights to extraterritorial jurisdiction. At a stroke, the Chinese treaty ports with their "unequal treaties," along with the enclaves and concessions of the previous one hundred years, were ended. Hong Kong remained British as the island had been transferred to British sovereignty in perpetuity, but the remaining treaty ports such as Tientsin, Amoy, Foochow, Canton and most importantly, the enormous international settlement in Shanghai were all returned to the Chinese. Even Peking was affected, with the foreign embassies losing control of the Legation Quarter.

After their release, many internees returned to find their old homes had been looted, and the infrastructure their businesses relied upon had disappeared. Many British traders felt betrayed. They claimed the Government had specifically asked them to stay behind during the Sino-Japanese War to protect British interests, which led to their incarceration and subsequent loss of all their assets.[7] Sympathy from the Chinese side, however, was in short supply.

....

6 E.T.C. Werner, *More Memorigrams* (1948), page i.
7 Desmond Power, *Little Foreign Devil* (1996), p242.

While most of his American compatriots went home, Prentice stayed in Peking to reopen his dental practice at 3 Legation Street, where, remarkably, his furnishings and equipment had somehow been preserved.[8] After nearly thirty years in China, the last twenty of it living alone, it was the only way of life Prentice knew.

He had not long returned to Peking when officers from the OSS, the forerunner of the CIA, paid him a visit. They wanted to know what Prentice knew of David Laughlin. They were aware that Laughlin had been close to the Japanese back in 1941, not that it did him much good since he was interned until the war's end along with everyone else. They were also aware of the rumor that Laughlin was a drug addict. Prentice couldn't confirm this allegation.[9] What action the OSS decided upon is unclear, but Laughlin eventually returned to the US, where he died in 1982.[10]

Release from internment meant Werner was once again free to pursue justice for his murdered daughter Pamela. He was now in his eighties and had made plans to return to England, but before leaving he endeavored to secure the assistance of Major-General Chang Hsu-liang of the Nationalist Government, the new Chinese Minister for Foreign Affairs, in pursuing justice against his two prime suspects, Prentice and Cappuzzo. The Major-General listened politely to Werner before expressing "his willingness that the two accused men should be tried in his court" and requested that Werner supply him with the evidence.[11] Nevertheless, the Chinese Foreign Minister appears to have done nothing to follow this offer up.

By this time, Werner had reduced his list of suspects to in-

8 US National Archives, death of American citizen abroad, 393.113 Prentice, Wentworth Baldwin.
9 US National Archives, OSS report no. YKX YPX/694 of November 16, 1945 and report No. YKX YPX/140 of 17 November 1945.
10 National Cemetery Administration, US Veterans Gravesites, 1775-2006.
11 *More Memorigrams*, E.T.C. Werner, Edwin Snell & Sons (1948), p208.

clude just Prentice and Cappuzzo. Knauf and Pinfold were omitted entirely, as was Han, the Chinese investigating officer whom Werner had criticised so roundly in the past for being both corrupt and a "sexualist" in league with the murderers. Being mindful of giving offence to the Minister by accusing a fellow Chinese may have been behind Werner's restraint, but it does not explain his radical *volte face* in simply dropping suspects he had long considered guilty.[12]

By his own admission, Werner's documentary "evidence" consisted only of the twenty-three reports he had written and mailed to the Foreign Office before his internment. Clearly, this means that his "evidence" lacked witness statements and comprised only his strongly-held opinions. Not that he appeared to have seen the weakness in this. On the contrary, he remained bullish on the matter. Having no copies of his earlier reports, Werner enlisted the help of a young Acting Consul for Peking, John Boyce, a recent arrival, who had the job of serving British interests amid the post-war chaos and who could possibly have done without the demands of Werner to retrieve letters posted to London years before.[13]

Werner recorded these post-war events, adding them to the manuscript of his final book, More Memorigrams, a 1948 volume, in which he claimed that, a decade after the murder, he was now in the possession of "the note written on his office note-paper by (blank) to Pamela asking her to come to his flat… and… the small case of surgical instruments bearing (blank)'s embossed initials and blood-stained thumbmark."[14] The book's publisher almost certainly insisted on the suspects' names being omitted to avoid potential libel, hence the blanks.

....

12 ibid., p204.
13 ibid., p205.
14 ibid., p208.

True to past form, Werner made no reference to the current location of these new objects. Nor did he give any explanation as to where such incriminating exhibits had been hiding since 1937. In reality, they were almost certainly a figment of Werner's imagination, though it is possible that one of his Chinese agents had manufactured them in order to please him.

Back in Peking from Weihsien, it was almost inevitable that Werner would sooner or later come into conflict with those around him. He had taken up temporary residence in a Chinese college, and from there went to the Embassy to retrieve some of his property kept in storage in its stables since the outbreak of war. Remarkably, the Japanese had left the Embassy's collection of miscellaneous property largely unmolested. But to Werner's anger he found that his black stove had gone missing. He complained and made it known that the stolen stove was identical to the one now in the possession of an embassy staff member. There was a good measure of upset. Realizing, or being made to realize, that he had made an insinuation too far, Werner was forced to write as retraction of his suggestion of dishonesty. Describing himself "a man of peace," he added:

> I write this because long experience shows that absence of reply is interpreted as inability to reply - saying nothing is understood as having nothing to say. Hence misrepresentation and injustice. P.S. - I did not die at Weihsien.[15]

This last comment was perhaps addressing a local rumor. Much of the property stored in the stables belonged to the Embassy staff themselves, but as well as Werner's numerous possessions there were three meagre items belonging to the elusive Mr Pin-

---

15 UK National Archives, FO 562/14 Movable personal property stored in British Embassy Stables, Peking.

fold: a rattan suitcase full of clothing, a Japanese basket with cooking utensils, and a leather trunk containing papers, scrolls, books and some empty boxes. All of these items remained un-collected long after the war.[16] Fred Pinfold was not recorded as having entered any of the Japanese internment camps and there is no trace of his leaving China or arriving elsewhere. Given his age and low social status, it is possible that he died somewhere in China during the war, possibly anonymously, and possibly in the same manner in which he had long lived – alone.

Werner returned to Britain in late 1946, to a war-torn London beset with rationing and austerity. He immediately began demanding that the Foreign Office take further action on his daughter's murder.[17] By 1947, it might reasonably have been expected that Werner's quest was over, for an associate back in China wrote to the old man with news: Wentworth Prentice had died.

Prentice had been working in his Legation Street dental prac-tice on the afternoon of Tuesday, July 1, 1947 when he suddenly collapsed having suffered a large heart attack. A doctor was sum-moned to the flat but to no avail: Prentice was pronounced dead at the scene. He was only fifty-three.[18]

With Prentice's next of kin far off in the United States, it was left to the American Consulate staff to attend to affairs and des-patch telegrams to Washington. Prentice's body was taken to the Hopkins Memorial Hospital, the same hospital where he had begun work as a young missionary-dentist nearly thirty years before. A Western-style pinewood coffin was purchased and a burial arranged at the city's British cemetery – the same cem-

16 ibid.
17 E.T.C. Werner, *More Memorigrams* (1948), p206.
18 US National Archives, death of American citizen abroad, 393.113 Prentice, Wentworth Baldwin.

etery where Pamela Werner had been buried ten years before.[19]

The United States is far better at the retention of its state records than the United Kingdom, and its archives often preserve in minutiae the letters, telegrams, inventories and statements of account relating to the death of a US citizen abroad. In the case of Prentice, they help provide an insight into the man. He died intestate. In the comprehensive inventory of his belongings are listed his clothes, his shoes, his furniture, and even the contents of his kitchen cupboards. The numerous ashtrays itemized suggests that like most men of that time he was smoker, which may well have contributed to his early demise. There was no mention of his violin, but a portfolio of drawings and a collection of sixteen oil paintings were reported along with a radio phonograph and one hundred vinyl records — a not insubstantial music collection for the period. A protective tube contained his diploma. There was no mention of a bible, but a small collection of novels was noted including the semi-religious, semi-science-fiction *Star of the Unborn*, written by a Jewish author with Catholic sympathies. Lighter reading was represented by a copy of the fiction magazine *Weird Tales*. He also had copies of *TIME* and *Life* magazines, but they may have simply been reading matter for the practice waiting room.[20]

The consular staff saw to it that the various outstanding bills and accounts were settled, including money owed to Prentice by patients. One account was with an elderly missionary woman, for whom Prentice held a special "Weihsien Contract" — he providing her with a generous discount for having been interned at the camp with him.[21]

Approached by the Consulate, the head of the American

19 ibid.
20 ibid.
21 ibid.

Methodist mission in Peking agreed to act as Prentice's attorney, owing to the fact that Prentice had, as a consulate staff member put it, "during his lifetime [taken] a particular interest in the Methodist Mission here."[22]

Notably, the Consulate in Peking went to the trouble of sending Prentice's family a clipping from the local English language newspaper, probably *The Peiping Chronicle* (the article from the once-again renamed newspaper is unfortunately lost). The writer explained how "this tribute by one of his oldest and most prominent Chinese friends was felt to be an accurate expression of the general feeling among residents of Peiping about your father."[23]

There was nothing remotely sinister about Prentice's effects in the consular file concerning his death. Certainly nothing to support the claims that Werner continued to push in London, not that such a fact would have cut much ice with Werner, claiming as he did without any supporting evidence, that Prentice's habit of "showing charity to social outcasts" was merely a front for the man's association with other criminals.[24] By this logic, Prentice could do something or not do something and be damned either way.

Interestingly, there was one unusual item in the consular file: among Prentice's possession, staff had found a letter from an Alfred Lueckenhaus, a German national. In the letter, Luckenhaus named Prentice as his representative in relation to a power of attorney (an act which suggests that the dentist was a man to be trusted). Lueckenhaus, present in Japanese-occupied China throughout the War, was a writer and journalist who had worked before the War for German publications in both Britain and America. In 1946, American intelligence reports from China

22 ibid.
23 ibid.
24 UK National Archives, FO 371/23513/1510 Murder of Pamela Werner. Code 10 file 1510, letter from E.T.C. Werner to the British Ambassador to China.

named Lueckenhaus as being part of a wartime network of spies and informants that had worked across China for the Nazis. The veracity of such claims is now probably impossible to assess, and Lueckenhaus later went on to write several successful books, some on the subject of China. Whilst there is no suggestion that Prentice's association with Lueckenhaus was improper, the incident illustrates how mixed society was within the foreign community in China; people of all types rubbed shoulders and formed friendships, sometimes with those who would have been classed as official enemies.[25]

---

25 US National Archives, Strategic Services Unit report, March 1, 1946, German Intelligence Activities in China During World War II.

16

THE PEOPLE'S REPUBLIC

A NEW CHINA

DURING THE IMMEDIATE post-war period, in stark contrast to the thousands of foreigners in post-war China who were in a hurry to *leave* the country, Fred Knauf was determined to *return* to it. On his arrival in the US on the *SS Gripsholm* in December 1943, Knauf was given a period of leave from the Marine Corps Reserve; he immediately applied for the back-pay and pension owed to him for the period covering his confinement by the Japanese. Other servicemen on the boat did the same. In Knauf's case, the money due came to the considerable sum of $863. Knauf remained in the Marine Corps Reserves for the remainder of the War, serving for a spell in Honolulu before finally retiring from military service altogether a few months after the end of hostilities.[1]

Living thereafter in San Francisco, no distance from the Mare Island barracks where he had commenced his Marine Corps career, Knauf yearned for yet another return to Peking. His pension of $51 per month did not purchase a great deal in the US thanks to post-war inflation, but it could go a long way in China. And

1   National Personnel Records Center, St Louis, Missouri; official military personnel file for Fred Knauf.

besides, for Knauf, as with Prentice, Peking had long been the place he considered home.[2]

But Knauf's desire to return to his old haunts was stymied by the US Government which simply refused to grant him a passport. A frustrated Knauf enlisted the help of the Marine Corps Rehabilitation Office which wrote on his behalf seeking advice from the Passport Division:

> Thrice the subject named has requested the Passport Division, Washington D.C. that he be granted a passport and papers for the return to China. Thrice he has been refused with the notation that a passport cannot be issued to him at this time.

The reply Knauf later received was not what he desired:

> Please inform named man that travel to China is restricted at the present time except for essential cases, and his application to the Passport Division, State Department, does not fall within that classification.[3]

The unstable political situation in China, particularly the brewing civil war, was such that the US Government anticipated trouble and chose to avoid as much as possible having its citizens caught in the middle. After years supporting the Nationalist Chinese government against the Japanese and then against communist expansion, the US Government had begun to realise that it was probably backing the losing side. The communists were in the ascendancy.

Back in the UK Werner was in danger of bumping into George

2 ibid.
3 ibid.

Gorman, the onetime editor of *Caravan* and *The Peking Chronicle*, and for some years a figure of hate for the old man. After Gorman's arrest on his return to Britain in 1942, he was questioned by the security services and released without charge.[4] Perhaps there was insufficient evidence against him. Perhaps, having been arrested by the Japanese at the outbreak of war, there was little for which he could be held accountable. Or perhaps the British security services simply had more pressing concerns than those presented by an out-of-work journalist. In any event, though the authorities could have detained him for longer if they felt it necessary, Gorman was released from detention under Defence Regulation 18(b) and set free into the bombed streets of London.[5]

It may have surprised Gorman's detractors at the Foreign Office to learn that he soon found employment in the newspaper industry once again, in no less than London's Fleet Street. In about 1945, after spells on other London publications, Gorman joined the *London Evening Standard*, where he worked for many years with the team that produced The Londoner's Diary, a long-running society gossip column.[6] During this period, the *Evening Standard* was owned by Canadian-born Max Aitken, 1st Baron Beaverbrook. Beaverbrook was an influential newspaper owner, and also a successful business magnate and wartime politician, serving as a senior minister in Churchill's coalition government. It is unlikely that Beaverbrook or his editors would have employed Gorman if they had disapproved of his history. And it is equally unlikely that Gorman's background could have been kept secret in the world of journalists. So despite his close connections with militarist Japan, it seems that Gorman was not con-

....

4 Deborah McFarlane, *Britain & Japan; Biographical Portraits, volume VIII, compiled & edited by Hugh Cortazzi*, pp507-524 (2013).
5 UK National Archives, HO 45/25743 War: Defence Regulation 18B Detainees.
6 Deborah McFarlane, *Britain & Japan; Biographical Portraits, volume VIII, compiled & edited by Hugh Cortazzi*, pp507-524 (2013).

sidered *persona non grata*. He died in 1956, aged sixty-eight.[7]

The 1945 general election saw Clement Atlee's Labour Party replace Churchill's wartime coalition. As a result, the widely-respected Ernest Bevin, a former trade union leader from humble origins in Somerset and wartime coalition Minister of Labour, took over as Foreign Secretary from the Conservative Party's Sir Anthony Eden. The pair were very different characters with very different political attitudes, but that appears to have made no difference in the Foreign Office's subsequent dealings with Werner. As in previous years. it was left to someone junior in the depaartment to respond to Werner's persistent demands for action over the murder of his adopted daughter.

Giving his address as the *Athenaeum* (his London club in Pall Mall), Werner wrote to Bevin in early 1947 insisting that it was not too late for the British Embassy in Peking to raise a charge of murder in China. In response, the Foreign Office replied that the treaty of 1943 and the end of extraterritoriality meant that the Embassy no longer possessed such powers. This was probably legally correct. Werner, however, countered that this was nonsense as the Chinese were willing to assist and that the young Boyce, the last British Acting Consul he had met in Peking (and who had since died in post), had voiced no such opinion regarding extraterritoriality. Werner also wrote disparagingly of Boyce's predecessors in Peking, to which he received a reply politely informing him that "Mr. Bevin is unable to take cognizance of your remarks concerning former members of His Majesty's Foreign service."[8]

Further replies to Werner from the Foreign Office were slow in returning, but firmly insistent that there was nothing further the Government could do. Whitehall staff probably nurtured the

---

7 ibid.
8 E.T.C. Werner, *More Memorigrams* (1948), p207.

hope that Werner would simply give up and go away. However, in one letter, in what was clearly an effort to buy some time, they did concede that a letter would be sent to the Embassy in Peking requesting further information.[9]

Months passed with Werner receiving no further updates. Eventually, on a cold Monday in early December 1947, Werner called unannounced at the Foreign Office in Whitehall. Admitted into the ministry building, Werner was seated in an office, which, he noted disapprovingly, was more than amply heated by the largest coal fire he had seen since his return from China (coal remained rationed in the UK). There followed a long, futile conversation with Mr. John W. Davidson (1888-1973), then the Head of the Consular Department,[10] a man who had previously served for many years in China and who would undoubtedly have known of both Werner and the murder case. Present also, much to Werner's annoyance, was a second Foreign Office official who remained anonymous and silent throughout the entire interview. Werner saw this last as a "characteristic" attempt at "two-against-one" intimidation. It appears that Werner did not realize – but should have given his consular experience – was that the second man was almost certainly present to corroborate Davidson's subsequent account of the meeting and thus be able to refute any spurious allegations made by Werner in the future. In the event, Davidson appears to have parried and otherwise held firm to the extent that Werner emerged from the meeting thoroughly dissatisfied. In disgust, he recorded how the Foreign Office were simply continuing to "play tennis" with him over his concerns.[11]

At some point during these difficult discussions, and prob-

9   ibid.
10 UK National Archives, annual Foreign Office list.
11 E.T.C. Werner, *More Memorigrams* (1948), p215.

ably wishing to be seen as offering Werner some positive assistance, the Foreign Office suggested that he might want to consider employing a lawyer of his own to represent his claims in China. Werner retorted that such a course of action was way beyond his purse, which it probably was. Nevertheless, Werner did at one stage at least "consult" a London lawyer on the implications of the ending of extraterritoriality. He may also, however, have soon been forced to consult one concerning accusations of defamation of character, relating to accusations levelled at Werner himself. For in 1948 he published his final book, *More Memorigrams*, which included a lengthy account of the murder by suspects described as A and B. The print-run must have been small, small enough for Werner himself to pen a few minor corrections into each copy. But although copies of *More Memorigrams* were few in number, word of its publication nonetheless reached as far as Peking.

Wentworth Prentice was dead, but not so Doctor Ugo Cappuzzo who was still living and working in the Legation Quarter. Cappuzzo, now in his early forties, wasn't impressed by the contents of Werner's book, or how he was portrayed within it, thinly disguised as suspect B.

Cappuzzo's wartime experience had been very different to that of most foreigners as he was Italian. With Benito Mussolini's Fascist Government allied to both Japan and Germany, the Italian nationals in occupied China were more or less free to carry on life as before. In stark contrast to their former British and American friends, the Italians' status and standard of living remained high. But not for long.

The War in Europe and North Africa went badly for Italy. In the summer of 1943 the Allies invaded first Sicily and then the Italian mainland. In the midst of this crisis, the elderly King Victor Emmanuel dismissed Mussolini as prime minister and had him arrested, only for the dictator to be rescued from his mountain prison by the Nazis and reinstated as leader in the northern half of the country. The political situation in Italy was chaotic, with factions for joining the Allies and others for remaining with the Axis, leaving thousands of regular soldiers unsure of who they were fighting for.

Italians abroad similarly found themselves in the tricky position of having to choose sides. This was a dilemma that was keenly felt by Italians in occupied China, where the Japanese suddenly demanded that they declare their position after Italian sailors scuttled two of their own nation's gunboats and a liner in the Shanghai harbour in full view of the enraged Japanese watching from their naval headquarters only four hundred yards away.

For many Italians, the choice made was one of expediency. Civilians in Peking who declared for the winning Allies were promptly interned at Weihsien where they were kept isolated from the other internees in a tiny corner of the camp. Italian soldiers declaring the same fared worse and were removed to the Japanese POW camps. Though they must have sensed that they were on the losing side, those Italian soldiers and civilians in China who declared themselves for the surviving Fascist government remained at liberty, albeit rather tenuously and under a cloud of suspicion as the Italians generally had no more affinity for the Japanese than they did for their other allies, the Germans – a feeling which was mutual.

For the sake of expediency or otherwise, Cappuzzo, like a great many Italian diplomats, may have felt compelled to declare for his Government – whatever that may have been at the time. For in a later post-war letter to the Ministry of Foreign Affairs in Rome, Cappuzzo reminded the Ministry of how, unpaid though he had been, he had remained loyally in his post as embassy doctor throughout the chaotic period from September 1943 until after the war's end.[12]

In the wake of his encounter with Werner in his hospital waiting room in 1939, Cappuzzo may, like Prentice, have decided that the best policy was to ignore or shrug-off the old man's murder allegations, the knowledge of which appeared to extend no further than Peking where Werner's character was all too well-known. But to learn, ten years on, that the allegations had been published in a book proved too much for Cappuzzo. It was time to take legal action.

In a series of letters in late 1948, Cappuzzo sought the assistance of the Italian Consulate in London. Though Cappuzzo had not managed to obtain a copy of the new book himself, he had learned through a contact that within its pages Werner specifically described one of the two unnamed murderers – Suspect B – as an Italian doctor who had visited the island of Hainan not long after the crime. Understandably, Cappuzzo held that he was readily identifiable as Suspect B as he was the *only* Italian doctor in Peking during the relevant period. He wanted to seek redress for defamation against both Werner and the book's publishers. He even went so far as to forward a sum of money to London for this purpose. To what extent this action proceeded is unclear, but the answer is, probably not far. The print run for *More Memorigrams* was very small, it was a moot point whether Cappuzzo had indeed been defamed, and taking the matter to court would have been expensive and perhaps would only have succeeded in promoting the very rumors that Cappuzzo sought to extinguish.[13] In any event, Cappuzzo was soon overwhelmed by far greater troubles than mere defamation.

....

12 Archivio Storico Diplomatico, Rome, archive "Le Rappresentanze Diplomatiche e Consolari Italiane a Pechino 1870-1952, folder 186, file 9043 "Cappuzzo".
13 ibid.

Life for Cappuzzo in post-war China proved not nearly as agreeable for him as it had been in the 1930s. Italy was no longer the world player the fascists had aspired to make it. Much of the country was reduced to rubble and there was a great deal of political instability with a real possibility that the country's communists might win control.

In Cappuzzo's opinion, the staff at the Ministry of Foreign Affairs in Rome gave him an unnecessarily hard time. Economic necessity meant that Rome no longer needed a Peking Embassy doctor, and the Ministry wanted Cappuzzo out of his Legation Quarter home, the same home he had held rent-free since his arrival in the city over fifteen years before. The Ministry received reports that Cappuzzo may have unlawfully dispensed medical drugs and, most scandalously, had performed abortions, a procedure that remained unlawful in Italy.[14]

Cappuzzo somehow clung on to his state-owned residence, perhaps by reminding the Ministry of the significant amount of unpaid work he had done for both Italians and Chinese. The bad feeling didn't end there: Cappuzzo thought the Ministry unappreciative of his medical work, and in return the Ministry thought Cappuzzo arrogant and rude.[15]

Cappuzzo, who still made adventurous weekend motorcycle trips to tend to his six villages, was by then living alone. He had sent his wife and their growing sons home to Italy to further the boys' education. As it turned out, the sound advice would have been to accompany them.[16]

By late 1948, the Chinese communists backed by the Soviet Union, were finally winning their twenty-year war against the Chinese government led by Chiang Kai-shek (and supported by

----

14 ibid.
15 ibid.
16 ibid.

the United States). In February 1949, the communists marched unopposed into Peking, the city having been largely abandoned by its defenders. And from Tiananmen Gate on the October 1 of that year, Mao Zedong proclaimed the founding of the People's Republic of China.

What was left of the Nationalist forces escaped with Chiang Kai-shek to the island of Taiwan. Meanwhile, Cappuzzo and the few foreigners still in Peking very soon discovered that communist control was not simply another regime change that affected only the Chinese and left them untouched. Quite the contrary; it was to prove a game-changer for everyone in China. Under Mao, most foreign embassies were closed and, with the exception of the Soviet Union and its satellite states, diplomatic relations severed. *The Peiping Chronicle* ceased to exist. Political campaigns roiled the streets.

Having delayed too long, Cappuzzo was refused an exit permit to leave the country. He was also subject to a curfew and his movements were restricted to Peking. Forbidden from sending money out of China and home to his family, and deprived of contact with the outside world, Cappuzzo was trapped. Like other foreigners he was purposely made to feel humiliated. Soldiers and officials entered his home, rifled through his belongings, counted items down to the last shirt, laughing as they helped themselves to the vegetables he grew in the garden and wiped their boots on his furniture. On days when senior Communist Party members were scheduled to drive nearby, Cappuzzo, a despised and distrusted alien, was confined to a room in his house and unable to work.[17]

But Cappuzzo was soon to experience far worse. Many years later, he described his experiences during this period under the

17 Luke Anthony, *Chang-fu (Self-criticism)*, (edition 1997), chapter one.

communists in a book he titled *Chang-Fu*, which loosely translated as meaning *self-criticism*, a Communist Party term the meaning of which he only slowly came to understand. Using the pen-name of Luke Anthony and writing in English in the first person, Cappuzzo also substituted his own identity for that of a fictitious American doctor (possibly in the hope of gaining a readership wider than Italy's), but the book otherwise appears to be an accurate account of his treatment in a Peking prison.[18]

By 1951, large numbers of Chinese soldiers were fighting in support of communist North Korea against South Korea and a United Nations force led by the United States. The conflict developed into a major war. In July 1951, the Chinese communist security services rounded up an unknown number of foreigners remaining in Peking.[19] Cappuzzo was one of them. On an otherwise routine day amid the usual stifling summer temperatures, Cappuzzo was operating on an anaesthetized Chinese patient at his private clinic when Chinese officials in communist-blue suddenly burst into the room and, ignoring the Italian's protests, forced him out of the building at gunpoint. Furious and pleading for the life of his helpless patient, a handcuffed Cappuzzo was driven to a notorious Peking prison where he was destined to endure several years in captivity. No explanation was given.[20]

Weeks later, Cappuzzo was eventually told that his crime against the people of China was that of spying for foreign agencies. It transpired that everyone in the prison was accused of spying. There were a few other foreigners in the prison also, but most of the inmates were Chinese, either former Nationalists, property-owners or intellectuals.[21]

....

18 ibid.
19 Journal of the Royal Asiatic Society Hong Kong Branch, Volume 46 (2006), article by Keith Stevens, Henri Vetch (1898-1978) Soldier, Bookseller and Publisher.
20 Luke Anthony, *Chang-fu (Self-criticism)*, (edition 1997).
21 ibid.

But on day one, as yet ignorant of these facts and incredulous at his arrest, the newly-arrived Cappuzzo pleaded to his captors that a mistake must have been made, but no one was interested. Still more angry than afraid, Cappuzzo demanded to see someone in authority. With this, he was led still handcuffed to a heavy door and pushed inside.[22]

Cappuzzo had been duped into walking into a prison cell. Staring back at him wordlessly were six Chinese, more emaciated scarecrows than live men. Sitting cross-legged and half naked on the cell's one large bench, it was clear that none of them had washed in months; sweat dripped down their grimy and wasted flesh; their long hair and straggly beards thick with grease. Several of the men wore handcuffs or leg-irons. A bucket brimming with urine and spittle sat in one corner and a single 15-watt bulb glowed dimly high above, beyond which was a small barred skylight, the insufferably hot cell's only form of ventilation. The stench was overpowering.[23]

This cell and others just like it were to be Cappuzzo's principal environment for the next few years. The bare greasy bench, or *kang*, served as table, seat and bed for all. Food – starvation rations in the form of gruel and bread – was delivered through a hatch in the door. Once a day, the entire cell was frog-marched heads-down to an internal yard. Here, under the hot sun, the stench became still worse as, still in line, inmates in rows were given two minutes to strain together and empty their bowels into shallow ditches already full of faeces, worms and flies.[24]

But the appalling physical conditions of the prison were just one aspect of the punishment meted out. Shrewdly, the prison regime compounded the inmates' misery by setting them against

---

22 ibid.
23 ibid.
24 ibid.

one another. There were to be no friendships, no alliances. Each cell holding up to a dozen men was allocated a *tu-jan,* an inmate favoured with being chief of the cell. Reading aloud from Communist Party leaflets, the *tu-jan's* task was to prize confessions of spying from the others. It transpired that every inmate in Cappuzzo's cell had long since begun to realize the nature of their crimes and commenced the process of confessing. The same procedure was to begin with Cappuzzo immediately. As a newcomer, he also had to confess to his crimes, to his spying for the former Nationalist government and for foreign imperial regimes. If Cappuzzo confessed then *Chang-Fu*, in his benevolent mercy, would remove his handcuffs. At first Cappuzzo, who was fluent in Mandarin Chinese, assumed that *Chang-Fu* must be a senior prison official. Perhaps one to whom he needed to make appeals. Or perhaps he was one of the guards. Unseen and all-powerful, *Chang-Fu's* identity was a mystery. Cappuzzo naturally insisted on his innocence; he was not a spy and had nothing to confess. At this, the other inmates rounded on him, and together they *struggled* him - a term used to describe verbal and physical confrontation designed to cause pain rather than serious injury. Forbidden to sit or sleep, still with his hands cuffed behind his back, he was left to urinate in the trousers he arrived in.[25]

After a few weeks without a change in clothing, no means of washing and no outside contact, Cappuzzo was marched to appear before a People's Court. Three judges wearing the yellow uniforms of the People's Liberation Army sat behind desks in a long and otherwise empty room. Cappuzzo was made to stand before them in his handcuffs, a lamp shining in his eyes. And thus he remained overnight, those being the usual hours of the court.[26]

....

25 ibid.
26 ibid.

Despite the court panel's demands, Cappuzzo refused to admit to spying. The panel screamed in fury. Instead of shooting him as he deserved, *Chang-Fu* had been generous enough to provide Cappuzzo with food and water and yet Cappuzzo returned this generosity with nothing but lies. A second, tighter set of handcuffs was applied in addition to the first and leg-irons were fitted to his ankles. At daybreak Cappuzzo was marched, partially blinded, back to his cell where he was again *struggled* by his fellow inmates and made to stand upright all day while they berated him for his ingratitude toward *Chang-Fu's* clemency. The following night, with swollen and festering limbs, Cappuzzo was again marched before the People's Court.[27]

Not unnaturally, Cappuzzo feared that to admit to something he had not done – spying – would result in his execution. Only slowly did he realise that this was not the case. Everything was perverse. The prisoners were held incommunicado and had no means of defending themselves. No specific charges were brought against them. There was no examination of evidence. There were no sentences. The prisoners were at the prison because the all-knowing *Chang-Fu* knew them to be guilty and that they were miserable enemies of the Chinese people. Only by confessing could they hope to undeservedly win *Chang-Fu's* mercy and perhaps secure release to a forced-labour party where they might work to provide some form of service and recompense to the Chinese people. *Chang-Fu*, Cappuzzo eventually came to realize, was not a man at all; the words meant *self-criticism* or *self-examination*.[28]

In the face of such treatment, it was only a matter of time before prisoners submitted to what was required of them and eventually "confessed." But the confession had to be convincing,

----

27 ibid.
28 ibid.

and prisoners had to commit their accounts to memory. Prisoners had to give details of their activities going back over decades – subjects, dates, places, contacts, agencies. How many bags of rice they had spoiled; how many Chinese dollars they had sent out of the country. And they had to denounce others. They had to provide names of other spies. Again and again, they were sent back to be *struggled* and to re-write their inadequate confessions, or to start them all over again.[29]

Cappuzzo eventually came to realize that the confessions themselves were of no importance. The *Chang-Fu* purpose was simply to break the inmates psychologically. Whilst a proportion of inmates died – Cappuzzo shared cells with men with advanced tuberculosis, and some contrived to commit suicide – most somehow survived, albeit as human wrecks. What better way of instilling fear and control over an entire nation than to let the existence of such prison regimes be known. Prior to his arrest Cappuzzo had thought that as a doctor he would be safe from such treatment, and he had assumed that any new Chinese regime would surely see the value in doctors. But *Chang-Fu* wasn't interested in doctors. Crushing an imperialist foreigner, and being seen to do so, was what mattered.[30]

To safeguard against men forming any form of relationship with one another, inmates were moved randomly from cell to cell. Though the majority of inmates were Chinese, Cappuzzo occasionally found himself sharing a cell with another foreigner, often unrecognizable at first, whom Cappuzzo realized he had known years before. One such inmate was an elderly Catholic priest. Moved by the poor man's plight, Cappuzzo wanted to help him by displaying friendship and passing on advice on how best to survive, all of which was forbidden. An idea sprang to the Doc-

29 ibid.
30 ibid.

tor's mind. The priest spoke little Chinese, so Cappuzzo started berating him for his spying, as was required, not in Chinese, but in Latin, a language no one else in the room would understand. By this means, Cappuzzo disguised kind and supportive words as harsh reprimands. He was quietly congratulating himself on this subterfuge when to his horror a Chinese inmate also new to the cell stood up and reported him through the door to the guards. Cappuzzo was aghast. This new inmate spoke Latin and had been placed in the cell in the expectation that Cappuzzo and the priest would act just as they had. Cappuzzo and the priest were punished, with the priest later dying in the prison.[31]

Months became years. But in time and with greater experience, Cappuzzo's prison existence became more tolerable. After an adequate series of confessions, his handcuffs and leg-irons were removed (at one point his limbs had become so swollen and infected that he'd expected to die of septicaemia). Now, to his advantage, he was removed from his cell for hours at a time to teach foreign languages to various soldiers and officials. He was proficient in English, French and Spanish. His students were stony-faced and devoid of thanks, but as well as textbooks and extra food, Cappuzzo was given time and space to prepare for lessons. These language lessons may well have saved his life.[32]

On one occasion, Cappuzzo's cell was provided with a Chinese magazine article, the contents of which the inmates were required to discuss and agree on the merits of the justice it described. To his alarm, Cappuzzo read how six Peking foreigners – all men he knew – had been found guilty by a court of conspiring to kill Mao and other leaders of the Central People's Government by firing a mortar while they stood on a rostrum during a ceremony in Tiananmen Square. The plot had been foiled

31 ibid.
32 ibid.

by the diligence of the Public Security Bureau of the Municipal People's Government of Peking. All six men had subsequently "confessed" their involvement. Two of the six men, one Italian and one Japanese, had been executed by firing squad.[33]

The executed Italian, Antonio Riva, age fifty-five, had been born in China and had spent most of his life there. He had served with the Italian air force in World War One, becoming a flying ace with a number of kills to his name. After the war he had returned to China where he had been the Peking agent for a trading company, all of which was later made out to be cover for his spying against the Chinese people. The other man to be shot was Riuichi Yamaguchi, a history graduate and commercial trader from Kyoto.[34]

According to the article, Riva took possession of the mortar while Yamaguchi sketched the plans for its use. Many years later, one of their co-accused gave a different account: a communist security agent had approached Yamaguchi in the street asking him if the Japanese company he represented could provide fire-fighting equipment powerful enough to shoot water two hundred yards from a point of supply to the seat of a fire fifteen feet off the ground. Eager for a sale, Yamaguchi assured him that such a feat was possible and promptly completed a rough diagram of the same for the man's benefit showing the trajectory of the water to the target. With the sketch handed over, Yamaguchi was arrested on the spot for planning to assassinate Mao Zedong. The diagram was later produced as the main piece of mortar-fire evidence against Yamaguchi, even though it included side notes in Japanese referring to how water could be pumped from the canal.[35]

---

33 ibid.
34 School of Oriental & African Studies, MS 380730 Sir Lionel Lamb collection; The Trial and Conviction of US Spies in Peking, article in the supplement to the People's China, volume IV, number 5, September 1, 1951.
35 Luke Anthony, *Chang-fu (Self-criticism)*, (edition 1997).

Antonio Riva, a friend of Yamaguchi, was arrested the same day. Riva's foolish mistake was to keep a souvenir World War One French mortar in his home – he had once had to demonstrate a similar weapon's use. The mortar had not been fired in decades and was probably unfit for use, but that would have been of little or no concern to the court, which reviewed a photograph of Riva standing at his home next to the mortar.[36]

The other four men, all friends or associates of Riva and Yamaguchi, were arrested separately over the following months. They included two more Italians (one a local Roman Catholic bishop), a German, a Frenchman, and a Chinese. They were all found guilty in a military court where they were unrepresented and unable to defend themselves. The only thing the foreign community in Peking knew was that the men had suddenly disappeared. The first the outside world heard of the affair was via the Chinese newspapers announcing the men's guilt. Riva and Yamaguchi were shot on the same day as the trial.[37]

Reading the article in his prison cell, Cappuzzo had no doubt as to how the men's confessions had been obtained. Never mind that a mortar was an absurd choice for a murder weapon and that none of the men were trained in its use. Also never mind the difficulty of setting up such a weapon among a hostile Chinese crowd and that escape after the event would have been near impossible. And further never mind that for months after the first arrests, four of the men had made no attempt to hide or run or burn any correspondence.[38]

Cappuzzo's captivity ended abruptly and without warning. Suddenly after about three year's imprisonment, Cappuzzo was

----

36 School of Oriental & African Studies, MS 380730 Sir Lionel Lamb collection; The Trial and Conviction of US Spies in Peking, article in the supplement to the People's China, volume IV, number 5, September 1, 1951.
37 ibid.
38 Luke Anthony, *Chang-fu (Self-criticism)*, (edition 1997).

taken from his cell, given a haircut and a shave. He assumed he was being made presentable for public execution. He was marched to a room where his photograph was taken and he was again made to stand before a judge and read once more his manufactured confession. Still expecting a bullet, he was then taken to a huge hall where army officers in yellow uniforms sat behind a wide line of desks. Cappuzzo stood before them, trying to hold his nerves together, thinking only of his wife, when an officer announced with little in the way of preamble that he was part of an exchange. He was to be swapped for a communist prisoner held outside China.[39] In his book, which ends with his sudden release, Cappuzzo gives no details of leaving China other than saying that he did so on a Danish ship via the Yellow Sea. Nor did he relate how any of these arrangements came about or for whom he was exchanged.

During this same period, the early 1950s, despite British troops playing a role in the Korean war, Britain might reasonably have expected some diplomatic credit from China for having been among the first to acknowledge the new People's Republic. But the British Government closed all but three of its consulates in China after diplomatic buildings were searched by police who arrested some staff members on espionage charges. In addition, the Vice-Consul in Mukden was expelled for having objected to the Chinese digging rifle pits in the consulate compound.[40]

Britain's Ambassador to China was Lionel Lamb. But when Lamb returned to Peking in early 1951, he found a very different diplomatic climate to that he experienced as a vice-consul in the 1930s. Unable to confirm his role as ambassador with the Chinese, the British Foreign Office resorted to describing Lamb as "charge d'affaires ad interim," while the Chinese, with deliberate

....

39 ibid.
40 Hansard, House of Commons debate, vol 480 c 115W, November 13, 1950.

disregard, referred to him as a "negotiating agent" and the British diplomatic mission as "Mr. Lamb's office." Lamb was refused a permit to travel outside Peking and his efforts to communicate with the government were largely ignored. His only meetings were with low-level officials. Slighted and sidelined, Lamb kept abreast of what was happening in the country by reading the newspapers. In such circumstances, it was hardly surprising that the fate of missing foreign nationals held in secret prisons — men such as Cappuzzo — was often a mystery.[41]

Lamb's life as a diplomat in communist Peking would have been a peculiar and lonely experience. Compared with his previous service during the 1930s when thousands of foreigners lived, worked and socialized in the Legation Quarter, the walled enclave would have appeared noticeably empty, with its embassies either closed or run by only a few consular employees. Lamb knew that he could increase his staff by employing Chinese, but realised that would be of limited use as they would almost certainly be informers.[42]

A few years later, perhaps as a reward for his miserable stay in China, Lamb was appointed Britain's Ambassador to Switzerland,[43] a far more congenial posting. As a result, Lamb was not present to witness the wholesale changes the following years brought to Peking. Some of the Legation Quarter's grand embassy buildings survived with new Chinese government roles or functions. A few of them even remained, for a time, as foreign diplomatic missions, but the area's open spaces, the compounds and the glacis, gradually disappeared under sprawling redevelopment as the population of the capital of the new People's Republic of China swelled. Not that the Legation Quarter was

....

41 School of Oriental & African Studies, MS 380730 Sir Lionel Lamb collection.
42 Ibid., article from Newsweek magazine June 9, 1952.
43 UK National Archives, annual Foreign Office list.

singled out for such sweeping town-planning: over the following decades, the entire centre of the old city was steadily transformed. Most of the old city walls and towers, arguably Peking's greatest features dating back to the 15th and 16th centuries and even earlier, were torn down to make way for roads and railway lines, or to build air-raid shelters.

A short length of wall that *did* survive is that section along which Pamela's disfigured body was found. But the scene and that of Pamela's fateful route home has been transformed almost beyond all recognition by the nearby construction of a modern rail station (with a minor amount of trespass, it's possible to walk along the very stretch on which she was found, now surprisingly green with grass and a few trees). Owing to changes in house numbers, it's not possible to identify number 1 Kuei-chiachang, though much of the hutung exists as it was in 1937, a mixture of scruffy courtyards, old and new. Gone entirely, however, is the small British cemetery which was a place of "beautiful trees and flowers" and where Pamela, her adopted mother Gladys, and also Wentworth Prentice were all buried. Wentworth Prentice's

The stretch of the city wall where Pamela was found. Now landscaped and flanked by an isolated path constructed for the 2008 Olympics, but currently closed to the public

sudden early death in 1947 meant at least that he was spared the possible experience of a fate such as Ugo Cappuzzo's.

Cappuzzo survived his imprisonment, but his subsequent life is something of a mystery. In 1955, he sailed from Southampton on the south coast of England for Venezuela,[44] but beyond that his ultimate fate is unknown.

In the event, though he would not have known it at the time, Fred Knauf was lucky that after the war, the US Government refused to grant him a passport, so preventing him from returning to his old haunts in Peking. Knauf never set foot in China again, and remained living in San Francisco, presumably adapting to the fact that his US Marine Corps pension would no longer stretch to provide him with a handsome living complete with domestic servants. Still unmarried, aged sixty-eight, Knauf died of cancer in December 1961 at the Letterman General Hospital. An ex-serviceman, he was buried at the Golden Gate National Cemetery in California.[45]

44 Passenger list for the SS Antilles, leaving Southampton October 21, 1955.
45 National Personnel Records Center, St Louis, Missouri; official military personnel file for Fred Knauf.

17

RESUMING LIFE

PICKING UP THE PIECES

As FOR THE subsequent lives of others mentioned in this account, few were without drama, and many are worth recounting.

Detective Inspector Richard Botham's stay in China appears to have been a short one. At the time of the Werner murder, Botham was a comparative newcomer to the country, having only arrived in Tientsin in 1935 after service with the Metropolitan Police in London. After the police murder investigation had reached its inconclusive end, Werner wrote to the Foreign Office disparaging Botham, alleging that during his stay in Peking the young inspector had gone on drinking bouts with the Chinese magistrate Han, and that together the pair had accepted bribes and enjoyed the services of prostitutes. All damning stuff. Werner also claimed that as a result of such gross misconduct, Botham was dismissed from the Tientsin police by Dennis and returned to England in disgrace.[1] Any Werner claim as to a man's character has to be treated with scepticism, but Botham and his wife do appear to have left China by or before 1939 as they are not

---

1   UK National Archives, FO 371/23513/1510 Murder of Pamela Werner. Code 10 file 1510, letters from E.T.C. Werner to the British Ambassador to China, June 1939 & October 1939.

mentioned in later documents relating to Tientsin or the Pacific War. Perhaps Botham *did* drink to excess, as did so many men of the period. Perhaps he was "let go." Or perhaps life in China simply did not agree with the Bothams. Perhaps, like many, they found it hard to adapt: China was certainly not to everyone's taste.

Sergeant George Binetsky.
(Courtesy of George Binetsky &
Jodie White)

Nor did Werner have anything nice to say about Botham's colleague, Sergeant George Binetsky, the White Russian. Werner complained that Binetsky had failed to take fingerprints from Pamela's shoes at the murder scene[2] and had then broken a silver casket during the search of her bedroom.[3] Binetsky was probably as capable of making a error as the next man, but while searching the bedroom for evidence he may well have felt it necessary to force the lock or hasp of the casket in order to ascertain its contents. Such damage is sometimes unavoidable. As for his neglecting to take fingerprints at the crime scene (one that technically remained under the control of the Chinese police), in the 1930s fingerprints were only recoverable from a very limited number of surfaces. In any event, the wind and dust that winter day may well have destroyed any fingerprints that may have existed. True to form, and with no supporting evidence, Werner also went on to accuse Binetsky of diverting Botham's attention from local brothels, the people running them being fellow White Russians whom Werner suspected

....

2   ibid., letters October 1938 & June 1939.
3   ibid., letter of June 1939.

A Peking winter dust-storm

of being somehow involved in Pamela's murder.[4]

At the start of the Sino-Japanese War in 1937, the Japanese made a concerted effort to win north China's many thousands of White Russian exiles over to their side. One method was to make the case of a common enemy in the form of the Soviet government in Moscow. To this end, the Japanese sponsored the establishment of a social club in Tientsin's former German concession. Dubbed the "White House," it was run by several Russian exiles, each with a long history of violence. Tientsin's community of White Russians were invited by the Japanese to register their support. In effect, they were required to declare their allegiance to either the Allies or the Axis powers. There was a great deal of intimidation and worse, during which a prominent Russian disappeared from his home in the British concession. A week later, his badly mutilated corpse was found floating in a creek.[5] Nevertherless, Binetsky received much praise from his employers for

4   ibid.
5   Desmond Power, *Little Foreign Devil*, (1996), p124.

the way he "distinguished himself" in the crime's investigation.[6]

The next few years continued to be a dangerous period for Russian exiles, throughout which Binetsky remained loyal to his employers, the British Municipal Council. He was one of a small but significant group of Russians who bravely continued in their role as police officers. In 1939, Binetsky was rewarded for his loyalty by being given the status of a "British protected person."[7] Later still, some time prior to the attack at Pearl Harbour, Binetsky volunteered for and was accepted into the British Army. As a serving soldier, he appears not to have been in China when the Japanese arrested Dennis and others. Not so, however, Binetsky's wife, Nadejda, who was interned at Weihsien camp for the duration of the war.[8]

While his wife was a captive, Binetsky saw active service in the Burma Campaign. He was one of a number of White Russians attached to the 1st Battalion of the Gloucestershire Regiment, where he met with favour. During his time with the Gloucesters he and many of his compatriots were regarded as a tough and courageous asset with a profound hatred for the Japanese.[9] In August 1943, Binetsky was given an emergency commission and was later further promoted to the rank of captain.[10]

After the war, Binetsky reunited with his wife and returned to Tientsin where he was once again employed as a police officer.[11] This time, however, he worked for the Chinese government, as both the British Municipal Council and the British Concession no longer existed. In 1947, Binetsky very prudently applied to be-

....

6 UK National Archives, FO 366/2930 Payment of pensions to former employees of the British Municipal Council at Tientsin on account of their claims against the Chinese Government for service benefits. Code XR file 05.
7 ibid.
8 Weihsien Internment camp list, compiled by Ron Bridge.
9 Gentleman's Military Interest Club website, comments from veterans, June 4, 2006 & March 2, 2004.
10 London Gazette, 29 October 1943, page 4797.
11 Conversation with Binetsky family members George Binetsky and Jodie White, 2015.

come a full British subject; until this point he had been a stateless person. An exception to normal Home Office rules was made and his application was granted owing to his "special circumstances" and "because of the nature of the services performed." Thinking well of Binetsky, British colleagues went out of their way to vouch for him.[12]

Binetsky's certificate of naturalization arrived just in time, as his police career with the Chinese government did not last long. He was strongly advised to flee from China. The information came from Binetsky's new police superior, a Chinese general, who quietly warned him that the communists would soon take Tientsin and that he and a host of other foreigners had best not be there when they arrived.[13] As a White Russian who had previously worked for the British, Binetsky risked being either murdered by the communists, or handed over to the Soviets for them to do the same. In possession of his British passport, Binetsky and his wife were able to flee first to Hong Kong and then to the safety of Australia. There they settled and later ran a chicken farm in New South Wales. Aged fifty-nine, Binetsky died in Australia in 1966.[14]

The fate of senior Chinese police officer Han remains a mystery. He appears to have remained in his post and survived the initial 1937 transfer of power from Chinese rule to that of the Japanese occupiers. But perhaps not for long, as the Peking newspaper *Yih Shih Pao* of April 1, 1938 reports his removal from post, though without stating how, or why, or whether permanently. His position thereafter is unclear, for as late as 1941 Werner, alleging the man's corruption, wrote of Han as still being in office. But not by late 1945; on Werner's return to Peking from Weih-

---

12 UK National Archives, FO 372/5724 British naturalization of Captain George N Binetsky. Code 378 file 5552.
13 Conversation with Binetsky family members George Binetsky and Jodie White, 2015.
14 ibid.

sien, though by this time describing Han in glowing terms, he nevertheless wrote of him using the past tense, as if he were no longer on the scene. It is possible therefore that Han may have fallen foul of the Japanese after all, or equally possible that with the returning China administration he was dealt with for having worked with the enemy. Staying alive and well during this period was a difficult and often dangerous path to tread for any Chinese in public office. And a few years later, it was made even more difficult with the arrival of the communists, when Han and others like him with close associations with previous regimes would have been extremely vulnerable to being denounced as enemies. Cappuzzo shared his captivity with a good number of inmates having a similar background to Han.

After his arrival in Britain on an intern exchange ship in 1942, former Chief Inspector Richard Dennis worked for the Ministry of Food. He returned to the Far East in 1946, attending the International Military Tribunal for the Far East and the war crimes trial of senior Japanese military officers and government officials in Tokyo.[15] Very much overshadowed by the Nazi equivalent in Nuremberg, the Tokyo trial resulted in the jailing of sixteen senior Japanese military officers and government officials for life and in the execution of a further seven. Dennis's role in the affair is not entirely clear. As a victim, he may have provided evidence of his arrest and imprisonment, incarcerated in a wooden cage in Tientsin. But as a former police officer with experience of both the region and of evidence gathering, he may also have played a useful support role for the British legal team. While Dennis was in Singapore, his only child, a teenage son in the Royal Navy who he had not seen for many years, ran into him unexpectedly on the steps of Raffles Hotel. Neither had the slightest idea the

....

15 Diana Dennis, *All I Ever Wanted* (2015).

other was in the Far East. Both older and changed since they last met and wearing unfamiliar uniforms, it took a few moments for them to recognise each other.[16]

On his eventual return to the UK, and after several years of delay, Dennis and some of the other former employees of the – by then defunct – Tientsin Municipal Council received a modest *ex gratia* payment from the British Government for their loss of career, pay and pension.[17] Dennis married for a third and final time and with his new wife invested in a small hotel in London's Bayswater area: the Dennis Hotel. Later still, he became a land-lord of pubs in Buckinghamshire and Hampshire. He died aged seventy-seven in 1976.[18]

Richard Dennis's character and manner were very matter-of-fact. He was a man of few words and difficult to get to know closely, even for his family. He never wrote about his police ca-reer.[19] Indeed, there are no known diaries or papers for any of the police officers involved in the Werner murder case. While it is true that all British police officers were and still remain sub-ject to the Official Secrets Act and similar earlier legislation, thus restricting by law what they may divulge about cases they were involved in, they nevertheless tend to have the frustrating habit of never writing about their work even in the most general of terms. Having been required to write so many investigative re-ports, detectives perhaps have an aversion to penning any fur-ther words of their own. This is unfortunate, as had any one of the police officers involved in the Werner case written privately about the matter in any way, the answers relating to *who, where and why* would probably be a great deal clearer.

16 ibid.
17 UK National Archives, FO 366/2930 Payment of pensions to former employees of the British Municipal Council at Tientsin on account of their claims against the Chinese Government for service benefits. Code XR file 05.
18 a) Conversation with Diana Dennis 2015, & b) Reference to GRO birth & death records.
19 Conversation with Diana Dennis 2015.

The lives of the Foreign Office staff involved in the case were no less dramatic than those of the police officers, although for differing reasons. Sir Hughe Knatchbull-Hugessen, the British Ambassador to China in 1937, the man shot through the abdomen by a Japanese aircraft, was made Ambassador to Turkey, where he remained for much of the war. A lapse in security in that post gave Nazi Germany one of its greatest espionage successes. Knatchbull-Hugessen's driver, an Albanian named Elyesa Bazna (codename *Cicero*) regularly photographed his employer's secret documents which ought to have been kept secure in a safe. Thought by embassy staff to be dimwitted, Bazna reportedly took wax impressions of Knatchbull-Hugessen's despatchbox key and used a specially-constructed wire frame to support a camera. He then contacted a member of staff at the German Embassy in Ankara and offered the photographs for money. Apparently not entirely convinced by Bazna or his product, the Nazis paid him with counterfeit banknotes and thankfully appear not to have made the most of the information gifted to them in what was a major failure in British security. The Bazna case became known publicly in 1950 when one of the Germans involved wrote a book on the affair.[20] With a good deal of artistic license, it was made into a Hollywood movie with James Mason playing the part of the spy.[21] This disaster could have ended his career in disgrace, but somehow Knatchbull-Hugessen went on to become Ambassador to Belgium and then Envoy to Luxembourg. He died in 1971, aged eighty-four.[22]

Turning to the two British consuls at Peking in 1937: Nicholas Fitzmaurice at the time of Pamela's murder, and Allan Archer who succeeded him later in the year. Born within a few years of

20 Operation Cicero, Ludwig Carl Moyzisch, Wingate (1950).
21 Five Fingers, movie, directed by Joseph L. Mankiewicz, 1952.
22 UK National Archives, annual Foreign Office list.

Nicholas Fitzmaurice.
(Courtesy of Mary Thompson)

each other, both were "China Service" men who had each spent over thirty years in the country, and the Peking consular post they each occupied had a large degree of authority over all the other British consular posts in China.[23] Both men were roundly condemned by Werner in his letters to the Foreign Office as being incompetent and failing to identify or bring to book his list of suspects. Both men were promoted to consul-general. And both men later suffered at the hands of the Japanese on the outbreak of the Pacific War in December 1941.

At the time of the attack on Pearl Harbour, Fitzmaurice was serving at the southern port of Amoy, while Archer was far to the north, at Harbin in Manchuria (Manchukuo). Fitzmaurice, the son of a Sussex doctor, seeing the prospect of war, had sent his wife and two small children by ship to stay with relatives in New Zealand where, if and when war came, he hoped to join them. It was not to be. He and his vice-consul gave up their berths on a last boat out of Amoy for the benefit of two foreign Christian missionaries. As a result, Fitzmaurice and his vice-consul were placed under eight months of house arrest by the Japanese. Fitzmaurice was aware of Backhouse's Japanese revenge murder theory over his judgement in the Sasaki case. Were it true, now was their opportunity for further retribution. But throughout his captivity the subject appears not to have featured. Eventually the two men were shipped to Shanghai in the cramped hold of a cargo ship. There, a Japanese soldier demanded Fitzmaurice's

23 School of Oriental & African Studies, PP MS 52 P.D. Coates collection, letter from George Kitson, August 16, 1973.

signet ring, to which the exhausted yet combative Fitzmaurice declared that the man could have it, but he'd have to remove his finger also. The soldier backed down and Fitzmaurice kept both the ring and his finger. He had already lost all his personal papers and diaries, having destroyed them rather than allowing the Japanese access to the maps and notes they contained. Ten years earlier, as the newly-appointed consul in Kashgar, Fitzmaurice had twice travelled overland from Peking to his posting near the frontier with Kyrgyzstan and India, a journey through a wilderness of some three thousand miles. Rather than allow the enemy any advantage, Fitzmaurice consigned his experiences to the flames. Fourteen months later, an emaciated Fitzmaurice joined his family in New Zealand, after a circuitous route via South Africa and Australia. By then in his mid-fifties, his health never fully recovered: his captivity had left him with partial sight in one eye. In October 1943, Fitzmaurice and his family sailed back to the UK. He retired to Hampshire where he died in 1960, aged seventy-two.[24]

Allan Archer, meanwhile, was in Japanese custody for the duration of the War. Why he missed out on a release or exchange is unclear. Suffering from rheumatism, he retired in poor health from the "China Service" in 1946. He was honoured by being made a Freeman of the City of London, and later occupied himself by volunteering for the laborious task of revising Rugby School's register, a type of "who's who" for the famous Warwickshire public school.[25] Archer was a former Rugby school pupil, where he had been a contemporary of the poet Rupert Brooke. But he did not finish his literary endeavour, dying suddenly of a heart attack soon after emigrating to South Africa in 1950, aged

24 Interview with Mary Thompson (nee Fitzmaurice) 2016.
25 Rugby School Register 1911-1946, revised and annotated by Alan Maude and Allan Archer, George Over 1957.

sixty-three.[26] Longevity tended not to be feature among "China Service" staff.

At least Fitzmaurice and Archer left China, if not in good health, then without suffering violent injury, for consular duties could place a man firmly in the line of fire. Arthur Blackburn, for instance, described as the "mildest of men" (notwithstanding Werner's 1913 accusation of him spying on his wife while she dressed), suffered a hole in his knee, a fractured jaw, and the loss of part of one ear when his Hong Kong residence was bombed by a Japanese plane. Lucky to have survived these injuries, he was then interned in a camp for six months after being released from hospital.[27]

Leaving to one side Werner's angry allegations of both Fitzmaurice and Archer being incompetent, what else can be gleaned about them? Fitzmaurice was too nice and too soft, was the blunt opinion of one junior colleague in a candid list he later wrote describing "China Service" staff and their foibles.[28] Another colleague considered Archer "very clever and capable," but said he was handicapped by a "difficult" wife, that generally being an euphemism for something worse.[29] The suitability or otherwise of a man's wife could make or break his Foreign Office career.

Robert Howe missed the worsening conflict in China owing to his transfer back to London and the Foreign Office in 1938. During World War II, he was posted firstly to Riga, and then Ad-

---

26 UK National Archives, annual Foreign Office list.
27 a) "An account of personal experiences of my wife and myself at Hong Kong during the Japanese attack and afterwards", Sir Arthur Blackburn, 1942, Journal of the Hong Kong Branch of the Royal Asiatic Society Vol. 29 (1989), pages 77-93, & b) School of Oriental & African Studies, PP MS 52 P.D. Coates collection, letter from Mrs. Isabelle Blackburn to her father, 1941.
28 School of Oriental & African Studies, PP MS 52 P.D. Coates collection, notes on conversation with Sir Colin Crowe, February 1977.
29 School of Oriental & African Studies, PP MS 52 P.D. Coates collection, letter from Sir Alwyne Ogden, September 14, 1975.

dis Ababa. Regarded as possessing a quiet determination and a cool head, the man from humble beginnings in Derby was assigned to what became the most challenging role of his career – Governor-General in British Sudan, upon which appointment he received a knighthood.[30] Howe was in Sudan for seven difficult years (1947-1954) and gained many friends and admirers for the calm and gracious way he negotiated his way through the politi-

Eric Teichman

cal conflicts that eventually resulted in Sudanese independence from both Britain and neighboring Egypt.[31] The "man for a tight corner"[32] retired with his wife to her family home in Cornwall, where they had first met at the beginning of the Great War. There, as well as pursuing his love of horse-riding, he became a justice of the peace and a local church warden. Cheerful and active to the end, Sir Robert Howe died in 1981, aged eighty-seven.

Less fortunate in his retirement was Eric Teichman, the "China Service" diplomat and adventurous traveller, who, after thirty years' service, retired for the first time a few months before Pamela Werner's murder. He published his *Affairs of China* the following year, a guide to the country that was so well thought of, it was considered a must-read for new consular arrivals. During World War II, at the request of the Foreign Office, which recognized his expertise, Teichman agreed to come out of retirement and return to China as a much-needed advisor to the newly-appointed British Ambassador, working with the

30 UK National Archives, annual Foreign Office list.
31 *The Times*, obituary, July 2, 1981.
32 Sir Berkeley Gage, *It's Been a Marvellous Party*, p55.

Chinese Government in the territories outside Japanese control.[33] Teichman spoke Chinese fluently, but in an almost comic fashion, pronouncing the language with an incongruously clipped British accent. He was also somewhat deaf, leaving an alarmed colleague with memories of him dictating confidential despatches at full-volume in a temporary embassy that possessed nothing more than paper thin walls.[34] "Tei" Teichman retired for a second time in 1944 and returned home to Honingham Hall in Norfolk, a large mansion house within an even larger estate that he had inherited from his father. On a cold afternoon in December of that year, only a few months after his return from China, Teichman heard what sounded like poachers shooting guns on the estate grounds and went to investigate. He came across two American soldiers from a nearby airbase trespassing with semi-automatic weapons. Teichman had scarcely managed a word of protestation before one of them shot him dead through the head at near point-blank range.[35] The two offending American soldiers were soon arrested, and one of them appears to have had mental health problems for he explained in matter-of-fact way that he'd seen a crow and shot it, then likewise a cow and finally an old man, and shot him too.[36] Eric Teichman was sixty years of age. He had survived decades of adventurous travel, disease, revolution and conflict in China, only to be needlessly murdered in rural Norfolk. The soldier was found guilty of murder and hanged on May 8, 1945, which also happened to be VE Day.[37]

As for E.T.C. Werner, after his return to the UK he took up residence in a small nursing home in the seaside town of Margate on the north coast of Kent, which must have provided as sharp a con-

33 *The Times*, reports of January 9, 10, 11, 13 & May 14, 1945.
34 Sir Berkeley Gage, *It's Been a Marvellous Party*, p107.
35 *The Times*, reports of January 9, 10, 11, 13 & May 14, 1945.
36 Sir Berkeley Gage, *It's Been a Marvellous Party*, p107.
37 *The Times*, reports of January 9, 10, 11, 13 & May 14, 1945.

trast as was possible to his former life in Peking. While continuing his campaign to have the killers of his adoptive daughter brought to justice could have been expected of Werner, there is no record of his having done so following his post-war visits to the Foreign Office and the publication of the 1948 book that Cappuzzo so resented. Or at least, no record of any activity has survived.

The redoubtable Werner, aged eighty-nine, died of heart failure at his Margate nursing home on February 7, 1954. He was not buried locally, but cremated in accordance with his wishes. His ashes were laid to rest with those of his sister, Alice Werner, in a crematorium garden in London. It is not known if any distant relatives attended the ceremony, or indeed whether there was any ceremony to attend, for he left instructions that he wanted "no Christian or other burial service." His only request was for someone to read a poem composed by his sister Alice.[38]

A few weeks after Werner's death an obituary by an unnamed author appeared in *The Times*. As well as charting his consular career and listing his many Chinese publications, the article described Werner, both euphemistically and with a good measure of understatement, as "an individualist" who hated living with "the herd."[39]

Werner's will was proved at the High Court of Justice the following May. Rather oddly, and with no explanation as to why, Werner had given instructions for his estate, valued at over £7,000, to be divided between three British children's charities. In addition to this, he also left several minor items (some cutlery, a clock and a wristwatch) to various married ladies in different parts of the world, people with whom his connection is unclear. To one, he left his typewriter, complete with its carbon paper and ribbons. It was probably the same machine he used in China to

38 Will of E.T.C. Werner, dated 28 August 1953.
39 *The Times*, obituary, February 16, 1954.

British cemetery, Peking, before and after the 1948 destruction. (UK National Archives)

type his many reports on Pamela's murder sent to the Foreign Office. But the will, brief as it was, made no mention whatsoever of any items connected with either his wife or his adopted daughter. Nor, sadly, of any personal papers, exhibits or documents relating to evidence of the murder of Pamela.[40]

Thus with the death of E.T.C. Werner in 1954, so too ended any active interest in the murder of a young woman in far-off Peking seventeen years before and a world war apart: an unsolved crime that occurred within a community that no longer existed, in a country that was now closed to outsiders, and a matter for which effectively no police force had responsibility. The case was to remain that way, without further examination, for over fifty years.

In late 1948, Chinese government troops destroyed much of the small British cemetery where Pamela was buried, levelling it to improve the defensive line of fire against the expected ar-

40 Will of E.T.C. Werner, dated August 28, 1953.

rival of communist forces.[41] By 1954, the cemetery and the land surrounding it had been requisitioned by the local communist authorities. The British Embassy discovered that the graves had been disinterred with the remains being reburied at a new, unconsecrated site some seven miles outside the city. The waterlogged coffins had been discarded and bones placed in bags before reburial. The matter was a *fait accompli*; it was too late for the Embassy to protest. Staff appealed to London for funds so that the new graves could be marked with concrete crosses, but the enterprise was considered too expensive and no assistance was forthcoming. In the circumstances it was unlikely that any particular grave could have been identified with any degree of certainty. Whether Werner, in Margate, was aware of these events is unknown.

In a way, the disappearance of the British cemetery epitomises the disappearance of the China that Pamela knew, the China of foreigners in enclaves and concessions, the China in which Pamela lived her entire, abruptly-shortened life and would have undoubtedly considered her home.

---

41 UK National Archives, FO 369/4090 Maintenance of military graves in Peking and naval graves at Chunking; damage by Nationalist troops to British cemetery in Peking. Code 210, file 305.

18

THE SUSPECTS

SORTING SHEEP FROM GOATS

So WHO DID murder Pamela Werner? And what may be deduced with any degree of certainty from the available evidence?

George Gorman, writing as editor of *Caravan* a month after the crime, rather boldly listed a number of possible scenarios, many of them reflecting the stories circulating amongst Peking's foreign society. Perhaps the most scandalous and sensational of these was that Pamela was the "victim of a sex ritual" involving rumors of "exposure parties". A titillating suggestion for his readership. But in the Werner case there is no evidence to support such a scenario. Vices, sure enough, are to be found in cities across the world, but the Peking sex-ring alluded to in Gorman's article was described as little more than a rumor relating to "some years ago". But Werner, as elsewhere, appears to have been influenced by such speculation, reporting that "there is a clique of sexualists in Peking,"[1] and the "sadist sexualist" Prentice as "holding sexual orgies"[2] (that Pamela may have been at-

1   UK National Archives, FO 371/23513/1510 Murder of Pamela Werner, Code 10 file 1510, letter from E.T.C. Werner to the British Ambassador to China, October 1938.
2   UK National Archives, FO 371/23513/1510 Murder of Pamela Werner, Code 10 file 1510, letter from E.T.C. Werner to the British Ambassador to China, June 1939.

tacked by "a sadist" was another Gorman article theory). These lurid Werner allegations went unsupported by evidence. Nevertheless, the question may be posed: was there a sex-ring or similar in Peking? The answer is possibly, or possibly not. What *is* certain is that it is not possible to draw any worthwhile conclusion from speculation that such a group existed, twinned with speculation that it was involved in a murder, i.e. speculating about compound speculation.

Despite the passage of time, the evidence this book has unveiled shows that it is still possible to meaningfully examine events surrounding that January night, and in more depth than Gorman covered in his magazine. It is also possible to evaluate the likelihood of various individuals being implicated in the crime.

Before examining as-yet undescribed police suspects, it is pertinent to consider to what extent any of the men described thus far have a case to answer.

The three men behind Werner's theory of orchestrated abduction and rape – Messrs Knauf, Prentice and Cappuzzo – can be eliminated on the simple basis that there is no evidence supporting their involvement that stands up to reasonable examination. The most that can be said about Werner's charges against the three men is that they did live in the same city on the date of the crime. Apart from Prentice attending to Pamela's teeth six years before, when she was a child, there is no evidence that any of the men met or knew of her prior to her death.

Werner's "evidence" against the men, such as it was, stemmed purely from Werner himself. His account of what happened must be deemed to be a product of his own imagination, of his desire to find guilt in men of his own choosing. Entertaining his prejudices, he first selected his suspects and then paid Chinese agents to find evidence to support his theories. In so doing, he acquired only unsubstantiated hearsay and supposed eyewitness testimo-

ny that literally changed with the passage of time and circumstance. Tellingly, though they had ample opportunity to do so, at
no stage did the British or Chinese police show any serious interest in Werner's list of suspects, all of whom remained in Peking
and made no attempt to flee. Werner's claim that this was due to
the ability of an ex-missionary dentist and his deviant friends to
bribe their way out of a murder charge is beyond credulity, and
would have required men on modest incomes to possess a sinister influence far beyond their true positions in life.

The case of Fred Pinfold was different. Arrested early in the
investigation, the strange Mr Pinfold would undoubtedly have
been placed under close scrutiny by the police. From what can
be gleaned from newspaper reports of the time, the original
grounds for his arrest were that he had shown a close, possibly
ghoulish, interest in the crime scene in its aftermath, with blood-
stains later being found on his clothing. These were not strong
grounds for an arrest, but were nonetheless worth probing by
the police who it appears gained nothing further. Pinfold was
released, and it appears for good. It may be concluded with some
certainty that if the police in a high profile case had a man in
their custody and released him with no further action, and displayed no further interest in him as a suspect, then they probably
had good reason, i.e. there was no supporting evidence of his
involvement. Werner's later claim that Pinfold was nefariously
connected to his own list of suspects of Prentice, Knauf and Cappuzzo, is just that: another contrived Werner invention without
supporting evidence.

Likewise George Gorman, another man on the periphery of
the police investigation, the widely unpopular journalist and
newspaper editor who provoked so much of Werner's ire, can be
similarly dismissed as a suspect. Pamela's suggestive diary entry
and her visit to his home on the day before her death would have

undoubtedly attracted close scrutiny by the police. Once again, however, the connection appears to have led the police investigation nowhere. As with Pinfold, the finding of the diary entry must have at least made the police consider Gorman as a potential suspect. It is therefore inconceivable that they did not look closely into the matter. If the police in 1937 found no evidence to support any further interest in Gorman, then it's highly likely that it was because there was simply none to be found.

The assertion, clandestinely delivered to the British Embassy, that the murder was politically motivated and conducted by the Japanese is almost certainly another example of Backhouse's many elaborate frauds. The motive behind this claim was probably Backhouse's desire to curry favour with the British authorities and maintain his reputation as a source of intelligence. In this respect he appears in some measure to have succeeded – at least some of the Embassy staff in Peking believed his secret information. But although well-crafted (a hallmark of all his frauds), Backhouse's murder account doesn't stand up to careful scrutiny. Leaving aside its messenger's history of contrived deceptions, it required an irrational approach by the Japanese; killing as an act of political revenge makes little sense unless it is recognised as such at the material time, which it was not. It also required a display of courage by the isolated Backhouse that was entirely uncharacteristic of him (he reported that the Japanese would "get" him if he gave them away). His explanation that he feared being guilty of being an accessory after the fact if he did not pass on the information was, in the circumstances, without foundation, something he, an intelligent man, would have known. Backhouse later undermined his tale by changing his position and agreeing with Werner that the latter's Prentice-Cappuzzo theory was correct and that having conducted his own investigation he himself had independently arrived at the same conclusion. These positive statements went beyond mere humouring, especially when combined with the incorrect information he supplied to the old man about Cappuzzo and his embassy home. Backhouse's integrity is further harmed by later reverting to an altered version of his original account when relating it to Hoeppli, the Swiss Consul. The conclusion: it is highly improbable that Pamela Werner was murdered at the hands of the Japanese.

And what of the involvement of the British diplomat? It is an example of a good story that improves with the telling. That Pamela Werner was murdered by someone at the British Embassy, specifically the unfortunate First Secretary D. J. Cowan, was a claim, whispered rather than spoken, based on little more than Legation Quarter gossip and rumor – the linking of a prominent figure with a prominent crime, thus adding colorful scandal to a shocking tragedy. In the complete absence of any primary supporting evidence whatsoever, it should be assessed as such.

In the case of Cowan, as with Prentice and the others, he was, at least, in Peking at the time of the murder, which is almost certainly more than can be said of another high-profile victim of unbridled rumour, Sydney Yeates (1893-1955), a man so unconnected to Peking and the murder that he has escaped attention until now and is only mentioned in order to dismiss him as a suspect.

Sydney Yeates was the British headmaster of the Tientsin Grammar School during the years Pamela attended. He had held the position for ten years.[3] With the start of a new school term, Yeates would surely have been in Tientsin on January 7, 1937, a hundred kilometers from the scene of the murder. Nowhere at the time is it suggested otherwise. It appears that he may have attended Pamela's funeral in Peking, but the report in *The Peiping*

---

3   School of Oriental & African Studies archive library, MS 380697 John Emmitt Woodhall Collection.

Chronicle is unclear on this point, and he may only have sent a wreath.[4]

Two months later, Yeates unexpectedly retired from his position at the school and returned for good to the UK with his wife and daughter. This fact, and this fact alone, appears to have been enough in the eyes of many of his former pupils to somehow link him with the murder. Yeates' leaving, owing to unspecified "health problems," was not so sudden as to prevent him from

Sydney Yeates, TGS headmaster

presiding over the school's speech day in late March 1937, with the school chairman thanking him for his skills of guidance.[5] None of which suggests flight from a serious crime.

As with so many men of this period, it is possible that the "health problems" Yeates was experiencing related to alcohol.[6] Yeates, in the opinion of some pupils, was a harsh disciplinarian, quick with his use of the cane,[7] whereas for others he had seemed quite reasonable, almost affable, lending errant boys copies of *Illustrated London News* to read instead of punishing them.[8]

Whatever his actual health concerns or true character, on his return to Oxford, Yeates found employment as a headmaster's secretary at a local school where he had been a pupil as a boy. He

4 "Last Rites Held for Miss Werner", *Peiping Chronicle*, January 16, 1937.
5 School of Oriental & African Studies archive library, MS 380697 John Emmitt Woodhall Collection.
6 Conversation with former pupil Findlay Mackenzie, 2014.
7 Correspondence with former pupil Desmond Power 2013-2015.
8 Conversation with former pupil Findlay Mackenzie, 2014.

died in 1955, aged sixty-one.[9] He was replaced as Headmaster at the Tientsin Grammar School by John Woodall, later present when the school was forcibly closed by the Japanese.

So persistent was the school gossip connecting Yeates with the Werner murder, that sixty years later, former pupils were still writing speculatively about the possibility on the internet. Another fiction spread about was that Pamela had been a boarder with the Yeates family at the time of the murder. Pamela had, in fact, lodged with the Mackenzies, and prior to that with other missionary families. The casual hearsay that Yeates was guilty of murder was even published as though established fact in an otherwise respectable biography of one former school pupil.[10] Such is the enduring nature of rumour.

Yeates' name, however, was not sullied by schoolchildren alone. Two years after the murder, Werner, though never once suggesting the headmaster was involved in Pamela's murder, reported to the Foreign Office that the real reason for Yeates leaving the school was the discovery of "improper conduct" by Yeates towards Pamela, about which the school authorities had reputedly kept Werner in the dark.[11] Yeates therefore joined the long list of men whom Werner had down as sex offenders and deviants. But, as with all such Werner accusations, and once again made by Werner alone, it was unsupported by evidence.

The gossip among TGS pupils linking Yeates with the murder only developed on the headmaster's departure, which was fully two months *after* the police would have begun looking into Pamela's life at the school. For in the absence of someone being caught red-handed or witnessed running away from the crime

9 City of Oxford High School magazine, 1955.
10 Jacob & Aaron Avshalomov, *Avshalomov's Winding Way; Composers Out of China - a Chronicle*, ppp66-67: "No one could have dreamt that this sedate Principal would some years later be found guilty of luring an unsuspecting student to her shame and gruesome death".
11 UK National Archives, FO 371/23513/1510 Murder of Pamela Werner. Code 10 file 1510, letter from E.T.C. Werner to the British Ambassador to China, October 1938.

Pamela, front row, second from the left, TGS hockey team

Pamela second from left, TGS netball team

scene, identifying the places Pamela frequented and those persons closest to her would have been priorities for the police in the days immediately following the murder. Perhaps topping the list was her school, where Pamela spent the bulk of recent years and where the majority of her friends and associates were to be found. And, most importantly, where any boyfriends were likely to be discovered.

Among the many flowers *The Peiping Chronicle* reported at Pamela's funeral were some marked as being simply "from Michael."[12] The rest of the wreaths were more formally ascribed.

Michael Horjelsky was Pamela's boyfriend at Tientsin Grammar School at the time of the murder, according to fellow pupil Desmond Power. Horjelsky was several years Pamela's junior, perhaps an illustration of her relative immaturity, as well as maybe Michael's relative maturity. Power remembered Horjelsky as being the school's sports star. Popular, good-looking and possessing an athletic physique, Horjelsky excelled at football, swimming, and on the running track. A Polish jew by descent, he was often found at the local Jewish club, the Kunst Club. But Power noted that when he wasn't there, he seemed always to

Michael Horjelsky,
Pamela's boyfriend

be in the company of Pamela. They were together in the playground, at the pool, or skating at the local rink; the pair made for a good-looking couple, she very much the quieter of the two.[13]

But Pamela's relationship with Horjelsky was a relatively recent one. Previously, in early 1936, she had become involved with a fellow boarder at the large Mission House of the Mackenzies by the name of Gilchrist

12 "Last Rites Held For Miss Werner", *Peiping Chronicle*, January 16, 1937.
13 Correspondence with former Tientsin Grammar School pupil, Desmond Power, 2013-15.

Struthers. Like Horjelsky, one of her hosts' teenage sons Findlay Macken-zie was several years younger than Pamela, but in his case he was totally overwhelmed by her female presence. To the young Findlay, the alluring Pa-mela had "all the right apparatus" but he could hardly bear to look at her, a situation made all the worse for him by their living in the same house. The frustrated Findlay could only watch with envy as Pamela was swept off

Pamela in a school photograph

her feet by another newcomer to the house, Gilchrist Struthers.[14]

Struthers, a school pupil about Pamela's age, was the son of a respected Canadian missionary doctor. Findlay Mackenzie ob-served how Struthers was not very sociable with other boys, but very successful with the girls. At the time, Struthers, whose tal-ents were many and varied, was enterprisingly building himself a small boat at the Mission House, and still found space and time to conduct what Findlay recalled as "a passionate affair" with Pamela. Passionate in a missionary community, however, may not have meant much. How the relationship ended and how Horjelsky came on the scene is not known as Findlay left for a boarding school in Japan in the autumn of 1936 and only learned of Pamela's death on his return the next year.[15]

The police would undoubtedly have closely examined both of these youthful romances, and urgently: Horjelsky, Struthers, Werner, the Mackenzies, the school, friends at the rink, would all have been questioned on the subject. The police would want to know the true nature of the relationships, the levels of intimacy,

14 Conversations with Findlay Mackenzie, 2014.
15 ibid.

The YMCA hostel Pamela may have visited shortly before her death

whether there were any disputes or jealousies, and, most importantly, *where* precisely both young men were on the day of the murder.

While skating at the ice rink, Pamela had mentioned to the young Ethel Gurevitch that a boyfriend might visit from Tientsin. Also not to be forgotten was the account given by the Chinese member of staff at the YMCA, who identified Pamela from a selection of photographs presented to him as the same young woman who called at the hotel a day or so before the murder and asked after room rates. The staff member may of course have been mistaken, in which case the event was an investigative red herring. But he may have been correct in his identification, in which case Pamela may have been making plans for a friend, probably Horjelsky, to stay there whilst visiting her in Peking. Or finding somewhere where they could meet privately, although the YMCA would most likely have excluded female visitors to rooms. Either way, the plan would have involved one of them staying somewhere other than the Werner home.

If the police were satisfied that Horjelsky and Struthers were in Tientsin or elsewhere on January 7, 1937, and possessed some form of solid alibi, then that would probably have ended any interest they had in them. Perhaps that's what happened; without the case papers we shall probably never know. But there does exist at least one small element of doubt. Intriguingly, on January 12, five days after the murder, the society page of *The Peiping Chronicle* mentioned Mr. and Mrs. R.G. Struthers – Gilchrist's uncle and aunt – as returning home to Weihwei in Honan province having stayed in Peking for a "short visit on business."[16] Gilchrist's uncle was another respectable missionary doctor. There was no mention in the column of any other family members. The Struthers visit was probably a coincidence, but it is the sort of thing the police should have examined closely, if they were aware of the relationship.

Michael Horjelsky, TGS swimming team

Gilchrist Struthers appears later to have left China with his family prior to the start of the Pacific War and thus avoided Japanese internment. So too did Michael Horjelsky, but he did not survive the War. Returning briefly to Tientsin after his release from Weihsien camp in 1945, Desmond Power was surprised to come across Michael Horjelsky's el-

16 *Peiping Chronicle*, society column, "Dr. and Mrs. R.G. Struthers of Weihwei, Honan returned to their home yesterday after a short visit to Peiping on business", January 12, 1937.

derly father still doing business in the same real estate office he had run before the War. Power asked after Micheal, and was told by Horjelsky that his son had "got away to the States before Pearl Harbour, went to college there, joined the USAAF, got posted to a squadron of B24s, took part in the raid on Ploesti, was shot down and killed."[17]

"Operation Tidal Wave" was a huge US bombing raid on German-held Romanian oil fields at Ploesti in August 1943 involving over 170 B24 bombers. It was a disaster for the Americans, with over fifty planes and in excess of six hundred crewmen lost, the USAAF's worst-ever casualties from a single mission. Horjelsky doesn't appear to feature on lists of those involved but, that notwithstanding, there is no reason to doubt the word of his father.

Convinced as Werner was that he "knew" the correct identities of the killers, in writing his investigation reports he does not appear to have shown the slightest interest in Pamela's Tientsin boyfriends, past or current. Obsessed as Werner was in promoting Pamela as dying to protect her virtue, the idea of her having male friends may not have sat well with him. He appears to have either ignored or discounted entirely the subject of boyfriends and romances, as though they never existed. The police, of course, would not have have been so blind and would have been very much alive to that side of Pamela's life. Though not a scrap of British police investigatory material survives – no notes, no interviews, no exhibits, no closing reports – Werner nevertheless inadvertently helped to provide an insight into police thinking at the time by, rather typically, writing to the Foreign Office complaining about it.

But before introducing these and other more salient aspects of the murder investigation, there is one more figure to consider

---

17 Correspondence with former Tientsin Grammar School pupil, Desmond Power, 2013-15.

and that is E.T.C. Werner himself.

That Werner may have killed Pamela is not as far-fetched as it may first appear. A large percentage of murders, especially those involving female victims, are committed by someone known to the victim or by a member of their family. Pamela's body was found within a few hundred yards of the Werner home. Werner knew her likely route home that evening. He had a history of becoming violent after losing his temper, as the episode in Foochow demonstrated and then again more recently by breaking the nose of a male Chinese friend of Pamela for showing too close an interest in her.

According to his own account of events on the evening of the murder, Werner had gone looking for Pamela in a state of anxiety. It is therefore possible that he came across her on her way home. Werner described passing the very spot where her body was later found, placing himself squarely at the scene at an early stage. Werner then turned up at the same spot the next morning, as offenders often do, only for him to feel faint and pass out, something which may have been opportune. All of the above amount to circumstantial rather than direct evidence, but they illustrate how close Werner was to critical events.

As for motive, Pamela was no longer an obedient child who could be moulded and controlled, but a young woman with a developing mind of her own. The Mackenzie children, with whom Pamela lived in Tientsin during her final year of life, remembered having the distinct impression that she did not get on with her father, but put a brave face on this unhappy aspect of her life.[18] Pamela also had a boyfriend whom Werner may or may not have known about, or perhaps may only have just discovered. Werner had been extraordinarily insecure in his relationship with his

---

18 Conversations with Louise McLean (nee Mackenzie) and Findlay Mackenzie, 2014.

long-dead wife, Pamela's adoptive mother, jealously accusing his consular colleagues of all manner of imagined improprieties. Given his nature, it is perhaps likely that Werner felt similarly about his adopted daughter. Loss of control and anger may have been cause alone for violence.

Werner's reputation for eccentricity was such that it led to at least some in Peking society suspecting that he had killed Pamela, for Werner's name was one of those included in the foreign community rumor mill, as was noted by the American journalist Helen Foster Snow in her memoirs: "One party believed it was done by Werner himself, who was far from normal".[19] Given the circumstances, there was more reason for it to have been Werner than the likes of Cowan or Yeates. Indeed, all things considered, Werner made for a better suspect than the men he himself openly accused of the crime.

Against this, however, there are a number of factors that weigh substantially against any Werner involvement.

While it is feasible that Werner, walking alone and encountering Pamela riding home, could have struck out at her recklessly and repeatedly in a fit of pique with a heavy object, enough to fracture her skull and kill her, it is nevertheless a scenario that fails to match fully the particulars of the murder scene. It provides no explanation for the worst of the mutilations performed on the victim's body, injuries that went far beyond any mere loss of temper by Werner: the evisceration of the victim was an act Werner could have no real motive for inflicting. Neither does this Werner-as-murderer scenario account for the evidence of the victim having recently had sexual intercourse, unless of course Werner somehow knew of this, or suspected it, and this was part of his cause for anger. It would also suggest that Pamela was

19 Hoover Institute Library & Archives, Nym Wales papers (Helen Foster Snow) 1931-1998, Sian Incident, box 17.

consensually sexually active, which while possible, was unlikely given the sexual mores of the time and the risk of unplanned pregnancy. Having committed an atrocious crime, Werner would then have had to return to his home, probably spattered with blood, and display nerves of steel in order not to raise the suspicions of his servants and to be able to face down the police the next morning. And he would have had to maintain this charade for the months and years that lay ahead. A tall order even for a man as obstinate as Werner.

Telling, perhaps, is the fact that at no stage did the Chinese or British police appear to regard Werner as a suspect. Without the police records, there is no way of being certain on this point, but the several consular letters between Archer and the Ambassador on the subject of the murder, candid though they are in their description of Werner, contain not the slightest suggestion that Werner might actually have been involved. Unless kept in the dark by the police, the letters between these two men would surely have read differently if there were genuine suspicions that Werner might be culpable.

In January 1947, precisely ten years after the murder, and within a few weeks of his return to England from China, the tireless Werner posted an *in memoriam* entry in The Times newspaper: "In ever-loving memory, on her birthday, of our darling daughter, Pamela, who was murdered in Peking. She gave her life in defence of her honour."[20] By the word *our*, Werner was presumably referring to his long-dead wife, for otherwise he remained very much alone, any interest in the murder by others having long since ended: by now Werner had no real cause to keep with his task. The following year, he published *More Memorigrams*, a book which even risked him being sued for libel over

....

20 *The Times*, notices, January 15, 1947.

his determined finger-pointing.

Were Werner's many years of campaigning a case of a man suspiciously protesting too much about the guilt of others? That is an idea that cannot be ruled out entirely. But all things considered, while it cannot be shown with certainty that Werner had no hand in Pamela's death, given the known facts, his involvement appears to be highly unlikely. When Werner died seventeen years after Pamela's murder, still obstinately holding to his view on the guilt of the men he had selected as suspects, his mindset was surely attributable to his natural intransigence rather than as cover for his own culpability. Werner's character was such that he simply could not brook being wrong, no matter how palpably wrong he was. As his wife, Gladys, once said: "Once my husband gets an idea into his head there is no changing his mind." Neither, it appears, could he ever lay an idea to rest.

19

THE OFFENDER

CUTTING TO THE CHASE

BY ANY REASONABLE STANDARD, the preceding chapters illustrate how Werner could not be taken at his word. To quote one "China Service" colleague trying to verify points made in an obituary that Werner wrote for an acquaintance: "I don't feel inclined to rely on a mere Werner statement."[1] But in his remarkable ability to find conflict in nearly everything and then commit the matter to paper, Werner could often be relied upon to quote the opposing person's position on any given matter, i.e. the position with which he disagreed, often vehemently. Ironically, in his efforts to dismiss the word of others, Werner appears to have been at his most accurate in his reporting. Once or twice in his long and accusatory reports to the Foreign Office, while dismissing the police lines of enquiry as nonsense, Werner very helpfully reveals an aspect of police thinking that was otherwise lost.

In November 1938, Werner reported that Dennis: "... has expressed in writing his determination 'not to budge one inch' from his conclusion that the murderer was a former Chinese ac-

....

1 School of Oriental & African Studies archive library, PP MS 52 P.D. Coates Collection, letter from Coates to Sir Alwyne Ogden, June 6, 1978.

quaintance of Pamela when, in 1923, we were living in the north city." (Werner must have meant 1933).[2]

Werner then continued: "Dennis strenuously affirmed his conclusion that the murderer was one of Pamela's former Chinese school friends."[3]

And then further still: "Dennis' unswerving conviction that the murder was committed by one of two Chinese students, one in Mukden and the other in Honan."[4]

From Werner's reports it would appear that the two men met several times, or at least corresponded, with Werner trying to convince Dennis about the merits of his star witness, the rickshaw coolie whom his agents had produced. As the most senior British police officer on the case, it would have been Dennis's role to deal with complaints and allegations from Werner. Given Werner's absolute certainty that he was right and everyone else wrong, Dennis's exasperation comes as no surprise. Dennis was probably drawn into saying or writing to Werner more than he ought to have done. It is generally unwise for police to announce the identity of a person they are after to anyone outside the investigation team, no matter what their personal interest. An exception may be made if an individual's knowledge or help is required in locating someone, which was not the case here. Nonetheless, telling Werner about his still outstanding suspect is what Dennis appears to have done.

In late 1941, in his last report to make it out of China before the attack on Pearl Harbour, Werner went one step further and gave a name for one of Dennis's two Chinese student suspects:

....

2 UK National Archives, FO 371 23513/1510 Murder of Pamela Werner. Code 10 file 1510, letter from E.T.C. Werner to the British Ambassador to China, October 1938.
3 ibid., letter, December 1938.
4 ibid., letter, March 1939.

I have discovered that Han Shou-ch'ing, the former student
at the Kao Teng Shih Fan College, in the south city, whose
nose I broke for him... was hanging around the Legation
Quarter during the first week in January 1937.[5]

Werner then continued:

"Han Shou-ch'ing (who some five years before had returned to his father's home in Mukden, and was married,
after which he came back to Peking) was later murdered
by some Japanese, but his death was due to quite another
matter and had nothing whatever to do (as falsely alleged
to me by the British Consul in 1940) with the murder of Pamela Werner. I now know that Han Shou-ch'ing was really
killed, and that the rumour that he had changed his name
and succeeded in escaping is false."[6]

These revealing snippets of information about Dennis's two
student suspects were part of much longer letters by Werner in
which he was trying to convince the Foreign Office of the guilt
of Prentice, Knauf and Cappuzzo. Whether the students were
alive or dead, killed by the Japanese or not, Werner was simply
dismissing the possibility that they were viable suspects. It is of
great help that he took the trouble to do so, for as a result he supplied the name of the man who was probably the police's chief
suspect, that of Han Shou-ch'ing from Mukden (today called
Shenyang) in Manchuria. Han Shou-ch'ing, it should be noted,
is not to be confused with that other Han, the chief of Peking
police, Han Shih-ching.

....

5   UK National Archives, FO 371/35815 Murder of Pamela Werner. Code 10 file 714, letter
    from E.T.C. Werner to the British Ambassador to China, December 1941.
6   ibid.

Dennis would have got his information from the men work-ing directly on the case, Botham and Binetsky, and quite pos-sibly from the Chinese police also. For Dennis to come out with dogmatic words and phrases such as "unswerving conviction" and "not to budge one inch from his conclusion," it follows that he must have been very sure of the reliability of the intelligence obtained by his officers. He would not otherwise have repeated it so loosely, even when pushed to the limits of his patience by Werner.

There is now no way of knowing the nature of the intelligence Dennis and his colleagues possessed, still less testing its accu-racy, but a former acquaintance of Pamela from a Peking school or college such as described, would fit well with many of the known facts.

In his 1941 report, Werner wrote that some years before the murder, he broke the nose of the student suspect Han Shou-ch'ing for showing too much interest in Pamela. It was, he ex-plained, as a result of this altercation that Werner went to the trouble of sending her to Tientsin to continue her schooling: "students were in the habit of waiting at the [school] gate and enticing the girls to go with them to tea, cinemas, or even to their rooms".[7] Given the length of Pamela's stay at the TGS, this vio-lent altercation would have been in the early 1930s when Pamela was in her middle teens and attending one of a number of Catho-lic schools in Peking.

Ordinarily, Werner would not be expected to recall or have any interest in the name of a Chinese youth, no matter what his background. How then, several years after the murder, and at least five years after the nose-breaking event, did he come to write reporting the name Han Shou-ch'ing? It could be that he

....

7   E.T.C Werner, Memorigrams, Shanghai Times, 1940, page 143

only learned of the name through the police, post-murder, as a result of their enquiries. Or perhaps became all too aware of it at the time of the nose-breaking incident, something which may have involved considerable local brouhaha or even trouble with the local authorities. Or perhaps he discovered it from the school or college as result his own enquiries into unsuitable suitors (Werner could be very determined over such matters). Or perhaps he learned it from Pamela herself, who may have liked Han, or thought him amusing, or been innocently attracted to him. She may even have drunk tea with him. Han may have persisted in his efforts over some period of time. Infatuation can overcome all manner of cultural boundaries (such relationships were roundly condemned by both Chinese and foreigners). The strong picture produced by the wording of these reports by Werner is of a college student loitering by a school gate, an interloper. But the description of a *former school friend* is also mentioned. It's a loose term which may refer to any number of circumstances, up to and including Han being at some stage a fellow pupil of Pamela. In the 1930s, as a result of nationalist government policy, religious schools, Catholic ones included, were open to children of all or no religion, Chinese and foreigners alike. Although most schools remained either all-male or all-female, it is just possible that at some stage Han and Pamela were at school together, and that they may have known each other over some period of time.

As to which secondary school these events occurred, a few years after her death Werner described Pamela as having attended the Catholic St. Michael's school in the heart of the Legation Quarter. George Gorman, however, in his *Caravan* article of February 1937, wrote of Pamela as having been a pupil at the "White Franciscan convent in Peking". Gorman may have been correct, for of the two schools the latter appears the more likely candidate. The Marist Brothers at St. Michael's ran a boys' primary school for local Chinese, teaching in Chinese and French only, and no girls. The Franciscaine Sisters, meanwhile, ran a small *pensionnat* all-girl's school - for foreigners and Chinese, both primary and secondary - within the *Institution du Sacré-Coeur*, a gated building, outside and to the north of the Legation Quarter (at the time the Werners lived in the north of the city). The sisters taught in Chinese, French, and English. A Chinese student may have found "waiting" outside the *pensionnat* a good deal easier than a venue inside the Legation Quarter, where Chinese access was strictly controlled.

Pamela returned to Peking from Tientsin on December 26, 1936, allowing adequate time for a former school friend and would-be-suitor to learn of her presence in the city. Ice-skating appears to have been a longstanding pastime of Pamela's. The visit to the French rink on January 7 was her second visit there in two days. None of these arrangements had been made in secret and could easily have been overheard or guessed at. A bicycle was her regular means of transport. In such circumstances, it would not have been difficult for someone acquainted with her to predict where Pamela might be on January 7, using which route, and at what time.

Pamela's body was discovered a short distance from her home and on the most direct route from the French rink. It also happened to be the only way home with which she was familiar. The strong likelihood is that she was killed at the very spot she was found. The theory of her being abducted initially and then taken elsewhere to be murdered, only to be dumped at a spot a few hundred yards from her home, rather than somewhere else in the city, is far-fetched at best and one of the more fanciful of Werner's many fixations. The simplest explanation is usually the right one and moving bodies around can be risk-laden and messy.

The suspect may have approached Pamela as she left the

French rink, alone. Being previously acquainted, Pamela may have trusted him, or liked him, or felt sorry for him, or may have been too polite to tell him to go away. She may not have had the slightest idea of the danger he posed.

The pair may then have set off together in the direction of Pamela's home. They may have walked or cycled. Or the suspect may have simply followed Pamela having been initially rejected

L'Institution du Sacré-Coeur and its entrance gates
(Annales des Franciscaines Missionaires de Marie, September 1934)

345

by her. Or he may not have engaged her in conversation at all.

The site where the assault took place was dark and remote. The depth of the ditch where the body was found afforded good cover. It was a spot without witnesses. The location suggests at least some degree of forethought, the suspect either suddenly seizing an opportunity or planning one in advance.

The motive for the crime was probably a mixture of frustrated sexual desire and long-standing infatuation. Pamela was either bludgeoned in order to subdue and rape her, or raped and then bludgeoned after the act.

Whichever was the case, the offender would have realized that he was known personally to Pamela and therefore identifiable if she survived to tell of events. The injuries that caused Pamela's death, blows to the head with a blunt object, are consistent with someone either thinking ahead, or more likely improvising by using a handily available object such as a length of timber, a rock, or piece of masonry.

The removal of Pamela's clothing is consistent with a sexual motive, even allowing for the fact that underwear was left in place, or perhaps replaced. As for the cold and dark, the primary offence would have required little in the way of ambient light and, given enough desire in a young man, sex, however basic, is perfectly possible in cold temperatures.

Such a scenario, thus far, is reasonably straightforward and could have been committed by virtually any young male, of any race or background. But what made this crime so peculiar and extraordinarily shocking were the mutilations and the removal of organs.

Of these, the most infamous was that the victim's heart had been cut from her body and removed from the scene altogether. From newspaper reports of the coroner's hearing it is uncertain whether other organs were in fact missing or merely damaged

View showing Pamela's wall route home from the Legation Quarter

or displaced. What is evident is that there was a determined and successful attempt to access the thorax and remove the heart: ribs were broken and displaced and a large hole made through the diaphragm. The removal of the heart would seem to have been a definite goal.

Werner laid great stress on his belief that the intention of the murderers was to *dismember* the body prior to disposing of it. But this is not borne out by the evidence. Dismemberment the world over commonly involves cutting a body into six manageable and transportable pieces - four limbs, the torso, and the head. The removal of organs is generally unnecessary. None of the wounds on Pamela's body were consistent with this common form of dismemberment, or even its preparation (which would have required cutting tools heavier than simply knives). It is true that the coroner's hearing recorded a deep wound to one of the victim's arms, but this described damage to muscle rather than the shoulder joint, that being the point at which dismemberment might have been attempted. In any event, it makes no sense to dismember the body if the intention was to bury it at the place at which it was found, as Werner claimed. For if the intention was to conceal the body by burying it, why not bury it whole and spare yourself the trouble and risk of dismembering it?

Contrary to providing evidence of dismemberment, the peculiar mutilations found on Pamela's body suggest a different motive altogether, one that may be attributable to Chinese cultural practices of long-standing which involved the removal of the heart from a dead body.

Perhaps understandably, relatively little has been written about what may be seen as a grisly and disturbing aspect of Chinese culture, but in the 1930s the American journalist Edna Booker recorded Chinese soldiers cutting out the hearts of dead enemies and eating them.[8] A generation or so before that, there were notable instances where high profile Chinese murder and execution victims had their hearts removed as an act of revenge.[9] In what remains a rare contribution to the subject, the modern historian Professor Key Ray Chong wrote extensively on such disturbing practices, discussing the place of ritual cannibalism in Chinese history. Key explained how, unlike in other societies, Chinese cannibalism was not related to any formal religious act, but rather to two opposing emotional drives: loyalty and affection on one hand, and hatred and revenge on the other, i.e. cannibalism may be an act of love, or, equally, its opposite, one of hostility.[10]

On a related theme, Key also discussed how many human body parts have long featured in traditional Chinese medicine.

8 Edna Lee Booker, *News is My Job: A Correspondent In War-torn China*, (1940), p103.
9 Jung Chang, *Empress Dowager Cixi: The Concubine Who Launched Modern China* (2014), p347.
10 Key Ray Chong, *Cannibalism in China* (1990), pages viii & 176.

This last may not have played a part in the case of Pamela Werner, but it further illustrates how the removal and use of human body parts was an accepted practice for at least some sections of Chinese society. In the 1920s, Werner himself commented on such beliefs in his book *Myths and Legends of China* describing how children were known to be murdered for body parts for traditional medicine,[11] and how the mutilation of a corpse was said to "maim it permanently during its existence in the otherworld."[12]

Seen in this cultural light, the removal of Pamela's heart starts to become less mysterious. What was a purely barbaric and abhorrent act to the foreigners of the Legation Quarter, may have seemed justifiable and natural to one particular love-spurned and resentful Chinese young man.

Then there are the other injuries found on the body. The gratuitous slashes to the face and torso may be consistent with the anger, resentment and violence generated by the moment. The deliberate removal of one entire ear resembles trophy-taking. Feral dogs, of which there were many reports, may have accounted for the loss of the other missing body parts, those perhaps removed in the search for the heart. Only the deep wound to the arm remains less readily explained, though it may be attributable to the overall level of force used throughout the crime.

At the time, much was made by both Werner and the newspapers on the apparent anatomical and surgical skills of the offender. This need not have been the case. Many people of the period would have been familiar with the slaughter and butchery of animals, possessing a far more hands-on approach to the rudiments of life than, say, the average resident of the Legation Quarter. Certainly the offender would have required at least one medium-sized sharp knife. Again, this last may suggest plan-

11 E.T.C. Werner, *Myths and Legends of China* (1922), p26.
12 ibid., p56.

ning and forethought on his part, though not necessarily so, for a sharp knife or cutting tool in a bag with other basic utensils such as a lamp in winter may have simply been routine items for many people to carry. These items may have been all that was required for the task, even in a ditch in the dark.

It's right to note that such attitudes and practices would be wholly unexpected in a Chinese student of the wealth and class that enabled him to receive a private education. From the little that can be gleaned from Werner's references to him, i.e., "a Chinese acquaintance of Pamela"; "a former Chinese school friend"; "whose nose I broke for him", Han Shou-ch'ing was probably one of the Chinese college students Werner complained of as being in the habit of "waiting at the [school] gate and enticing the girls to go with them to tea, cinemas, or even to their rooms."[13] If Werner was correct, the young man also harked from Mukden in Manchuria (from where his family may well have fled the Japanese invasion of 1931), attended the Kao Teng Shih Fan college, and later returned to Mukden and married. Typically, leading a sheltered and privileged existence, such an individual would be unlikely to be familiar with violence and mutilation. However, outside these scraps of information, nothing is known of the suspect Han Shou-ch'ing's family or background, his mores and customs, his life circumstances or mental state. And whatever his social status, his involvement in the crime accords with the known circumstances; Chief Inspector Dennis told Werner in very clear terms that he was convinced of the fact, something he would not have done without evidence and/or good intelligence. Policing reveals only to clearly how people from right across the social spectrum are capable of extraordinary acts of unexpected and shocking violence, acts that frequently beggar

....

13 Memorigrams, E.T.C Werner, Shanghai Times (1940), page 143

belief. Bizarre crimes; bizarre offenders.

The theft of Pamela's belongings can be all but ruled out as a motive ahead of the primary offence of rape and murder. Various items, including the skates and bicycle were missing from the scene, but these could have taken by any opportunistic passer-by at any time before the arrival of the police, especially if left some distance from the body. What cannot be entirely ruled out is the possibility, admittedly remote, that it was a passer-by who took body parts from the corpse, that Pamela was in a sense a victim twice, i.e. firstly raped and murdered, then subject to theft of body parts by another who later came across the scene. After all, like the skates and bicycle, human body parts may well have had a commercial value. Though perhaps unlikely (the theft of body-parts is not as easy as taking an abandoned bicycle), the twice-a-victim scenario is by no means impossible.

For the sake of completeness, comment should also be made about Pamela's stomach contents which were described by Dr Van Dyke as being semi-digested Chinese food consumed some four hours before her death. Though featuring in press reports of the coroner's hearing, the food's presence is unlikely to be of significance. Pamela appears to have been in the habit of eating at least some forms of Chinese food – as was described by the Werner's cook at the inquest – and would have had ample opportunity to eat at any number of local shops or street vendors that afternoon. Pamela snacking mid-afternoon, that being about four hours before leaving the rink, would account for her not being hungry at the Gurevitch's tea. Though unlikely, it is also conceivable that it was Han Shou-ch'ing who provided Pamela with the food, food that they then ate somewhere together. Unlikely because, if the estimated digestion period was correct, a post-rink meal would thereafter have required a four-hour time period before her death, necessitating an unaccountable delay that led Werner into imagining the involvement of all manner of people, places, transport, abductions and contrivances. Unlikely also because a shared meal would probably have attracted witnesses – genuine ones – who weren't forthcoming despite the availability a police reward.

Why, then, did the British and Chinese police, with all the time and resources available to them, fail to find and arrest Han Shou-ch'ing of Mukden, previously a student of the Kao Teng Shih Fan College, or the other former school friend of Pamela who was also a suspect? Why were they not apprehended? There is no sure way of knowing, but an explanation might be found in the scale of the task.

The offender had the great advantage of not being seen or caught committing the offence and was able to make good his escape from the scene. Generally, unless the guilty party is caught in the act or gives himself up, murder investigations are rarely without gaps and delays as police attempt an exercise in recovery after the fact, as they try to work out what may have happened, who saw what, where and when. It may have been days, weeks or even months before Dennis and his colleagues assembled the intelligence or evidence that led him to "strenuously affirm" his belief in one of two particular Chinese suspects, albeit that within a few days of the murder several British and Australian newspapers reported among their small print that the police officer "Han is following up the clue that Pamela was friendly with a Chinese student."[14] These newspapers also published a measure of purely speculative material on the case, but the several lines in reports relating to Colonel Han and his hunting for a Chinese student strongly suggest an early Chinese police source for the information.

....

14 Reported in various newspapers, among them *Gloucestershire Echo*, January 9, 1937.

Whatever time advantage the offender may have possessed, he would have had good reason to want to flee Peking as soon as possible. China is an immense country in which to hide for a Chinese person, and if the perpetrator was Chinese, he may have gone to ground long before the police even began looking for him. The police, however, did appear to have the name of at least one individual they were after. They would also have had access to the records of the college Han Shou-ch'ing attended, the Kao Teng Shih Fan in the south city. The college would have been at least partially fee-paying, and any Chinese students would have probably come from reasonably affluent Chinese families, families that ought therefore to be readily traceable in hometowns such as Mukden. The offender may have been able to hide or disappear, but a family would be less able to do so, which may explain the origin of Werner's conflicting information relating to Han Shou-ch'ing's alleged death, a point that needs exploring.

Werner's information was that Han Shou-ch'ing had been killed by the Japanese, and he disputed the British Consul's claim that his death was related to Pamela's murder (a subject and conversation of which we unfortunately have no further details). Whatever the truth of the matter, by 1940 both Werner and the British Embassy were of the opinion that Han Shou-ch'ing was dead. Perhaps that was correct, and perhaps not. One absolute certainty is the immense pressure the offender would have been under. A Chinese perpetrator would have realized that raping and murdering a foreign woman in Peking would bring the world down upon him. Nothing illustrates this point better than the fact that for several hours after the body's discovery it excited relatively little attention; Chinese corpses in the streets of Peking were commonplace. But once it was established that the corpse was that of a foreigner, the Chinese police chief Han was immediately on the scene along with the British authorities and all the influence they could bring to bear. In no time at all, the murder was the talk of China. It must have seemed to the offender that everyone was pursuing him, motivated by a substantial reward for information leading to his conviction.

Being purportedly dead may have been a clever ruse to keep the police from further pursuit, especially if, say, the assertion was supported by family members under an almost equal pressure and desperate to preserve a sense of family honour and face. Being killed by the occupying Japanese was a claim that was both plausible and had the added advantage of making such a death virtually impossible to confirm or investigate further.

One of the two students mentioned by Dennis via Werner's letters, the anonymous youth from Honan, is effectively lost to any further investigation, but it is conceivable that more is to be discovered of the other suspect, Han Shou-ch'ing. Writing prior to the advent of the pinyin romanization system, did Werner translate the name accurately? Have the records survived the years of war, the Japanese occupation, and later, the purges and upheavals of China since 1949? The chances now of his correct identification are remote.

There is a further complication. The reader may recall that the name Han Shou-ch'ing closely resembles the one provided by Backhouse to the Embassy in his Japanese assassination letter of 1938, that of Tan Shou Ching (as reported by Consul Archer). Backhouse described Tan Shou Ching as a former friend of Pamela who enticed her to her death at the hands of the Japanese, and said he also had a grudge against her father, Werner. Given the similar name and circumstances, Backhouse could well have been referring to the Han Shou-ch'ing, named quite independently by Dennis. On the other hand, Backhouse's frauds usually carried at least elements of truth or known facts in their construction. Han Shou-ch'ing or Tan Shou Ching: one could have been misheard and the variation in spelling can only make further identification of the individual concerned even more challenging.

The Backhouse Japanese-revenge theory also describes the student as having merely an entrapment role in the affair, leaving the murder, mutilation and sexual violence to the Japanese - then a militaristic society with the potential capacity for the extreme acts found in the Pamela case (and, to boot, with no qualms about attacking a white foreigner). This may appear plausible, and tallies with the reasonable presumption that the Chinese student was the cosseted son of a wealthy family. Against this however, the Backhouse theory - if the baronet can be believed, which is highly problematic - requires a complex political conspiracy involving many participants: chains of command, orders, intelligence, schedules, authorisation, victim-selection, team-selection. All of which would have required time and planning, both of which may have been short given that Pamela only returned to Peking on December 26. It all amounts to a tall order. And all in order to murder a victim that few people of note would have known of, and then go to the further trouble of dumping the body near the home address. To which must be asked: what kind of political revenge is it if no one recognizes it for what it is until pointed out by Backhouse a year after the event? Fiendish mysteries have a tendency to attract fiendish solutions; the simple and direct are by far the more likely.

Given the evidence available, both now and at the time of the murder, it may said with virtual certainty that none of the men featuring as suspects in this book would be found guilty of the crime were they to be tried in a criminal court. In the UK, similar to the majority of justiciary systems, including the foreign and Chinese courts of the time, a defendant is presumed innocent until proven guilty and the standard or burden of proof is set very high at "beyond reasonable doubt." As a result, the cases against all the named suspects, such as they are, would not have got as far as seeing the inside of a court as they lack sufficient evidence to support even the prospect of a prosecution.

Criminal courts aside, an approach that may be of greater help in forming an assessment of the various men and their connection or otherwise with the murder would be to use a different standard of weighing matters, one commonly used in civil courts to establish culpability, i.e. *on the balance of probabilities*. In other words, what is the probability that a particular individual was involved or not involved in the murder? This approach can be expressed in percentage terms.

Given an assessment of the evidence available it might reasonably be concluded that the chances of Knauf, Prentice and Cappuzzo being involved in the death of Pamela Werner are one percent, at the most. And only as much as that low figure because at the relevant time, all three men lived in and frequented that part of Peking where the crime occurred, as did thousands of others.

It is difficult to put a figure to Backhouse's Japanese revenge theory. If accepted, in its wholeness, as another of his carefully constructed frauds, then it scores zero. But it appears to have contained at least one element of probable truth – Backhouse hit upon the name of a student named Tan/Han and his problems with Werner – and so must score a percentage figure accordingly. The question is whether he heard that name on the Peking grapevine or from the Japanese, as he claimed. It should be remembered that Backhouse lived among the Chinese in the Tartar city, with whom he could speak directly in their own tongue; he may have heard more than foreigners did in the Legation Quarter. He may have woven a genuine suspect into a story of his own. But the fact that Backhouse later varied his murder theory, first for Werner, then for the Swiss consul, twinned with his long history of elaborate deceptions, renders him a hopeless witness and makes the task of sifting fact from fiction virtually impossible.

The headmaster, Yeates, reasonably presumed to be at the Tientsin Grammar School at the time of the murder, scores zero. As do the two boyfriends, Michael Horjelsky and Gilchrist Struthers, as they were likely in Tientsin, given the total absence of rumor or speculation about them.

Pinfold, Gorman, and Cowan lived in Peking and were in the city on the night of the murder. They also had some form of connection to the victim, or to the scene or, as in the case of Cowan, had alarmed a colleague by demonstrating how the offence could be committed. The chances of these individuals being involved therefore is perhaps the low figure of two percent. In Pinfold's case, his arrest may score him a little higher, perhaps three or four percent.

Controlling, bad-tempered, a minor history of violence, difficulties with the truth, in close proximity to the body, and appearing at the scene of the crime, Werner must be higher on the list of suspects. These factors are to a large extent circumstantial and none make for direct evidence. But on a scale of probabilities they might reasonably score Werner as much as five percent or more.

But none of these men rate as highly as Han Shou-ch'ing and the other unnamed Chinese former friend of Pamela whom Werner reported Richard Dennis was focused on.

The substance of the evidence the police possessed for one or the other's involvement is now unknown, but if Dennis, the senior police officer overseeing the case, felt strongly enough to tell of his firm belief in one of the two being guilty of the crime and strenuously affirming this conclusion, then his statement must carry considerable weight. In addition to this, Dennis's statement also best fits the known facts relating to both the murder scene and the victim's movements and circumstances over the previous few days. When these factors are weighed together, it might reasonably be said that the chances of one of the two Chinese suspects being involved in the murder is as high as fifty percent or more, i.e. the chances that one of them was involved is greater than their not being involved. Of this pair, the recurring name of Han Shou-ch'ing comes under the greatest suspicion: his waiting for Pamela at the school gate; his previous assault by Werner; his rumoured name-change; his success in "escaping"; his unconfirmed and mysterious death; the British authorities' enduring interest in him, as late as 1941.

In conclusion then: a judgement in the case of Pamela Werner. To the question: in the event of a trial, would the former student Han Shou-ch'ing today be found guilty of rape and murder? The answer is no, he would not: more than eighty years after the crime, that high bar of "beyond reasonable doubt" is never going to be achieved, not without recourse to the evidence of the day. But leaving law and the courts aside, after a reasoned and impartial assessment of all the known circumstances: did he kill Pamela Werner beside the wall on that cold night in January 1937? Was he responsible? The answer is yes, most likely he was. Dennis - the man overseeing the police investigation, with the intelligence and facts before him - was convinced of the fact. Additionally, Han Shou-ch'ing knew and had the connection to the victim. And he had the motive: infatuation, resentment, passion, rejection, revenge; all powerful drivers for unhinged and extraordinary acts, such as those seen by the wall road. Combine these factors with his convenient disappearance, name-changing, and tales of death: it all points strongly to him being the offender.

POSTSCRIPT

I FIRST READ of the Pamela Werner murder in *Midnight in Peking*, written by Paul French and published in 2011 (full disclosure: Nicholas Fitzmaurice was my wife's grandfather), and I am grateful to him for bringing this fascinating to case to my attention and that of the world. The book's conclusion, in line with the conclusion of her adopted father, Edward Werner, was that the murderers of Pamela were Prentice, Knauf and Cappuzzo, A cold case solved, or so it appeared. Except that I wasn't convinced. Something, I felt, was wrong. As an experienced police officer, I could not conceive how the police of the day had failed to identify so many of the leads the old man had reported upon.

My curiosity aroused, I checked into the book's supporting evidence. Its principal source was Werner's reporting on the crime, contained in his letters sent to the British Ambassador in Peking and to the Foreign Office in London. I called at the UK National Archives in London and examined them, and it quickly became clear that the Werner reports were in no way objective and were written by a man possessing a strange mind. Crucially, nowhere did they contain any primary or admissible evidence. Without corroboration of any kind, they could not be taken seriously. For the large part, they were little more than rants. Unfortunately this was not made clear in *Midnight in Peking*. In presenting and supporting Werner's case and conclusion, the book failed to mention his many contradictions, changes of mind, improbable scenarios and outlandish allegations.

I looked up other sources referenced in *Midnight in Peking*, and I found many to be simply wrong. For instance, the book contains references to *These are Strange Tales* by Anthony Abbot, a 1948 American publication providing short, third-hand accounts of popular crimes. *Midnight in Peking*, in a chapter entitled "Of Rats and Men," quotes what it says are a number of lines from *These are Strange Tales*, but which actually appear nowhere within it. For example, there is a police interview scene:

> "'Let's talk about the Western Hills nudist colony,' Dennis
> said and Pinfold blanched."

There is actually no mention of either Dennis or Pinfold in *These are Strange Tales*, and no police interview. There is also no evidence to suggest that the two men ever met. *These are Strange Tales* is, anyway, in no way an historical record and does not purport to be so. It contains stories with lurid titles such as "The Phantom in the Attic" and "The Girl Who Plotted Her Own Murder." In its account of the Werner murder, entitled "The Vanishing Heart," the author concluded by presenting his own theory, which was that Pamela's murderer was a sinister, rich New Yorker who travelled the world. Possessing a cult of his own, he needed to deflower a virgin on a winter night and cook and eat her heart before dawn. *Midnight in Peking* nevertheless makes no less than nine references to the book as if it is an authoritative source.

Another *Midnight in Peking* passage describes how "The Americans had been concerned for the welfare of Prentice's youngest daughter, Constance. A file on her had been opened at the legation in 1931, but there was just one line it: 'Prentice, Miss - Nov. 28, 1931 - 393.1115/14 - Welfare of American in China, safety of.' There were no details in the file."[1] *Midnight in Peking's* narrative then states that Prentice's wife had fled China fearing that her daughter was at risk from her husband. All damning stuff for Wentworth Prentice, but entirely wrong.

I obtained a copy of the same file from the US National Archive. It was not empty at all, but contained a record of the rescue from bandits in another part of China of an adult Miss Prentice, a Christian missionary unrelated to the dentist and his family. It had nothing to do with Wentworth Prentice. The file was opened in 1931, and Prentice's wife had returned to the United States with the three children in 1926. None of them ever returned to China.

The book contains many other similar inaccuracies. For instance, in the chapter "Journey to the Underworld", it states: "If Detective Chief Inspector Dennis had not been barred from talking to Werner, he too would have learnt of the lie. Werner had proof of it, handwritten evidence in the form of a professional note he had received. It was dated 1 December 1936."

Werner did indeed claim to have a note from Prentice estimating the cost of Pamela's dental treatment. But Werner gave the date as December 1930, not 1936. The year-change in *Midnight in Peking* brought the dental examination to within a month of the murder, rather than a whole six years before. Furthermore, Dennis was not "barred from talking to Werner." Werner described how the two men had disagreed passionately on a number of occasions in terms that at least implies a meeting. He complained of how Dennis was dismissive of Werner's rickshaw witness, would "not budge an inch" in his opinion that Pamela was killed by one of her former Chinese school friends, and later "strenuously affirmed his conclusion".[2] The notion that a senior police investigator was

---

1 *Midnight in Peking,* chapter "A Respectable Man of Influence".
2 UK National Archives, FO 371/25315/1510 Murder of Pamela Werner Code 10 file 1510, letters from E.T.C. Werner to the British Ambassador to China, December 1938 & June 1939.

somehow barred from contacting a murder victim's father is not credible.

There are wrong attributions. For example, in *Midnight in Peking*'s chapter "The Wound that Wouldn't Heal," a passage reads: "But finally, in January 1943, someone in Whitehall read one of Werner's reports, and in a file memo noted: 'If British administration of justice in China is to recover its good name, a case of this heinous nature cannot be merely pigeon-holed, 'dropped' and forgotten. In any event, full, unexpurgated details must be made public in due course'."

The reader might infer from this that an outraged Whitehall staffer had come to agree with Werner's claims of injustice, but this was not the case. The sentence was in fact written by Werner himself; it was in one of his letters. It was not written by, repeated, nor commented upon by anyone else.[3]

There are also a number of incriminating passages in *Midnight in Peking* that are without source or reference. Here is another short section from the book's chapter "A Respectable Man of Influence" continuing on from the quote erroneously attributed to *These Are Strange Tales*:

> "What about the nudist colony? Dennis insisted. What about nude dances? But Prentice didn't even flicker. The nudist colony was respectable; naturism was well established in Europe and America. The detective chief inspector shouldn't be such a prude; some of Peking's most solid and reliable citizens were members. If anything inappropriate was occurring, surely the Chinese police would have objected by now, after several summers? The gatherings in Prentice's flat were simply like-minded men enjoying cultural activities in

3   UK National Archives, FO 371/25315/1510 Murder of Pamela Werner Code 10 file 1510, letter from E.T.C. Werner to the British Ambassador to China, March 1939.

a private setting."

The book provides no source for the above interview. In fact there is no evidence that Dennis interviewed anyone in the case, let alone Prentice. At his rank, it would not have been his role. Nudism, naked dances, parties at his flat: these were all accusations raised only by Werner in his letters. In *Midnight in Peking*, they take the form of a police interview.

Another example of a Werner remark taking full form in the book occurs in the chapter "Of Rats and Men." Dennis is depicted as being summoned to an urgent meeting with members of the school board: "Peters looked to Affleck. Affleck looked to the legal advisor Kent, who gave the nod, the consul laid out the events. The previous term, Pamela Werner's father had approached the school board and claimed that his daughter had been subjected to unwarranted sexual attentions while boarding at the school house - unwarranted attentions from headmaster Sydney Yeates."

Again, the book gives no source for this meeting, let alone such details as head-nodding. There is no evidence for it having happened. Werner, among the many allegations in his letters, once made a brief accusation that Yeates had been dismissed for improper conduct toward Pamela but, as usual, offered no further details. In *Midnight in Peking,* this allegation becomes an actual event.

And a further example. Aping Werner, *Midnight in Peking* is dismissive of the student Han Shou-ch'ing as a suspect. He gets a mention, but only briefly. Here is an excerpt from the chapter "The Hunters":

> "After a long search, Werner's detectives had found former classmates of the married student Han Shou-ching, whose nose had Werner broken with his cane. The students

remembered Han Shou-ching and Pamela being friends,
nothing more. He'd been deeply upset by her murder and
had told the students that the day before, he had met her by
chance outside the American drugstore on Hatamen Street.
Pamela felt bad about her father lashing out at him, and he
suggested they have dinner the following evening."

Once again an important passage goes without a source, its
detail and provenance a mystery. But the result is that the book's
narrative spotlight remains on Prentice and the other foreign men.

There are many other simple errors of fact. In the final chapter,
Fred Knauf is incorrectly given the first name of Joe, and is
described as having suspiciously "seemed to slip away from both
the Japanese and history." Not so. He was interned by the Japanese,
and his return to the US and life thereafter are well documented.
The book deals similarly with Cappuzzo, "who had left for Italy
shortly after Werner questioned him, returned to a country at war
with Great Britain". Once again, no source provided and in reality,
the archives easily reveal how Cappuzzo remained in China
throughout the war and into the early 1950s.

In summary, the *Midnight in Peking* account was, to me, unfair
and inaccurate in its analysis and incorrect in its conclusions. It
purports to be history but is not. So I decided to investigate the
crime myself. Who did murder Pamela Werner? What really
happened that night in Peking in 1937? What might still be
discovered?

I spent three years at the task and found that there was far more
to the murder than Werner's version. A wealth of material was
available on my doorstep in London: at the National Archives in
Kew, the School of Oriental & African Studies in Bloomsbury, and
the British Library in Euston. Other sources were further afield, in
the United States, China, Canada, Australia, Singapore, to name

but a few. "Search, and search again, and you will find," became a maxim. "Ask nicely and people will assist," was another. Both the British coroner and police case papers were lost, but not so the large quantities of routine paperwork generated by the British consular service in China; I sifted through it. Like Werner, many foreigners wrote memoirs and letters on their time in China; I located copies. Public servants and soldiers generated service records; I obtained them. A few people from the period were still alive; I tracked them down. The dead had living descendants; I spoke with them. There were experts in the period such as Yin Wenjuan of Capital Normal University in Beijing, and several of her students who helped trawl through archives in the city; I benefited greatly from their kind help and knowledge. It was often a case of thinking laterally: who might have been where? What might they have recorded? Where might it be found? Doggedness can be a virtue. Discovering the files relating to Edmund Backhouse frauds of the 1930s, unseen as they were by Hugh Trevor-Roper, was perhaps the most rewarding of my finds. Backhouse's report that Pamela was a victim of Japanese political revenge was missing entirely from *Midnight in Peking*. The controversial baronet was such an extraordinary character and reading his murder theory for the first time, having prior knowledge of its context, was very satisfying. Finally identifying and tracing the elusive Pinfold was also very rewarding, as was finding the sad account of the diplomat Cowan, both of which were again missing from *Midnight in Peking*.

My efforts delivered a wealth of new material. The final result was a complex tale played out in a complex period. The combined evidence points strongly to the offender being the student Han Shou-ch'ing. But historic murder investigations are rarely simple, or absolute in their results. That is their nature.

ACKNOWLEDGEMENTS

Many people have contributed to this book and I am deeply grateful to them all. The project would certainly not have been possible without their help. Indebted as I am, I would like to make a special thank you for the kind advice and assistance provided by:

Peter Bazire
George Binetsky & Jodie White
Ron Bridge
Julia Boyd (& publisher I.B. Tauris)
Betty Clementi
Brother Colin Chalmers FMS, Rome
David Cliffe (Berkshire Local History Association)
William Cowan
Diana Dennis (author of All I Ever Wanted)
Capital Normal University Professor Yin Wenjuan
Capital Normal University students Gao Wei and Du Bing
Graham Earnshaw
Greg Leck (author of Captives of Empire)
Findlay Mackenzie & Louise McLean
Deborah McFarlane (author of George Gorman (Britain & Japan; Biographical Portraits))
Jessica Murphy (Reference Archivist, Francis A. Countway Library of Medicine)
Merryn Myatt
Federica Onelli (Archivio Storico, Rome)
Erik Martin

Eric Politzer (Royal Asiatic Society (New York)
Desmond Power (author of Little Foreign Devil)
John Powers (NorthChinaMarines.com)
Mary Thompson (nee Fitzmaurice)
Malcolm Williams (City of Oxford School Association)
Colonel Christopher Woodbridge (US Marine Corps)
Lord Young of Cookham & Helen Winnifrith

I would also like to express my gratitude for the excellent work of the staff of the following:

The National Archives (UK)
The School of Oriental & African Studies library archive
The British Library
The Norwich Free Academy, Connecticut
Francis A. Countway Library of Medicine, Harvard Medical School
The National Personnel Records Center (National Archives)
The National Archives & Records Administration (USA)
United Methodist Archives & History Center, Drew University, New Jersey
Harry Ransom Center, University of Texas at Austin
Hoover Institution Library & Archives
National Library of Australia
Library & Archives Canada
Marine Corps Association & Foundation
The Times newspaper (London)
Pharos Tribune Logansport newspaper
B.H. Media Group
Oxford University Press (China)
Orion Publishing Group
Faber & Faber Ltd

Finally, I thank my wife Sue for all her patience and support; and for her skills in editing and somehow transforming my often juvenile grammar into something readable.

Copyright matters

I am grateful to many individuals, publishers, and institutions for their kind help in matters of copyright. Reference is made to the following in accordance with copyright conditions of use:

The quotation from a Dance with the Dragon by Julia Boyd in chapter two is reproduced with permission of IB Tauris and Company Limited via PLSclear.

The P.D. Coates quotation in Chapter 3 is reproduced by permission of the Oxford University Press (China) Ltd. From the China Consuls by P.D. Coates, copyright Oxford University Press (China) Ltd. All rights reserved.

The quotation from *The Bee* in Chapter 8 is reproduced by permission of BH Media Group.

Efforts to trace the copyright holder(s) to *My Boy Chang* by Hope Danby were unsuccessful (supporting correspondence with Orion Publishing Group available).

Other materials included are done so in the belief that they are either out of copyright or used within the bounds of fair usage. We are happy to re-consider any items where this proves not to be the case.

Language Note

The spelling of Chinese names in English is messy given the various romanization systems used over the past century. In this book, I have generally used the accepted spellings of the times.

Select Bibliography

Abbot, Anthony, *These are Strange Tales*, John C. Winston Company, 1948.

Acton, Harold, *Peonies and Ponies*, Oxford University Press, 1983.

Anthony, Luke (Ugo Cappuzzo), *Chang-fu (Self-Criticism)*, Otium Ac Negotium, 1997.

Arlington, Charles, & Lewisohn, William, *In Search of Old Peking*, Henri Vetch, 1935.

Avshalomov, Jacob and Aaron, *Avshalomovs' Winding Way; Composers Out of China*, Xlibris, 2002.

Backhouse, Sir Edmund Trewlawny, *Decadence Mandchoue*, edited by Derek Sandhaus, Earnshaw Books, 2011.

Bickers, Robert, *Britain in China*, Manchester University Press, 1999.

Biggs Jr., Chester M., *The United States Marines in North China 1894-1942*, Mcfarland & Company, 2003.

Booker, Edna Lee, *News is My Job; A Correspondent in War Torn China*, Macmillan, 1940.

Boyd, Julia, *A Dance with the Dragon*, I.B. Tauris, 2012.

Buhite, Russell D., *Nelson T. Johnson and American Policy Toward China 1929-1941*, Michigan State University Press, 1968.

Chang, Jung, & Halliday, Jon, *Mao; The Unknown Story*, Anchor Books, 2005.

Cliff, Norman, *Courtyard of the Happy Way*, Evesham, James, 1977.

Coates, P.D., *The China Consuls*, Oxford University Press, 1988.

Danby, Hope, *My Boy Chang*, Victor Gollancz Ltd, 1955.

Dennis, Diana, *All I Ever Wanted*, 2015

French, Paul, *Midnight in Peking*, Viking (Penguin Books), 2011.

Gage, Sir Berkeley, *It's Been a Marvelous Party*, 1989.

Gilkey, Langdon, *Shantung Compound*, Harper and Row, 1966.

Greenway, J.D., *Fish, Fowl, and Foreign Lands*, Faber & Faber, 1950.

Harcourt-Smith, Simon, *Japanese Frenzy*, Hamish Hamilton, 1942.

Hewlett, Sir Meyrick, *Forty Years in China*, Macmillan, 1943.

Key Ray Chong, *Cannibalism in China*, Longwood Academic, 1990.

King, Paul, *In the Chinese Customs Service*, T. Fisher Unwin, 1924.

Klein, Daryl, *With the Chinks; 2nd Lieutenant in the Chinese Labour Corps*, Naval & Military Press Ltd, 2009.

Knatchbull-Hugessen, Sir Hughe, *Diplomat in Peace and War*, John Murray, 1949.

Ladds, Catherine, *Empire Careers; Working for the Chinese Customs Service 1854-1949*, Manchester University Press, 2013.

Leck, Greg, *Captives of Empire*, Shandy Press, 2006.

Lovell, Julia, *The Opium War; Drugs, Dreams and the Making of China*, Picador, 2011.

McCasland, David, *Pure Gold; a new biography of the Olympic champion who inspired Chariots of fire*, Discovery House, 2001.

McFarlane, Deborah (& others), *Britain & Japan: Biographical Portraits, volume viii*, compiled and edited by Hugh Cortazzi, Global Oriental in association with the Japan Society, 2013.

Peters, E.W., *Shanghai Policeman*, republished by Earnshaw Books, 2011.

Power, Desmond, *Little Foreign Devil*, Pangli Imprint, 1996.

Snow, Helen Foster, *My China Years*, Harrap, 1984.

Teichman, Sir Eric, *Affairs of China*, Methuen Publishers, 1938.

Trevor-Roper, Hugh, *Hermit of Peking; The Hidden Life of Sir Edmund Backhouse* (first published as: *A Hidden Life; The Enigma of Sir Edmund Backhouse*, Macmillan, 1976).

Wakeman, Frederic Jr., *Policing Shanghai 1927-1937*, University of California Press, 1995.

Waldron, Arthur (editor), MacMurray, John Van Antwerp, *How the*

Peace Was Lost; the 1935 Memorandum, Hoover Institution Press, 1992.

Werner, Edward Theodore Chalmers, *Autumn Leaves; an autobiography with a sheaf of papers, sociological & sinological, philosophical & metaphysical etc*, Kelly & Walsh, 1928.

Werner, Edward Theodore Chalmers, *Memorigrams*, Shanghai Times, 1940.

Werner, Edward Theodore Chalmers, *More Memorigrams*, Edwin Snell & Sons, 1948.

Werner, Edward Theodore Chalmers, *Myths and Legends of China*, George G. Harrap, 1922.

Wood, Frances, *No Dogs & Not Many Chinese; Treaty Port Life in China 1843-1943*, John Murray, 1998.

INDEX

ABOUT THE AUTHOR

BORN AND RAISED in London, Graeme Sheppard is a retired police officer with thirty years' service with the Metropolitan Police in London and in the Northeast of England. He received several commendations for crime detection, and his policing experience included a wide range of locations including London's West End, rural villages and inner-city housing estates.

His enthusiasm for history and eager eye for evidence has resulted in articles published in History Today. Other interests include paleoanthropology, physical fitness and playing the classical guitar. He now lives and writes in Hampshire, UK.